D0935023

COMPARATIVE STUDIES
IN KINSHIP

Comparative Studies in Kinship

JACK GOODY

STANFORD UNIVERSITY PRESS
Stanford, California
1969

Stanford University Press
Stanford, California
© *1969 by J. Goody*
First published in the United States in 1969
Printed in Great Britain
L.C. *73–76227*

To

M. F. and E. R. L.

Contents

Tables

FIGURES

Abbreviations

UDG	unilineal descent group
P/M	patrilineal/matrilineal
P-M marriage	marriage of 'patrilineal' man with 'matrilineal' woman
XCM	cross-cousin marriage
FZD	father's sister's daughter
MBD	mother's brother's daughter
ZDS	sister's daughter's son
FBD	father's brother's daughter
MZD	mother's sister daughter

Preface

THE major problems that face the comparative study of human society, especially as concern simpler societies, are two-fold. The first has to do with the reliability of its observations. Accounts of overt ritual activities present relatively few difficulties; some aspects of social life, such as divorce, residence and similar features are being subjected to crude numerical treatment. It is rather in the spheres of 'norms' and 'concepts' where fieldworkers often seem to lose sight of the criteria of evidence, of the differences between assertion and demonstration, or indeed of any idea that replicability (or the possibility of replicability) is a desirable goal. Moves in the right direction are being made by certain American fieldworkers[1] but meanwhile one should recognize that the standards of anthropological observation, the levels of cultural scholarship, are often remarkably low. This situation needs remedying at once and advances can be made only when we abandon (or at least reduce) our commitment to wholistic studies. To think that anyone can cover 'a culture', even a pre-literate, 'homogeneous' one, in a year or two is a figment of the anthropologist's imagination and not one that he would be prepared to extend to an understanding of his own personal situation. It has been possible in the past only because of the great paucity of written knowledge about pre-literate and partly literate peoples.

Secondly, social anthropology (which Radcliffe-Brown referred to as 'comparative sociology') needs to progress from its phase of 'descriptive analysis' and get into the business of comparing, not social systems or societies or cultures as such, but specified variables under different social conditions. This is our experimental method, crude as it may be. It doesn't replace 'intensive investigation' but it is a necessary adjunct to the undirected collection of diffuse data that is often described as 'fieldwork'. Indeed even intensive fieldwork of the Trobriand or Tallensi kind is full of implicit comparisons, if only because of the language in which the societies are described.

The solution to both these problems presents a major challenge to social anthropology, since it questions the concentration on (though not the utility of) intensive fieldwork and the adequacy of anthropological 'methods'. My own view is that rather than be tied to a single approach, one needs to use the best available techniques to answer one's questions and solve one's problems, and these methods should not be too readily defined in 'disciplinary' terms. Inevitably new approaches will develop in the course of asking more pointed questions than the usual catch-all village study. At the moment nothing marks the anthropological method more than the lack of it. For example, one has only to compare recent Anglo-French discussions of 'systems of thought' to see that something is wrong at the ground level;[2] the methods of documentation clearly leave so much to be desired that serious discussion is often little better than speculation, 'pseudo-anthropology'.

The problem also presents a major challenge to the social sciences as a whole. The present division of these subjects is a reflection of a time when Western Europe and America dominated the world scene, economically, culturally, intellectually. That time is past. We cannot afford a sociology that concentrates upon Euro-American societies in the hope that all others will industrialize and turn out much the same. As fieldworkers we cannot afford an anthropology that dwells exclusively on the tribal world. We must create the conditions for the emergence of a truly comparative sociology.

In the early days of European sociology the subject was essentially comparative; the works of Montesquieu, Comte and Spencer deal with the whole range of human societies. On the anthropological side writers like Tylor and Frazer leant heavily towards the simpler cultures and to the 'survivals' of these that they perceived in other places. The wider comparative perspective was retained by legal writers like Maine and Vinogradoff, a man who spoke of his work in jurisprudence as 'comparative sociology'.

In this century, the two great sociological thinkers, Emile Durkheim and Max Weber, have continued to work on a wide canvas of this kind, attempting both to formulate and test their theories by means of the comparative method.

It is a strange contrast to recall the kind of opprobrium that has been showered on comparative research in the last few decades, and even now occasionally emerges from the pen of distinguished social scientists.[3] The reasons are not hard to seek. For specialists in the sociology of simpler societies, intensive fieldwork became the order of the day; such detailed studies brought to light the grave deficiencies of the materials that had too often formed the basis of comparative work. Meanwhile specialists in 'western' societies became increasingly divorced from the study of 'other cultures'. In America, which since the first World War has played such a leading part in the development of the social sciences, this split was institutionalized in the form not only of University departments but also of general theory, 'society' coming to be the domain of the sociologists and 'culture' of the anthropologist.[4] The professional dichotomy had much to do with the kind of colonial situation that America faced; sociology was for the immigrants, anthropology for the natives. The sort of radical division of the realm of human behaviour that resulted seems less profitable, less suggestive, than it did; certainly the fields of sociology and anthropology are becoming increasingly interlinked; as the simpler cultures become more complex, the division seems less and less relevant; and as techniques diffuse between disciplines, the 'anthropological' approach gets increasingly difficult to differentiate from the 'sociological'. So that the chances for the development of a truly 'comparative sociology' become somewhat more rosy.

To such an ambitious programme this book makes a very modest contribution. The first chapter, specific stimulus for which came from two years of teaching and examining in the social sciences at the University of Ghana, develops the argument of this programmatic preface. The second is a specific attempt to use the method of limited comparison to throw light upon a phenomenon of general interest in social life, the incest taboo.

The remaining essays are attempts to look at certain aspects of kinship behaviour from a comparative standpoint. There are of course many varieties of the comparative method and I don't propose to go over the ground well covered by Lewis and others.[5] Here I am mainly concerned with limited comparisons of a few societies, either because they are critical or well known, and also with comparison on an inclusive regional basis, using an area I know well from personal experience, that of northern Ghana. The two final chapters deal with specific aspects of the study of the kinship systems of archaic and modern societies, making use of cross-cultural and historical data to try and throw light on particular problems.

In later, largely unpublished work, I have tried to use the *Ethnographic Atlas* (1967) in order to test some of the propositions suggested here in a more systematic fashion.[6] Of course, one is always faced with the fact that becoming more comprehensive usually means becoming less intensive; but certain problems are best dealt with in one way, others in another. What I have aimed to do in each of the essays is to try and treat specific problems in a way that attempts to test 'theory' against 'evidence', to replace 'assertion' by 'demonstration'. In this one can have only a modest success. But it seems to me important to supplement both the one-society speculations of the functionalists and the universalistic formalism of the neo-structuralists, even in such limited ways as this.

I should like to thank the following for permission to reprint papers published in their journals or collections:

The editor, *British Journal of Sociology*, for 'A comparative approach to incest and adultery' (1956: Chapter 2); the editors of *Man* and the *Journal of the Royal Anthropological Institute* for 'The mother's brother and the sister's son in West Africa' (1959: Chapter 3), 'Cross-cousin marriage in northern Ghana' (1966: Chapter 8), 'The circulation of women and children in northern Ghana' (1967: Chapter 7), and 'On nannas and nannies' (1962: Chapter 10); the editor, *Current Anthropology*, for 'The classification of double descent systems' (1961: Chapter 4); the editor, *Past and Present*, for 'Indo-European Society' (1959: Chapter 9); the editors of *Mélanges C. Lévi-Strauss*, for 'Inheritance social change and the boundary problem' (1968: Chapter 5); the editors of *From Tribe to Nation in Africa: Studies in Incorporation Processes* (edited by Ronald Cohen and John F. Middleton, published by the Chandler Publishing Company, 1969), San Francisco, for 'Marriage policy and incorporation in northern Ghana' (in press: Chapter 6); the editor, *New Society*, for 'Prospects in Social Anthropology' (1966: revised for Chapter 1).

It is an impertinence on my part to include chapters written with my wife, Esther Goody. I have to thank her for her generosity in allowing me to do so, as well as her help with all of these essays, from the first to the last. But it is also the case that much of what one writes owes more to others than footnotes care to specify. I have tried to make some of my more immediate debts clear and do so again in dedicating this book. But many remain unthanked, unacknowledged.

JACK GOODY

St. John's College, Cambridge
May 1968

NOTES

1. See W. H. Goodenough (ed.), *Explorations in Cultural Anthropology*, New York, 1964.

2. See, for example, the introduction to *African Systems of Thought* (eds. G. Dieterlen and M. Fortes), London, 1966, and the review article by A. I. Richards, 'African systems of thought: an Anglo-French dialogue', *Man*, 2 (1967), 286–98. See also my review of M. Griaule, *Conversations with Ogotemmêli* (Fr. ed. 1948), in the *American Anthropologist*, 1967, 239–41.

3. For example, E. E. Evans-Pritchard, *The Comparative Method in Social Anthropology*, given as the L. T. Hobhouse Memorial Trust Lecture (1963). As in the parallel case of the Frazer lectures, the invitation to give a memorial address often becomes an opportunity to discuss the endeavour in which the memorialized was engaged.

4. Some of the theoretical formulations emanating from the early years of the Harvard Department of Social Relations seems to be influenced by an (unconscious) desire to share out the social sciences between sociology (society), anthropology (culture) and psychology (personality). For example, in *The Social System*, Talcott Parsons isolates 'three modes of systematization of action, Personality, Cultural Systems with special references to systems of Value-orientation, and Social Systems' (1951: ix); see also *Toward a General Theory of Action* (eds. T. Parsons and E. Shils) 1951.

5. See the useful anthology, *Readings in Cross-Cultural Methodology*, ed. F. W. Moore, Human Relations Area Files, New Haven, Conn., 1961.

6. Adoption in cross-cultural perspective, *Comparative Studies in Society and History*, 1969, **11**, 55–78; Inheritance, property and marriage in Africa and Eurasia, *Sociology*, 1969, **3**, 55–76.

CHAPTER ONE

Comparative Sociology and the Decolonization of the Social Sciences

The Background

B O T H sociology and anthropology have grown out of the attempts of man to make sense of his social environment, the behaviour of his fellow men, the variations between different societies and the changes that have taken place over time. In the Greek world, Aristotle examined some 150 possible constitutions; in the prolegomena to his *History of the Berbers*, the Arabic writer, Ibn Khaldun (1332–1406), worked out a general theory of social development; in China Ma Tuan-lin produced a *Comprehensive Study of the History of Civilization* (1320); in Europe Montesquieu classified and compared the range of human societies in *Spirit of the Laws* (1748), while Vico concerned himself, in the *Scienza Nuova* (1725) with examining the cycle of man's spiritual development in history. In the nineteenth century the task was pursued not only by sociological precursors like Comte and Spencer but also by a number of writers who specialized in the institutions of simpler societies. The information about remote lands resulted from colonial expansion and was subsequently incorporated into studies of human behaviour. Men like Waitz, Klem, Morgan and Frazer attempted to discern general similarities in the social action, physical, verbal and speculative, of different societies. With the help of the archaeological evidence that began to make its impact in the post-Darwinian era, they attempted to arrange these facts in an over-all pattern of the growth of human society.

There is no doubt that in this endeavour they had some considerable success. Both Tylor and Frazer described various institutions, such as divine kinship, ancestor worship, homoeopathic magic, which not only had a widespread distribution, but which Western European readers felt threw light on their own experience, their own social situation; intellectually *The Golden Bough* was one of the most influential books of this century.

The factual basis on which these reconstructions were built was provided by the accounts of students of European folklore interested in the strange 'non-rational' elements in their midst, and by travellers, missionaries and the like who took notes on the customs of the pre-literate peoples among whom they worked.

At the beginning of this century the process of professionalization, the growth of academic interest in 'other cultures', and the scientific advantages of getting the evidence for oneself, led to more extended journeys to out-of-the-way places, Haddon to the Torres Straits (1898), Boas to the Canadian Northwest (1899), Radcliffe-Brown to the Andamans (1909), Malinowski to the Trobriands (1914). Partly under the pressure of the fieldwork situation itself, partly under the influence of other social sciences (especially the French sociology of Emile Durkheim), British anthropology became specifically 'social', increasingly concerned with the exploration in depth of existing non-European societies with a view to describing and analysing the way they worked.

From the beginning, then, there were two main aspects of anthropology, the cultural-historical and the collection and analysis of information about particular societies. 'Social' anthropology concerned itself primarily with the second; it was essentially a child of European colonialism. Just as the wide-ranging interests of Greece and Rome gave us the human geography of Herodotus and notes by Tacitus on the Germanic tribes, so too the Western European conquests of the firearm era brought Lafitau on the Iroquois, Schoolcraft on the Chippewa, Spencer and Gillen on the Australian aborigines. A little later they took Radcliffe-Brown to the Andamans, Malinowski to the Trobriands, and their pupils to a whole variety of colonized peoples, the Azande, Nuer, Dobuans, Murngin, Tallensi, Kachin, Lozi and Tikopians. Anthropology, like trade, followed the flag, and the flag was planted there through superior fire-power. The anthropologist arrived as a representative of a technologically advanced society to put the local inhabitants under the sociological microscope.

The Field

The most authoritative recent account defines the field of social anthropology as 'that branch (of sociological studies) which chiefly devotes itself to primitive societies'.[1] It goes on to point out that it is generally assumed that social anthropology is also distinguished by its methods, which involve intensive fieldwork and the study of 'societies as wholes'.

If the social anthropologist studies contemporary primitive societies (and it is clear that these are the only ones he can study by observation, and as a whole), then his subject matter is rapidly dwindling before his eyes. The Nuer now elect Members of Parliament, the Navaho have their oil wells, the Tallensi their primary schools—and everywhere there is the bicycle, lorry, tin roof and wage labour. If one is taking a 'wholistic' approach, trying to see 'a culture', a society, in the round, then peasant villages must nowadays be seen as part of a rural-urban network, which includes a national government, police force, industrial complex and educational system. But social anthropology, heavily committed to its primitive subject-matter and its intensive approach, has failed to make a satisfactory adjustment to a situation where societies are no longer primitive and the networks much larger than those of earlier times. And one of the major problems here has been that the methods of social anthropology have also become a question of faith rather than reason, an end rather than a means.

The Method

Partly because of the impending disappearance of 'primitive societies' and the marginal contemporary interest of those that remain, many social anthropologists now tend to define themselves by the techniques they use rather than the people they study. The fieldworking anthropologist (and most British universities would not give advanced degrees to any other variety) settles down in camp, village or township, attempts to learn the language of the people and finds out as much as he can about their social life. It is, in effect, the single-handed community study of uncomplicated societies. The technique has been christened 'participant observation', and it can of course be applied in any relatively small-scale situation; for this reason, social anthropology has been referred to as 'microsociology' (Raymond Firth, *Elements of Social Organization*, 1951), but the title has also been given to social

3

psychology, especially the intensive study of 'human groups'. In any case, the northern Nigerian kingdom analysed in Nadel's classic study (*A Black Byzantium*, 1942) can hardly be described as a small-scale society; nor can any state (as distinct from a South Sea Island) be studied by intensive fieldwork methods alone: wider surveys are needed, both in time and space, in order to provide a satisfactory picture of the system as a whole, though the use of intensive observations is still of value in the study of small networks and groups.

If the technical resources at the command of the social scientist were not so limited in scope, the notion of intensive fieldwork by participation would seem so obvious as not to be worth mentioning, let alone be used to define a distinct field of study. Though some 'sociologists' have in fact worked in this way (notably William F. Whyte in *Street Corner Society*, 1943), there is no doubt that it deserves wider use in Western societies where it can supplement the more usual techniques of doorstep conversations and more formal interviews. There is also no doubt that it has made the social anthropologist more of a 'craftsman' than many of his sociological colleagues, and one whose theoretical interests are constantly tested on the touchstone of empirical research. It also makes him something of a jack-of-all-trades, since the collection of data is only partly structured and includes the acquisition of at least background knowledge on all the various facets of the culture, religious, legal, domestic and political.

But the attachment to 'total immersion' in fieldwork is becoming less valuable, except as a means to the salvation for the anthropologist—one man on his own making sense of a whole cultural universe. In the first place, as we come to know more about human societies, attention needs directing to particular aspects of their social organization; and it needs directing in a more problem-oriented way. For most anthropologists, problems arise after the research has been completed, not before—and the excuse that there is insufficient knowledge to formulate critical questions in advance is wearing thin.

I have noted that intensive fieldwork in a single village was not necessarily the best way of understanding a society like the Zulu or the Ashanti, especially if one is interested in the pre-colonial system. There was always a contradiction between the functionalist claim that one was dealing in wholes, and the actualities of work in these more

4

complex systems; and it is notable that, in Eurasia, anthropologists have largely confined their attention to village life ('Village India', 'The Mediterranean Countryman'), leaving the macrocosm to others. Even in pre-colonial times such societies were hardly 'primitive', partaking as they did (and this is true of more of the world than the anthropologist cares to remember) in the literate traditions developed in urban centres. In such a situation, full understanding of the social system can be derived only by the analysis of a wide network of social relations, by consulting written records and by methods of observation that take into account the considerable status differences that exist.

It is clear that as non-European societies become more and more stratified by income and differentiated by job, as the result of educational development, political independence and economic advance (and most of them have long since passed the point of no return) information about social behaviour needs to be gathered by more systematic methods than the social anthropologist has hitherto employed. In any case his methods were usually based upon the virtual absence of recorded information, upon convenient assumptions of homogeneity, and finally upon the hypogamous union which the anthropologist contracted with 'his people', either because he was a representative of the colonial nation, a manifestation of 'white power', or because he was a scholar from the city deigning to live among the people. It was his status as an elevated stranger, a friendly conqueror (combined with the more open way of life) that enabled him to walk into almost any house, to ask almost any question, to attend almost any ceremony, public or private. But as economic advance fragments familial groups and leads to a greater emphasis on privacy and individual achievement, so the doors close and there will inevitably be a shift towards those techniques favoured by students of Western societies, the stratified sample, the formal interview, the carefully prepared questionnaire, the problem-oriented research, supplemented of course by participant observation and armchair cogitation.

The Use
The study of 'other cultures' is moving in two main directions. On the one hand those involved in field research, of whatever kind, are becoming sociologists of developing nations, increasingly concerned in the

5

problems of such societies, similar in type to the problems sociologists face elsewhere. On the other hand, those whose primary interest lies in primitive societies have either to withdraw to remnant peoples such as the Bushmen of the Kalahari or to turn to the analysis and interpretation of what has already been written, in other words, to history.

The utility of the first branch of study seems self-evident, as a means of learning to live with one's neighbours, as the necessary basis of a comparative sociology and because of the practical implications of the sociology of development for the Third World. Nearly every country in Africa is planning a major hydro-electric scheme which involves the resettlement of large numbers of people. Less attention is given to their social problems than to the growth of weeds on the new lakes, yet such a situation is an opportunity for testing hypotheses on family organization as well as carrying out research of a socially useful kind.

But how about the study of primitive or quasi-primitive societies, either by the fieldwork methods which have been used in the past, or by the historical procedures that will obtain in the future?

Let us leave aside, not because I dismiss its value but because it justifies too much, the acquisition of knowledge for its own sake. I also set apart (again not unsympathetically) the search for knowledge of the primitive that has its origin in a withdrawal from the contemporary world. In the same way that writers in nineteenth-century England turned backwards to the Middle Ages, and others too found solace in the pursuits of the countryside (while continuing to profit from the life of the towns), so 'the noble savage' still has its more sophisticated worshippers in the twentieth century, and is exploited by those who have failed to find their philosophical or religious home in any of the contemporary creeds or anti-creeds.

Apart from these essentially personal quests, what is the social function of social anthropology? Is there any greater utility in knowing about the varieties of human culture than in the variations in non-human species, the territorial activities of robins, the maternal behaviour of macaques, the distribution of delphiniums? Certainly it is more urgent to gather information about the ways of humans than those of animals, because human habits, being learned, change rapidly when the social environment changes under new processes of social conditioning;

in one generation the child of an Italian immigrant becomes a hundred per cent American. Whereas in animal societies, where behaviour is passed down largely by a genetic code, the process of change takes place over a much longer (evolutionary) time span.

From one standpoint the very fact that the simpler human cultures are so liable to change, and all are undergoing such changes at this moment (where is the village without its transistor?), means that anthropology can offer little direct help to men of different cultures in learning to live in the same world, since people whom they have studied are already changing, or have become of peripheral relevance to the social life of their nations. So that one of the claims of anthropology in the colonial period (that it assisted colonialist and colonized to understand one another, i.e. the rulers to govern) has little to be said for it at the present day.

It was reluctance to have anything to do with the colonial governments of which they disapproved that made many anthropologists refuse to acknowledge that their work had any social functions other than 'scholarship'. What they did claim, implicitly at any rate, was that their intensive studies threw light upon other quasi-primitive societies, since they tried to isolate mechanisms (e.g. the workings of the clan or the feud, of bridewealth or dowry) which were widely found in other groups. In this they certainly succeeded.

There is also no doubt that the study of simpler societies does help illuminate the more distant past. The value of such knowledge is grossly inflated by many historians and pre-historians, who on the one hand disclaim any attempt to generalize their data and at the same time suggest that their writings throw some light on current events. But this end can be achieved only by classification, 'measurement' and comparison. Used in this way, as in the work of Durkheim and Weber, the study of past societies can generate interesting hypotheses and subject them to a crude kind of testing. More systematic testing can be carried out with the aid of the *Human Relations Area Files*, although this collection of data on the world's societies is (characteristically) hardly available outside America. The realization that the study of primitive societies is, in many respects, no longer a subject for field research will encourage a re-awakening of the interest in comparative studies that has been dormant in this country throughout the 'fieldwork' era, and more scholars will turn again to exploit the rich deposits of intensive studies in order to analyse long-term processes. It is time that 'evolution', 'cause' and 'change' ceased to be dirty words in the 'study of man'.

On a more fragmentary level, the academic value of field studies for the historical disciplines is obvious. Investigations of hunting communities have assisted archaeologists to reconstruct aspects of prehistoric society; the analysis of pre-industrial peasants has been used by Lévi-Strauss and others to throw light on the overall development of human thought; Robertson Smith, the great editor of the *Encyclopaedia Britannica*, used ethnographic material to explain features of the societies of biblical times; Maine and Frazer did the same with the archaic societies of classical times and the peasant customs of Western Europe. All this was already happening in the seventeenth century; the French traveller, de la Crequinière, looked for Indian parallels to Jewish and classical customs, for, he wrote, 'the knowledge of the customs of the Indians, is in no way useful in itself . . .'

But is that so? Is the study of pre-industrial societies merely a scholar's subject, a walled-in academic garden? Not altogether. For a student in the modern world, a knowledge of the range of human behaviour that different societies permit, reward or prohibit, is some safeguard against the ever-present danger of cultural *hubris*, of thinking that one's own is the only proper way of doing things. Such attitudes, unleavened by understanding, have catastrophic implications. This detergent function of the study of other cultures has a more serious aspect for the social sciences generally, including those that concentrate upon industrial man.

Since many aspects of human behaviour cannot easily be examined by the experimental methods of the 'hard sciences', comparison with other societies is an essential means of testing propositions and theories about mankind. Malinowski looked at Freud's concept of the Oedipus complex against the background of his fieldwork in a society that was less father-centred than the Jewish community of Vienna before the first World War, and found a different set of intra-familial tensions. The conflicts that arise under various kinds of family structure, the forms that aggression takes (whether witchcraft or murder), have been an important theme of recent kinship studies.

Only by comparison can we find out which elements of behaviour are given in 'human nature' and which man himself creates. Margaret Mead, for example, has insisted (perhaps over-insisted) that women's roles have a greater flexibility than many cultures suggest. Our ideas upon what is possible in human organization are often extremely hidebound, conditioned as they are mainly by a knowledge of the recent past, by political beliefs that are rarely subject to comprehensive review, by pop. sociology and psychology. While the study of pre-industrial societies cannot be of much help to constitution-makers in, say, Nigeria, it can point to general mechanisms (such as reciprocity or rotational succession) that should be taken into account in the organization of human affairs under particular conditions, mechanisms that are sometimes easier to discern in other, simpler societies, than in more complex ones. It has also contributed, not insignificantly, to the study of roles, networks, recruitment, socialization, succession, stratification, all recurrent topics in sociological analysis. In addition, there are a number of institutions, mainly in the domestic and religious spheres, which extend across the whole gamut of human cultures in rather similar forms; to subjects like the incest taboo, the rites that centre around the main junctures of communal and individual life (birth, marriage and death), the cross-cultural viewpoint has brought significant advances.

Anthropologists have usually avoided any consideration of the social function of their work. The fact that Everest exists has been enough reason to climb it. But there is more to be said for the subject. It seems doubtful whether the study of man can make much general progress without taking into account the totality of human social organizations. The distinction between sociology and social anthropology is basically a xenophobic one. Sociology is the study of complex societies, social anthropology of simple ones; sociology of Euro-America (with brief excursions into Asia), anthropology of non-Europeans; sociology of whites, anthropology of coloureds. As non-European societies become increasingly complex, so the distinction becomes increasingly meaningless as far as fieldwork is concerned. Soon one will only be able to study simple, 'indigenous' societies from travellers' accounts and the unpublished field notes of earlier anthropologists; the sociological fieldworker will have the choice of doing research in this continent or that, but his problem will not be basically one of choosing between literate (sociology) and pre-literate (anthropology) societies, for there will no longer be any such distinction; nor yet between one technique and another, for one must surely choose the technique not because academics proclaim that this is the way sociologists behave, but because one wants to solve a problem, intellectual or pragmatic.

The Prospects

The current division of the social sciences is a product of European colonialism, not of the problems to be tackled. Sociology and social anthropology are both sub-divisions of comparative sociology, the one concentrating upon European (complex), the other upon non-European (simpler) societies. But since the latter are now becoming increasingly complex, three main interlocking fields of comparative sociology emerge:

1. the sociology of developed societies,
2. the sociology of developing nations,
3. the sociology of simpler societies.

In the first two branches, both field and historical research are feasible. The third is becoming a branch of the historical sociology of pre-industrial societies, which includes the study of archaic, medieval and oriental societies; in the traditional preserve (though not the only one) of those describing themselves as social anthropologists, only documentary research will be possible; indeed it is already the case, certainly in the political, military, and religious fields, that the study of primitive societies is largely social archaeology. And throughout the anthropological world, the supply of old men is running perilously low; without their memories, primitive societies, in the strict sense, would no longer exist.

The suggested reorientation will place a greater emphasis than hitherto upon the interdependence of these branches of comparative sociology. A sociological 'theory' which is distinct from a 'theory' of social anthropology is conceivable only to the extent that zoological theory differs for sheep and for goats; the base must be common to both. By and large, the same is true of social psychology, another of the apartheid disciplines. Indeed a common background (as yet too divorced from research activities) is already emerging and there is a certain measure of convergence, anyhow in the work of American sociologists and British anthropologists.

We have today few polymaths whose activities cover the whole range of sociological interests, whether in advanced, developing, archaic or primitive societies. Sociologists tend to concentrate on work (industry), or the family, or religion, or politics. In the study of simpler societies, there is a similar tendency to concentrate on one subject, law, kinship, economics. Hence another development, cross-cutting the tripartite division already outlined, is the promotion of a truly comparative analysis of these various branches of knowledge. On the basis of fieldwork studies, modern social anthropologists like Evans-Pritchard and Gluckman have made important contributions to the sociology of religion and law respectively, just as their nineteenth-century predecessors did as a result of armchair speculation. The process of specialization should lead not to the elaboration of a series of sub-anthropologies (e.g. 'political anthropology') but rather to a political sociology that does not limit itself to the party politics of the Western world. In such an enterprise the sociology of developing nations will be of particular importance. Equally, the social institutions of such societies will make more sense given some understanding of the base on which they were built.

Like many of the processes surrounding the loss of empire, the adjustment involved in the decolonization of academic studies is radical and painful. 'History's' difficulty with the other continents is typical of the humanities in general. As British academic society has only recently accepted nineteenth-century sociology, it is unlikely to welcome a reorganization on the basis of comparative sociology, giving full recognition to the sociology of the Third World. University departments possess more inertia in face of change than almost any other type of bureaucratic organization. But such developments seem bound to come in the long run, beginning, as do so many innovations, on the periphery —in the academic institutions of the developing nations where the old divisions are particularly inappropriate; for their 'other cultures' become our 'sociology'. Indeed such a programme is already in motion. Instead of having the sociology of the family and the anthropology of kinship, the University of Ghana has been developing courses which include the study of matrilineal households in Ashanti, the mother-centred families of the West Indies, and the kinship patterns of urban Europe, East and West.

The re-orientation has many advantages, theoretical and practical. Equally there will be some loss. The sociology of primitive peoples will become more speculative, more 'intellectualized', as the opportunities for first-hand research dissolve. In the analysis of cognitive systems (the universe of knowledge) there could be some gains. Equally, there is a potential loss in the search for gimmicks (dressed up as 'models') from other fields (economics, linguistics, or computer technology) to cover up the poverty of one's sociological clothing.

But such are the inevitable effects of the rethinking which the decolonization of the social sciences is bound to involve.

NOTE

1. E. E. Evans-Pritchard, *Social Anthropology*, London, 1961.

CHAPTER TWO

A Comparative Approach to Incest and Adultery[1]

In an article entitled 'Changing Emphases in Social Structures' (1955), Murdock maintains that sciences first go through a classificatory stage and subsequently arrive at a second phase in which an attempt is made to analyse the 'dynamic processes which give rise to the phenomena thus classified' (1955: 361). As far as anthropology is concerned, 'the initial classificatory task has by now been substantially accomplished in the field of social structure' (361).

This thesis, which has been propounded on other occasions by other writers, seems to me not only to take a naïve view of scientific discovery, but definitely to mislead those from neighbouring fields of study into thinking that anthropological terms necessarily have some primary referent which is accepted by the large majority of anthropologists. That is by no means the case. In the first place, there is often a considerable measure of overt disagreement. Secondly, even where apparent agreement is found, the ambiguity of the terms themselves may conceal a number of different usages.

Partly this derives from the fact that the continuous analysis in depth of different societies calls for more precise conceptual discriminations than were previously required. And partly too it is related to the fact that the terms often employed by social scientists are those which we use as members of a particular society to refer to our own institutions. Such concepts may turn out to be quite inappropriate for the purpose of cross-cultural analysis. The English 'family' is an obvious case in point. From the sociological point of view, the term has at least four analytically separable meanings. A statement of the kind, 'the family is a universal institution among all human societies', is meaningless without further elaboration.

In sum, these concepts cannot be regarded as having been defined once and for all time, leaving anthropologists now free to get on with other types of activity. A refinement of concepts is a product of onward-going research; it proceeds hand in hand with it. The depth analysis of societies through long periods of residence by trained observers is a necessary concomitant of the sharpening of concepts for cross-cultural studies.

The particular concept in which I am interested here is that of 'incest'. I want also to mention the related ones of adultery and fornication, as I shall later be concerned with them as categories of heterosexual offence. The everyday meanings given by the *Concise Oxford Dictionary* are as follows:

1. Incest Sexual commerce of near kindred.
2. Adultery Voluntary sexual intercourse of married person with one of the opposite sex, married (double adultery) or not (single adultery).
3. Fornication Voluntary sexual intercourse between man (sometimes restricted to unmarried man) and unmarried woman.

These particular definitions are by no means standardized. For instance, the *Encyclopaedia Britannica* (11th Edition) and *Webster's Dictionary* both define incest as 'sexual intercourse between persons so related by marriage or affinity that legal marriage cannot take place between them', a formula which assumes an identical range in prohibitions on heterosexual intercourse and prohibitions on marriage.

It is these everyday usages which have formed the basis of the anthropological concepts. Malinowski, for example, appeared to treat the incest taboo, the prohibition on sexual intercourse, and exogamy, the prohibition on marriage, as being but two sides of a coin.

Murdock, on the other hand, adheres more closely to the *Concise Oxford Dictionary* when he defines incest and adultery:

> When it (heterosexual intercourse) takes place outside of marriage between two persons of whom at least one is married to another person, it is called *adultery*. If its participants are related to one another by a real, assumed, or artificial bond of kinship which is culturally regarded as a bar to sex relations, it is classed as *incest* (1949: 261).

14

Radcliffe-Brown, while retaining the criterion of kinship, offers a more restricted definition of incest. He writes, 'Incest is properly speaking the sin or crime of sexual intimacy between immediate relatives within the family, father and daughter, mother and son, brother and sister' (1950: 69).

Such extensive controversies have raged around the 'incest taboo' that it may perhaps appear impertinent to raise the question as to whether all these writers are in fact discussing the same range of phenomena or looking for explanations of the same set of prohibitions. But when we put the definitions of Murdock and Radcliffe-Brown side by side it is obvious that such doubts are not altogether misplaced. It is clear for instance that in terms of Radcliffe-Brown's definition, Murdock's 'second factual conclusion' . . . 'that incest taboos do not apply universally to any relative of opposite sex outside of the nuclear family' (1949: 285) is tautologous. Equally, on the basis of Murdock's formula, it is difficult to decide whether sexual intimacy with the father's wives other than one's own mother would constitute incest or adultery, particularly in societies like the Tiv or Bedouin where kinship is universal. The difference between the two definitions is this, that though both apparently see the regulations as 'grounded in the constitution of the nuclear family' (1949: 284), Radcliffe-Brown attempts to limit the application of the term to the elementary family itself, while Murdock prefers to include all kin-based prohibitions, seeing these as 'extensions' of the primary taboo. Murdock's emphasis is in line with Malinowski's stress upon the elementary family and with his dogma of 'extension of sentiments'. Both definitions are clearly based upon the institutions of our own society, where prohibitions on intercourse, like prohibitions on marriage, are bilaterally organized within limited ranges of kin. But are these necessarily adequate for the analysis of non-European societies?

In order to answer this question, let us examine the evidence from two societies characterized by unilineal descent, one by matrilineal, the other patrilineal descent. I have selected for this purpose the Ashanti and Tallensi of Ghana, for which the main sources on incest are Rattray (1929) and Fortes (1936, 1949) respectively. These societies were chosen partly because of the high standard of the available reports and partly because of my own familiarity with the area. The Trobriand and the

Nuer material will be used as a check upon the results obtained from an analysis of the examples from Ghana. In each case I want to examine both the explicit verbal categories of the actors themselves and the classifications implicit in the system of sanctions. These will be compared with the concepts employed by the observers.[2]

The Matrilineal Case

In his treatment of sexual offences among the Ashanti, Rattray distinguished what he calls sins or tribal offences (*oman akyiwadie*) from household offences (*efiesem*). The former demanded the intervention of the central authority and the execution of the guilty party, although in some instances compensation was allowed. The latter 'were settled by the persons directly concerned or were decided by argument before any Elder, without reference to the "house-father", who stood entirely aloof' (1929: 287). The offences falling under these two categories were discussed separately. I have listed them together in the table opposite.

From this table it can be seen that among the Ashanti sexual offences can be categorized in two ways, firstly according to the different names used by the Ashanti themselves, and, secondly, according to the different sanctions employed. I shall consider first the classification according to the nature of the sanctions.

This reveals three classes of offence. In the first class falls *mogyadie*, intercourse with a woman of the same clan, punishable by death; this includes intercourse with full siblings and maternal half-siblings and with the mother; it excludes intercourse of father with daughter. But there is another type of offence, which though not given the same name, is also punishable by death; this is *atwebenefie* (1), intercourse with a member of the same patrilineal sub-group, which of course includes that between father and daughter. Terminologically this constitutes a different category, but in respect of the nature of the sanction it must be associated with *mogyadie*. Both are cases of intercourse with members of the same descent group. The terminological distinction indicates that it is intercourse within the matriclan which is the major prohibition here while that within the patrilineal sub-group is subsidiary. This is consistent with the nature of double clanship among the Ashanti.

The second class of offence consists basically of intercourse not with

16

TABLE I
HETEROSEXUAL OFFENCES AMONG THE ASHANTI[3]

	Offence		Sanction
	Ashanti name	Definition	
Tribal:			
A i	mogyadie 'eating up of one's own blood'	SI* with female member of matriclan (abusua)	Death for both parties
A ii	atwebenefie (1) 'vagina near to the dwelling-house'	SI with female of patri-clan (ntoro) sub-group	Death or expulsion from matriclan
A iii	baratwe	SI with 'unclean' woman	Death
A iv	di obi yere (1) 'eat a man's wife'	(a) SI with chief's wife (b) ahahantwe (1), SI with unwilling married woman in the bush	,, ,,
Household:			
B i	di obi yere (2)	ahahantwe (2), SI in bush with: (a) unmarried woman (b) married woman (c) own wife	Ridicule Adultery payment plus sheep Ridicule
B ii	,, ,, ,,	SI of chief with subject's wife	Special adultery payment
B iii	,, ,, ,,	SI by master with wife of a slave	,, ,,
B iv	atwebenefie (2)	SI with wives of matriclan SI with wives of patriclan sub-group SI with wives of military company SI with wives of guild SI with affines (wife's mother, wife's sister)	,, ,, ,, ,, ,, ,, ,, ,, ,, ,,
Household: C	di obi yere (3)	Residual—SI with any married woman not falling in any of the above categories	Ordinary adultery payment

* Sexual intercourse. In treating household offences, Rattray explains that 'adultery' may include various forms of 'intimacy' besides actual intercourse. Since it was not always possible to distinguish from his account where this distinction was relevant, I have included these under the heading of intercourse.

members of the same descent group but with the wives of fellow members, as well as with other classificatory wives. It also includes some prohibitions on intercourse with affines which might tend to confuse the social position of the wife herself. The punishment for this class of offence varies. It is never death, but consists of some variant of the adultery payment.

The third class of sexual offence is with wives of other men, and the sanction here is the simple adultery payment.

The threefold typology on the basis of sanctions is an indication of the weight placed by the society on these various offences. The first class brings together offences relating to the structure of descent groups, both matrilineal and patrilineal (A i & A ii), offences relating to the hierarchical organization (A iv *a*) and 'ritual' offences relating to the cult of the Earth (A iv *b*) and to the fertility of women (A iii).

When we look at the terms used by the Ashanti themselves, we find there is another threefold typology, if we exclude the category *baratwe*, which represents a different method of classifying these offences. Intercourse within the matriclan is sharply differentiated terminologically from intercourse within the patriclan, the latter falling into the same category as intercourse with the *wives* of members of the matriclan and of other social groups. In this way it is assimilated to what I wish to call group-wife offences to distinguish them from intra-group offences. This is clearly related to the overwhelmingly greater importance of the matriclans in the social system. The third category is residual in that it consists essentially in sexual intercourse with people other than the members or wives of members of the descent groups, and of a few other quasi-kin groups such as guilds and military companies. Thus the concepts of the Ashanti themselves concerning heterosexual offences closely reflect the system of social groups. Intercourse with a daughter falls into a different category from intercourse with a sister, although for us both would be classified as 'incest'.

Now let us turn to Rattray's own use of the terms 'incest' and 'adultery' to see how he meets this situation. 'Incest' he uses simply to translate *mogyadie*, 'eating of one's own blood', that is, sexual intercourse with a matriclanswoman. He applies the term to none of the other offences, even those also punishable by death. The term 'adultery' he uses to translate all the household offences, 'eating a man's wife' (*di obi yere*, 2 and 3) and *atwebenefie* (2)—'a vagina near to the dwelling-house'. He also uses it to translate those offences called *di obi yere* (1) which fall under tribal jurisdiction and are therefore punishable by death. This consists of two offences only, intercourse with a chief's wife, and the worst type of sexual sin against the Earth, the rape of a married woman in the bush. His difficulty arises with category A ii, that is, *atwebenefie* (1). In his original list of offences, he translates this neutrally as 'sexual intercourse with certain individuals other than those related by "blood" ' (304)—i.e. females of the same matriclan. On the following page he writes:

> *Atwe-bene-fie* means literally (having sexual intercourse with) 'a vagina that is near to the dwelling-house', and the offence, as the title implies, consisted in committing adultery with the wives of certain persons with whom the existing *ménage* necessarily compelled close social intercourse or constant physical proximity . . . (305).

The term 'adultery' has now replaced the neutral circumlocution previously used. However, when we examine the list of *atwebenefie* offences we find that those included under 'tribal sins' (i.e. *atwebenefie* (1)) are not defined by the affinal relationship to ego. The women are forbidden not because they are someone's wives but because they are female members of the same patrilineal sub-group. For such an offence adultery seems a misleading translation.

The point at issue is this. In English usage the term 'adultery' is defined in relation to the marital status of one or both participants and is in effect residual to the category 'incest'. The term 'incest' is defined bilaterally, in keeping with other aspects of the social system. Heterosexual offences among the Ashanti do not fall into these categories, and in trying to translate these simply by the English words 'incest' and 'adultery' Rattray was faced with an impossible task. The English concept 'incest' refers to heterosexual intercourse with persons within a particular range of kin, whether they fall within that range by birth or by marriage. When a male ego marries, the immediate female kin of his wife are assimilated to his own kinship chart by becoming sisters- or mothers-in-law. Intercourse with affines is defined as incestuous, and placed in the same conceptual category as intercourse with consanguineous kin.

Thus, whereas the Ashanti differentiate between intra-group offences and group-wife offences, the European system does not have to do this because at marriage the spouses are assimilated, for many social purposes, into each other's natal groups. There is no distinction, in the context of heterosexual offences, between group-member and group-spouse.

This interpretation is strikingly confirmed in another matrilineal case, that of the Trobriands. Malinowski discusses incest in considerable detail in his book *The Sexual Life of Savages* (1929). First let us ask what Malinowski means by incest. 'Incest within the family and breach of exogamy', he says, is the meaning of the Trobriand word *suvasova* (389). As the family is bilateral, the term *suvasova* should therefore cover the intercourse of a man with his mother, his sister, or his daughter.

When we look at the Trobriand concepts themselves we find that this is not the meaning of the word *suvasova*. Malinowski himself makes this apparent in another context, although he continues to assume an equivalence.

> It must be clearly understood that, although father to daughter incest is regarded as bad, it is not described by the word *suvasova* (clan exogamy or incest), nor does any disease follow upon it; and, as we know, the whole ideology underlying this taboo is different from that of *suvasova* (447).

Suvasova corresponds precisely to the Ashanti concept *mogyadie*. It is the name for what I have called intra-group offences (intercourse or marriage), and has to be distinguished from intercourse with wives of members of the matriclan, such as brother's wife, which to judge from the example Malinowski gives (98) is not heavily sanctioned. The category *suvasova* includes intercourse with the mother, the daughter and the sister, the last being considered the most heinous, possibly because this was felt to be the most likely. The worst heterosexual offences in the Trobriands as among the Ashanti, in each case distinguished terminologically, are those committed with members of the same matriclan. Malinowski repeatedly insists that it is the brother-sister prohibition which is the basis of the 'incest' taboo in Trobriand society.

A Comparative Approach to Incest and Adultery

The Patrilineal Case

Let us now consider a patrilineal case, the Tallensi. According to Fortes (1949) the Tallensi have no word for incest. There is a term *poyamboon* which might be translated literally 'matters concerning women'. Fortes himself translates this as 'adultery', but on the basis of my own experience among the LoDagaa I would suggest that it covers a wider range of heterosexual offences than is usually indicated by this term.

If the Tallensi have no specific word for incest, what range of phenomena does Fortes include under this term and how does he differentiate this from other types of offence? Looking at his analysis, we find that incest consists in sexual relations within the 'expanded family', that is, the family group based upon the inner lineage (1949: 111). Thus, in the absence of an indigenous concept, Fortes has introduced what is essentially a bilateral classification, one that includes in the same category offences with a paternal aunt, a sister or a daughter (intra-group offences) as well as offences with the wife of a father, brother or a son (group-wife offences). But though he calls both of these offences 'incest' he emphasizes that they are differently thought of by the Tallensi. For the first category of offences is merely 'disreputable', while the latter is viewed with the horror usually taken as being characteristic of incest. Outside the inner (or medial) lineage this dichotomy becomes even more obvious, for a lover relationship with a female lineage member is in fact permitted, while intercourse with the *wife* of a lineage or even a clan member is still considered a wrong. Fortes claims that this latter offence is not incest, but 'the most reprehensible form of adultery. It does not bear the same moral stigma as the corresponding form of incest, nor does it carry religious penalties for the adulterer' (1949: 116). For Fortes, therefore, incest consists in sexual intercourse with female members of the inner lineage and with the wives of its male members, while adultery consists in intercourse with the wives of male members outside that range as well as with wives of non-clansmen.

There is then no Tallensi term for heterosexual offences other than one for 'matters concerning women'. Fortes uses the English terms 'incest' and 'adultery' to divide up this category. The way in which he does so is bilaterally oriented. 'Incest' is the offence of sexual intercourse within the 'expanded family', 'adultery' the offence of sexual intercourse with any married woman outside it.

An alternative method of treating this problem is to infer the implicit classification of offences among the Tallensi from the nature of their reaction to any breach. This in effect is what Fortes does when he insists that 'incest' with a sister or daughter falls in a different category of sexual acts from 'incest' with a wife of the lineage (1949: 114). This standardized procedure for the investigation of moral, ritual or legal norms gives the following threefold division:

i. sexual intercourse with a member of the same patriclan (up to the inner lineage only).
ii. sexual intercourse with the wife of a member of the same patriclan.
iii. sexual intercourse with the wife of a non-clansman.

I suggest that this classification has more inherent probability for three reasons. Firstly, it appears to fit better with the Tallensi emphasis on unilineal descent. Secondly, it corresponds to the classification I found among the LoDagaa of the same general area who are culturally similar to the Tallensi in very many ways. Thirdly, it is analogous to the classification which we have found among the Ashanti. Thus in both the matrilineal and patrilineal cases prohibitions on sexual intercourse are grouped together, depending upon whether they were:

i. with a member of the same descent group (intra-group sexual prohibition).
ii. with the wife of a member (group-wife prohibition).
iii. with another married woman (extra-group prohibition).

I suggest that a similar typology will be found in most societies characterized by unilineal descent, but has been obscured in anthropological reports because of the ethnocentric bias of the observers towards bilateral classifications. It is only possible to rectify this in the case of the Tallensi and Ashanti because of the excellence of the reporting and the fact that the authors have provided us with the terms used by the actors themselves. If we accept these three basic categories for heterosexual prohibitions and offences in societies characterized by unilineal descent groups, it would be reasonable to refer to the last as adultery, or more specifically non-group adultery. But what about the other two types of offence? Which of these should be called 'incest'?

The Classification of Heterosexual Offences

The whole lengthy discussion of incest has turned on the supposition that it is a type of illicit sexual intercourse which is characterized by a particular horror. In the Western European system it is true that the entire range of offences included under the category incest is so regarded. But in many other societies, this is not so. Even within the minimal domestic units, heterosexual offences may be differently classified both terminologically and with regard to the organized sanctions with which they are met. Furthermore, they are also distinguished by diffuse sanctions, by the reactions which they arouse in the other members of the community. Among the Tallensi, offences between brother and sister (intra-group offences) are merely 'disreputable', while group-wife offences are met with 'horror'. On the other hand, and this is a point of fundamental theoretical interest, among the Ashanti the reverse is the case. It is the intra-group offences which are dealt with by death, while the group-wife offences are treated as a heightened form of extra-clan adultery. I would claim that it is a mistake in either of these societies to class both these types of offences together as 'incest', because they are treated in such markedly different ways in terms of the sanctions employed, and, among the Ashanti, in terms of the actor categories themselves. Equally it would be difficult to classify either the first or the second types as incest on the basis of the internal reaction to them, as this varies so markedly in the two societies. I suggest that the word incest be retained for the category of offences inside the group and that it be divorced from the criterion of 'horror'. The group-spouse category should be associated with adultery rather than incest, for at the core of the prohibition lies the fact that the woman is *married* into the group; the taboo depends upon her married status. If she were not married, intercourse with her would be neither incest nor adultery but rather fornication, an act which may not be negatively sanctioned at all. For the group-wife category I therefore suggest the somewhat clumsy phrase, 'group-wife adultery'. Let me now schematize the threefold categorization of offences which we found among the Ashanti and the Tallensi. The terminology I suggest seems to me more appropriate for the cross-cultural analysis of heterosexual acts outside marriage (see table below).

There are three points about this table which require explanation. Firstly, it is constructed from the point of view of an ego of either sex, whereas previously I have often taken the male ego's vantage point, in speaking, for example, of offences with the wife of a group member rather than the spouse of a group member. In certain respects it would

TABLE II

THE CLASSIFICATION OF HETEROSEXUAL OFFENCES

Offences that are	*Offences with*	
	Unmarried person	*Married person*
Intra-group	Incest	Incestuous adultery
Extra-group	Fornication	i. Spouse of group
		(group-spouse adultery)
		ii. Other married person
		(non-group adultery)

have been preferable to have retained the earlier standpoint. For this was not merely a reflection of my own sex role; it corresponds to ethnographic reality. Although in European law adultery is defined as sexual intercourse where one of the partners is married, in most other societies it is only considered adultery when the woman is married. This is the case in Roman law. The reason for this is that in general marriage confers relatively exclusive rights on a man over the sexual services of a woman. It is most unusual to find that the woman acquires similar rights over the male, even in matrilineal societies. However it seemed preferable to construct the table to take account of this case, rare as it is.

Secondly it should be pointed out that in addition to the prohibitions on sexual intercourse which can be discussed in terms of the structure of descent or kin groups, there are also those attached to specific kinship positions. For instance, in English law, it is incestuous adultery to sleep with one's wife's sister. This is also true of the Nuer and of many other African societies. As Evans-Pritchard points out in this connection, these prohibitions are to be seen as preventing a confusion of kinship statuses, a disruption of the solidarity of the sororal group.

Thirdly, a further variable has been introduced into this table, namely that of marital status. I have already explained why this is essential in considering extra-group offences. But it may also be relevant in the case of intercourse with a fellow-member of the group. For instance, the LoDagaa of northern Ghana, among whom I worked, and who are in many ways very similar to the Tallensi, regarded intercourse with a clanswoman before her marriage, that is, before her sexuality had been alienated to a member of another clan, as being of very minor importance. But intercourse with the same woman after her marriage, what I have called 'incestuous adultery', is more severely treated.

For the comprehensive analysis of heterosexual offences, it is essential to introduce yet a further variable, not shown in the table, that of generation. Social relationships with a member of the same or alternate generation are usually characterized by relative equality and those between adjacent generations by super- or sub-ordination. This fact is likely to affect the severity with which the offence is treated. It will tend to be more severely treated where the relationship is characterized by authority, and especially where the male offender is of junior generation, for example, in the event of intercourse of a man with his father's wife. The same is true of other unequal statuses.

The Incidence of Horror

By breaking down the categories of incest and adultery in this manner, it is possible to offer not only a more adequate analysis of heterosexual offences in any one particular society, but also to begin to examine these offences on a cross-cultural basis. I have already called attention to the different incidence of 'horror' among the Tallensi and the Ashanti. In the former case it was offences with clan wives that were considered most heinous, whereas among the latter it was with the clan females themselves. The category heavily sanctioned among the Ashanti was relatively lightly treated among the Tallensi and vice versa. Why should the Tallensi represent the 'mirror image' of the Ashanti in this respect?

I suggest the following is the explanation of this remarkable reversal. The Tallensi are patrilineal; their classification of offences resembles that of many other patrilineal peoples. The category 'wives' is of fundamental importance to the descent group because it is through them that the continuity of the clan is obtained. Hence illegal intercourse with the wife of another member of the group is treated most severely.

The Ashanti are matrilineal. Social reproduction, as distinct from physiological reproduction, is obtained not through wives but through 'sisters', the female members of the clan.[4] Hence it is interference with *their* sexuality that constitutes the most heinous heterosexual offence. An interesting aspect of this explanation is that it accounts for the differential treatment of father-daughter and mother-son offences. In neither the patrilineal Tallensi nor in matrilineal Ashanti does the father-daughter relationship fall into the most heinous category, while in both societies the mother-son relationship does. In the Tallensi the mother is the closest *wife* of a clansman of *senior* generation, while in the Ashanti she is the closest *female clan member* of *senior* generation. This I suggest forms a more satisfactory explanation of the different treatment of these offences than the usual 'biological' one.

To put this difference in another way, in patrilineal societies the rights over a woman that are transferred at marriage include rights to her reproductive capacities as well as rights to her sexual services, whereas in matrilineal societies it is only the latter that are transferred. Indeed among the Ashanti, a male only acquires exclusive sexual rights by the payment of a special sum, known as the *tiri-nsa*, which is not intrinsic to the 'marriage' itself.

The rights over the sexual services of women are customarily vested in one man, except in the rare cases of polyandrous systems. But the degree of this exclusiveness varies. For example, the LoDagaa, like the Tallensi, regard intercourse with the wife of a patriclansman as being the worst form of heterosexual offence. Yet the junior of a pair of male twins, if unmarried, is said to have access to the wife of his elder brother. In this case, the social identification of the siblings is such that it overrules the individualization of rights to the sexual services of the wife. There is always an incipient contradiction in patrilineal societies centring around the fact that while rights to the sexual services of women are in general acquired by individuals, rights to their procreative capacities are to some extent vested in the clan as a whole. An offspring of a particular union is an offspring of the entire clan. This contradiction

26

is differently resolved in various societies. In Brahmin groups, for example, rights over women are so highly individualized that a widowed woman may not marry again. Among the Tallensi a man's exclusive rights in a woman cease at his death, and by the institution of widow inheritance are taken over by another member of the same patriclan. Fraternal polyandry, or polycoity, represents the extreme case of corporate rights over the sexual services of women, at the opposite pole as it were to the individualization of Brahmin society. The problem of plural access is different from, but not unrelated to, that of plural marriage.

The Nuer are an interesting case in this connection, both because of the nature of the material and because of the theoretical position adopted by Evans-Pritchard. Both Evans-Pritchard (1949, 1951) and Howells (1954) speak of the Nuer as having a word for incest, namely *rual*. Evans-Pritchard explains that this term covers offences with clanswomen as well as other kinswomen falling within the range of prohibited degrees of marriage, and further that the prohibition on sexual relationships derives from the prohibition on marriage. But he also adds that the same term is used to designate offences with women who are married to kinsmen. Evans-Pritchard brings this within the framework of his explanation of the incest taboo as derived from the rule of exogamy by asserting that such women are 'brought within the circuit of the incest taboo not so much as wives of kinsmen but rather as mothers of kinsmen' (1951: 45). This contention seems somewhat strained. Women married to kinsmen surely fall into the forbidden category by virtue of their marriage and their *potential* child-bearing capacity. The Nuer certainly regard the presence of children as increasing the dangers of incest, but there is no indication in the literature that they look with any approval upon intercourse with the wife of a kinsman who has not yet given birth to children, except in one or two rather special cases (Evans-Pritchard 1949: 97).

Evans-Pritchard then uses incest to translate the Nuer word *rual* and maintains that the Nuer include in this category sexual relations with women falling within the range of prohibited degrees as well as with women married to such kin. If this were the whole situation, then the Nuer would have very similar categories of heterosexual offences to those which exist in our own society. But this does not appear to be altogether the case, for he also writes that 'sexual relations with the wives of half-brothers, paternal uncles, and patrilineal cousins of every degree are regarded as being either incestuous peccadillos or not incestuous at all. The wife of a "bull" is, in a general social sense, the wife of all the "bulls" . . . She is "our wife" ' (1951: 45). It would appear from this statement that the term *rual* is not generally used for intercourse with the wives of agnates, other than the father, a full brother or a son. 'There is no incest', the Nuer say, 'among bulls' (1949: 92).

Howell's account confirms this. He includes intercourse with women married to kinsmen in his discussion of adultery rather than under the rules of incest and exogamy, and concludes with the following remark . . . 'the act is therefore tantamount to incest (*rual*)' (1954: 164). His use of 'tantamount' again appears to indicate that the Nuer make a verbal distinction between intercourse with kinswomen ('intra-group offences') which is *rual* and intercourse with the wives of kinsfolk which is 'tantamount to *rual*'. It is probable that Howell here means agnates rather than the entire range of kinsfolk, for Evans-Pritchard is quite definite that it is only intercourse with 'bulls' that could fall outside the category *rual*, while intercourse with the wives of other kinsfolk is included. The failure to be clear on this matter is yet another example of the way in which reports have been skewed by terminology that reflects the institutions of the society to which the anthropologist belongs rather than those of the society he is analysing. It must be admitted however that in so far as the Nuer classify offences with kinsfolk and the wives of kinsfolk in the same category, their concepts present a closer, albeit deceptive, approximation to our own than is the case with the other societies we have examined.

Let me now turn from the way in which the Nuer classify hetero-sexual offences terminologically to the sanctions with which a breach of the prohibition is met. The punishment of intercourse with women falling within the prohibited degrees of marriage is left to supernatural forces:

> there is no question of compensation, and the spiritual contamination which is considered to follow incest (*rual*) and which is manifested in physical disorders (*nueer*), sometimes resulting in death, falls equally on both parties and even upon their relatives (Howell 1954: 82-3).

A Comparative Approach to Incest and Adultery

The effectiveness of these sanctions varies with the genealogical distance between the two persons involved, for Howell later states that 'there is no great condemnation of sexual relations with distant clanswomen' (147).

The statement concerning intercourse with distant clanswomen strongly recalls the Tallensi situation. On the other hand, intercourse within the closer ranges of kin seems more heavily condemned among the Nuer. This is not easy to assess, as both authorities at times omit to state whether their remarks refer to a breach of the prohibition on sexual intercourse or a breach of the rule of exogamy. *Rual* appears to mean both these offences. Indeed it is possibly because of this identification that Evans-Pritchard, like Malinowski, regards incest as being linked so firmly with exogamy.

I now want to deal with the question of intercourse with the wives of kinsmen, or what I have previously referred to as group-wife offences. In a passage quoted above, Evans-Pritchard speaks of intercourse with the wives of agnatic kinsmen as being 'incestuous peccadillos or not incestuous at all' (1951: 45). It is clear that, if we accept the implication that such offences are excluded from the category *rual*, some differentiation in treatment is to be expected. The interesting feature of the Nuer case is that, according to Evans-Pritchard, group-wife offences are relatively lightly treated, a situation quite different from the other patrilineal case we have examined, namely the Tallensi. Before discussing a possible explanation of this phenomenon, it is necessary to turn to the other main authority on the Nuer.

Howell gives some additional information on intercourse with the wives of kinsmen, a subject which, significantly, he treats under the heading adultery rather than incest. I quote in full his main paragraph on this question:

ADULTERY WITH THE WIVES OF KINSMEN
The full rate of compensation is usually demanded unless the husband and the adulterer are on exceptionally good terms in other respects, or their relationship in the kinship structure is sufficiently close to modify feelings of moral indignation on the part of the husband. Although the wives of kinsmen are brought within the sphere of kinship by the process of marriage, and to have relations with the wife of a kinsman is in a sense tantamount to a breach of the rules of exogamy, this is modified by the feeling that a wife, acquired

29

by the transfer of cattle in which other kinsmen have limited rights, is theoretically the wife of all of them. Yet it is not considered correct that two kinsmen should have sexual relations with the same woman at the same period. There is no real conflict in these two concepts, but the attitude behind the payment of *yang kule* includes an idea that sexual relations with the legal wife of another man create an impurity, and that there is greater impurity if two men of the same kinship group have sexual relations with the same woman. It is felt that the wife of a kinsman is in some degree also a kinswoman, especially as a potential mother of kinsmen in the next generation. The act is therefore tantamount to incest (*rual*) (163-4).

It is difficult to compare the statements of the two authorities, for Howell speaks of the 'wives of close kinsmen' without indicating whether or not these kinsmen are agnates, while Evans-Pritchard is concerned specifically with these latter. But identity should perhaps be assumed from Howell's use of the phrase 'kinship group'. In any case the whole tenor of his remarks suggests that Evans-Pritchard's assessment of intercourse with the wives of close kinsmen as 'incestuous peccadillos' requires some modification. For although the greater part of the adultery payment may be waived, Howell specifically declares that 'adultery is an offence which brings greater spiritual dangers when the husband and the adulterer are kinsmen'. From this remark it would seem that Evans-Pritchard has perhaps neglected the spiritual dangers which intercourse with the wives of agnates involves.

Howell accounts for increased spiritual danger as well as the reduced compensation in cases of adultery with a group wife in terms of the conflict between the rule of exogamy and the corporate aspects of marital rights in women. He seems here to be falling into the error, also made by Evans-Pritchard, of confusing intra-group prohibitions (which have a direct relationship with prohibitions on marriage) and group-wife prohibitions (which clearly do not). And this confusion, deriving from Western European institutions, makes for some difficulty in interpreting the Nuer data.

Evans-Pritchard uses a similar explanation to account for the comparative leniency with which offences with the wives of agnates are dealt. This he contends can be easily understood by reference to 'the importance attached to children by the Nuer'. As it stands this explanation is inadequate, in that it could 'explain' intercourse not only with the wives of agnates, but also with any married women whatsoever. What Evans-Pritchard means is not the importance attached to children in themselves but the importance attached to children of the lineage, in other words to the continuity of the descent group. This relates to the argument I presented earlier. If we accept Evans-Pritchard's account of intercourse with agnates as a peccadillo, this is clearly a very different situation from the Tallensi one. Another variable is present. This is the extent of the corporate rights over the woman's sexual services. In any society with unilineal descent groups, there must be an incipient conflict between the individualized and corporate aspects of these rights. The Nuer, as distinct from the Brahmin and the Tallensi, tend to extend the corporate aspect to include rights over the woman's sexual services as well as her procreative capacity.

This interpretation receives support from the Nuer version of the common African prohibition on two members of a descent group having intercourse with the same woman. Among the Tallensi and the LoDagaa, this prohibition falls most severely on full siblings. Among the Nuer, however, the corporate character of rights over women receives greater emphasis and the situation is reversed; 'it is wrong for two kinsmen to court the same girl, *unless they are members of the same lineage*' (Evans-Pritchard, 1951: 45; my italics).

To sum up the Nuer evidence, two points emerge, despite some inconsistencies in the available data. Firstly, there does exist a somewhat similar differentiation of heterosexual offences to the threefold classification that was found in the other 'descent' societies. Whether or not there is any discrimination at the verbal level is not altogether clear, but there appears to be a valid distinction in terms of sanctions brought into play. The three categories are intercourse with the wife of a non-kinsman (simple adultery), intercourse with the wife of a clansman (or rather 'bull'), and intercourse with kinswomen and with the wives of kinsmen other than 'bulls'. The reference group is not merely ego's own patrilineal descent group; it also includes, as far as the last category is concerned, the mother's patriclan and other kin. But at the core of this range of kin lies the descent group. Secondly, although the evidence regarding the 'horror' reaction is ambiguous, it would seem that intercourse with the wives of patriclansmen is not regarded as severely as among the Tallensi or the LoDagaa. This does not I think invalidate the hypothesis that the differential incidence of the horror reaction to intercourse with group members and with group wives among the Tallensi and the Ashanti is related to the nature of the linearity of the major descent groups. What the Nuer material does is to bring out a further variable, namely the degree to which rights over women are vested in the descent group. Put in another way, this factor is the extent to which a distinction is made between rights over the reproductive powers of women and the rights over their sexual services. For where this distinction is emphasized, there appears to be greater individualization of the rights over sexual services.

Explanations of Incest

Once the distinction between intra-group and group-wife sexual offences has been understood the problems of the 'explanation' of incest, and of the relationship between incest and exogamy, can be seen in a new light. Explanations of incest fall into three categories. Firstly, there are those framed in terms of the internal relations of the group. These are associated with writers who have concentrated their attention on sexual prohibitions within the elementary family: Freud, Radcliffe-Brown, Malinowski, Brenda Seligman, Murdock, Parsons, and others. Secondly, there are those framed in terms of the external relations of the group, which are associated principally with Tylor, Fortune, and Lévi-Strauss. In the third category fall the biological, psychological-genetic variety. With this last I am not concerned here, although I am aware that they find their way into the formulations of some of the writers mentioned above. I take the two sociological hypotheses as my starting point not because I automatically assume that they will serve as complete explanations, but because for heuristic purposes it seems to me desirable to see how far one can get with these before employing theories which from the sociologist's standpoint are residual.

The two sociological theories are normally viewed as alternatives and a considerable literature has accrued as to their relative merits. Brenda Seligman has already summarized this discussion, herself coming down on the side of internal relations. Her argument is worth presenting not only because it gives some idea of how the discussion has developed but also because it deals fairly with both points of view. She writes:

Dr. R. F. Fortune ... considers that the barrier itself is adopted not because of its internal value to the family, but because the external value of the marriage alliance is essential to social structure (1950: 313).

She distinguishes two types of incest. 'One is the union of parent and child, the other is of siblings of opposite sex' (306). And she maintains that, while the marriage alliance might account for the brother-sister taboo, it cannot possibly explain the parent-child prohibition. There-fore, she concludes, it is the internal value of the arrangement which is the most important aspect of incest. 'With the prohibition of incest within the elementary family, the foundation of social structure is laid' (307). Thus she succeeds in categorizing heterosexual offences on generation lines and perceives that different explanations might be appropriate to each. But she fails to dichotomize either in terms of group members and group wives, or in terms of the structure of unilineal descent groups. The reason for this appears to be her commit-ment to the Malinowskian stress on the elementary family. If this is seen as the primary unit in relation to which the incest taboo functions, then the only possible breakdown of incest is by generation. The point elaborated in this paper is that, in the analysis of 'descent societies', a further breakdown is necessary, and exists within the actor frame of reference either in the terms used or in the sanctions employed. But the breakdown is made according to whether the prohibition is on inter-course with a group member or with a group wife; and the groups in question are in general based upon unilineal descent. It is from this point of view that explanations of incest and exogamy must be con-sidered.

Incest and exogamy are usually analysed as related prohibitions, the one on intercourse, the other on marriage. For example, Evans-Pritchard in his study of the Nuer maintains that the former is derived from the latter. Malinowski sometimes speaks of incest and exogamy as if they were entirely complementary. This point of view arises from a failure to make the distinction discussed above. For while the rule prohibiting marriage inside the group (exogamy) may be associated with the prohibition on intercourse within the group (intra-group prohibition), it cannot possibly be related, in any direct manner, to the prohibition on intercourse with the wives of the group, for these women must of necessity fall within the general category of permitted spouse. They cannot possibly be excluded by any marriage rule.

Exogamy, then, can only be related to the prohibition on intra-group intercourse. But as Fortes has shown, there need be no complete overlap even here. The Tallensi allow sexual intercourse with distant clansmen where they do not allow marriage. The reason is clear. Marriage affects the alignment of relationships between groups; it has to be publicly validated by overt transactions, and it provides a precedent for similar arrangements in the future. Sexual intercourse in itself does none of this, and therefore when carried on in semi-secrecy requires no realignment of social relations. And indeed, as Fortes has also shown, under certain conditions there may be advantages for the individuals concerned if the lover is forbidden as a spouse, for then these relationships are necessarily of limited duration. Within groups of more restricted span, however, intercourse between members can render other social relations difficult. This is especially true where the relationship is characterized by superordination, as for example between members of adjacent generations.

Although there is no inevitable overlap between the prohibition of intra-group intercourse and the prohibition of intra-group marriage, there is nevertheless a strong tendency for such an overlap to occur. Exogamy is frequently phrased in terms of kinship ... 'We cannot marry our "sisters".' So is the intra-group sexual taboo ... 'We cannot sleep with our "sisters".' It is true that the classificatory reference of the term 'sister' may not be the same in the two cases. This is so with the Tallensi. In the first instance 'sister' refers to clan females as a whole, in the second, to those belonging to the inner or medial lineage. But the principle of structural congruence acts in favour of the same referent in both cases. And indeed the prohibition on temporary sexual relations and the prohibition on semi-permanent sexual relations are patently not unrelated.

If therefore the rule of exogamy is to be related to the external value of the marriage alliance, as Tylor and others have suggested, I think correctly, then the intra-group prohibition on intercourse cannot be dissociated from it. The rejection of temporary sexuality within the group is in part a reflection of the rejection of permanent sexuality, and the latter is related to the importance of establishing inter-group relationships by the exchange of rights in women.

Let us now turn to the prohibition on intercourse with those who have married members of the descent group. This is spoken of by Seligman, Fortes, and many others as incest. Yet clearly the explanations of Fortune, Lévi-Strauss and others concerning marriage alliances have no bearing at all upon this phenomenon, because it is not intercourse with the women as such that is forbidden, but intercourse with them as wives of group members. Rights over their sexual services have been pre-empted by other males with whom one has prior relationships. These women are not necessarily consanguineal kin at all, with the exception of ego's mother; they are affines. Moreover, when the specific relationship with the member of the descent group ceases, then they may be legitimate sexual partners. In many cases one is in fact obliged to marry them when their husband dies, because of one's relationship with the dead man. Now this type of prohibition has nothing directly to do with marriage alliances, but rather with the other explanation which has been put forward, namely, the necessity of preserving the structure, not merely of the 'family', for there would then be no need for a rule of any extensive application, but rather of the descent group. For where rights of sexual access are individualized, conflict over females may be a cause of internecine dispute, and this prohibition renders such disputes less likely. It is indeed closely related to the taboo, found among the Tallensi and among many other African peoples, against more than one clansman having sexual relationships with one woman during the same period.

Conclusions

The current sociological explanations of incest are not, then, alternatives. Explanations in terms of external relations are relevant to the prohibitions on intra-group intercourse, while those in terms of internal relations are primarily relevant to the group-wife prohibition, although they also bear upon the intra-group taboo. Exogamy can be related to the former, but not to the latter.

This paper has attempted to establish a typology of heterosexual prohibitions to facilitate both cross-cultural studies and the depth analysis of particular societies. The typology depends in the first place upon a distinction between women who are considered to belong to the group and women who are married to its male members. In the societies with which the discussion has been mainly concerned, the reference group is the unilineal descent group rather than the elementary family. It is impossible to relate the concepts 'incest' and 'exogamy' when one term is held to refer to a bilateral group, the family, and the other to a unilineal one, the clan or lineage. It is impossible to account for the different sanctions placed upon these acts among the patrilineal Tallensi and the matrilineal Ashanti unless one introduces the system of descent as a variable. For the 'grisly horror of incest' is not a universal characteristic of all heterosexual offences with kinswomen and the wives of kinsmen. The reactions to a breach vary within and between societies. This is a fact which psychologists venturing into the cross-cultural field have often forgotten. Indeed, so concerned have they been with their own findings that they have tended, even more than anthropologists, to impose the categories derived from their own institutions upon the other societies with which they have been concerned. This is noticeable even in the type cases which psychologists have taken from classical Greek mythology. The nature of early Greek society makes it possible that their system of classification was closer to the patrilineal societies of Africa than the bilateral ones of modern Europe.

Like anthropologists, sociologists and psychologists dealing with our own society have patently failed to realize the ethnocentric nature of their categories. They have tended to treat 'incest' as an isolate instead of examining the system of prohibitions as a whole in relation to the social structure. Thus there is a quite disproportionate amount of literature devoted to 'incest' as compared to 'adultery', yet from the standpoint of social problems the latter would seem to deserve the greater attention. But the lure of the exotic has overcome the attraction of the mundane.

The study of 'incest' in any society must be related not merely to the analysis of marriage prohibitions or preferences, but also to 'adultery', so that it can be seen within the total constellation of sexual offences within that society. And this can only be done by accepting a breakdown of the monolithic category 'incest' into concepts more closely related to the structure of the society in question.

A Comparative Approach to Incest and Adultery

NOTES

1. An earlier version of this chapter was read to the Graduate Seminar of the Department of Social Relations, Harvard, in March 1956.

2. In the course of this paper I have reconsidered some of the data presented by my teachers, Meyer Fortes and E. E. Evans-Pritchard. What may appear as a criticism is in fact a compliment to their work. In the first place, their monographs on the Tallensi and the Nuer remain the most outstanding analyses of the social systems of non-European societies which have been written, and it is because of this fact that I am able to offer such a reinterpretation. In the second place, I am trying to carry their analysis a stage further within the framework of the general approach which they have done so much to develop.

3. In constructing this table I have followed Rattray's presentation of the offences except in the last category of section B (*atwebenefie* 2). Here is his list for this category (1929: 320):

Adultery with   i a brother's wife
           ii a son's wife
           iii wife's mother
           iv an uncle's wife
           v wife of anyone of same *fekuo* (company)
           vi wife of anyone of same trade or guild
           vii wife of one's own slave
           viii father's wife, other than the adulterer's own mother
           ix wife's sister, married or single.

In all these instances, the punishment is an adultery payment less or more than the standard amount. In addition, an animal has in some cases to be provided for a sacrifice; if a man has committed an offence with his wife's mother he then has to appease his wife with a gift. I have assumed that in i, ii, iv, viii, Rattray was referring to classificatory kin and have therefore reinterpreted the prohibitions in the way shown in the table. It should be added that the wives of fellow company and guild members are called 'wife'. Apart from affines, this particular category of 'vaginas too near' refers to classificatory wives, wives of group members.

4. This formulation was suggested to me in another context by Max Gluckman who told me that it originated with Radcliffe-Brown.

REFERENCES

Evans-Pritchard, E. E., 1949, 'Nuer Rules of Exogamy and Incest' in *Social Structure*, ed. M. Fortes, Oxford. 1951, *Kinship and Marriage Among the Nuer*. Oxford.

Fortes, M., 1936, 'Kinship, Incest and Exogamy of the Northern Territories of the Gold Coast' in *Custom is King*, ed. L. H. D. Buxton, London. 1949, *The Web of Kinship Among the Tallensi*. London.

Howell, P. P., 1954, *A Manual of Nuer Law*. London.

Malinowski, B., 1929, *The Sexual Life of Savages*. London.

Murdock, G. P., 1949, *Social Structure*, New York, Macmillan. 1955, 'Changing Emphases in Social Structure', *Southwestern J. of Anthrop.*, 11, 361–70.

Radcliffe-Brown, A. R., 1950, 'Introduction' to *African Systems of Kinship and Marriage*. London.

Rattray, R. S., 1929, *Ashanti Law and Constitution*. Oxford.

Seligman, B., 1950, 'Incest and Exogamy: a Reconsideration', *Am. Anthrop.*, **52** 305–16.

CHAPTER THREE

The Mother's Brother and the Sister's Son in West Africa

THE first section of this chapter consists of a critical review of recent discussions of the relationship of mother's brother and sister's son, with particular reference to patrilineal societies.[1] The second section offers definitions of certain terms used in the subsequent analysis. The third contains an examination of the 'patrilineal' case of the LoWiili and in somewhat greater detail of the 'matrilineal' case of the LoDagaba. The fourth section attempts an alternative explanation of certain of the customs which have been reported as characterizing the relationship in a number of patrilineal societies all over the world, especially the custom of 'ritual stealing'. And finally I comment upon parallel institutions in matrilineal societies in the light of the general hypothesis put forward.

I

(i) Radcliffe-Brown; the Original Hypothesis
In his essay 'The Mother's Brother in South Africa' (1924) Radcliffe-Brown authoritatively disposed of the explanation of the importance of the mother's brother in patrilineal societies as a 'survival' of matrilineal descent. He examined the reports of the relationships in Junod's material on the BaThonga of South Africa, and compared these with his own observations in Fiji and in the Friendly Islands (Tonga), noting in each case the power exercised by the sister's son over the possessions of his mother's brother, especially the custom of what Evans-Pritchard later called 'ritual stealing'. The essence of his alternative explanation is stated in these words:

Since it is from his mother that he expects care and indulgence he looks for the same sort of treatment from the people of his mother's group. .... The patterns that thus arise in relation to ... the mother are generalized and extended to the kindred (1952: 25).

The extension takes place in terms of what he calls 'the equivalence of brothers' (1952: 18), which was later to become the principle of the equivalence of siblings.

Radcliffe-Brown's analysis of the mother's brother-sister's son relationship in patrilineal societies underwent some changes as he developed his seminal contributions to kinship theory, in that additional hypotheses were produced. But the 'extension of sentiment' hypothesis was never abandoned.[2] It is repeated in his discussion of joking relationships (1952: 98–9), and again in the introduction to *African Systems of Kinship and Marriage* (1950). He writes:

> The mother, though she must, of course, exercise some discipline over her young children, is primarily the person who gives affectionate care. Just as the relation to the father is extended to his sibling group, so the relation to the mother is extended to hers (36).

As the earlier theory has been extensively adopted in later publications (e.g. Homans 1951; Homans and Schneider 1955), I shall begin by discussing why it appears inadequate to deal with my own field material.

In the first place, though Radcliffe-Brown noted the difference between what he called *avunculi potestas* and *patria potestas*, his hypothesis contains no explicit statement of why the generalization of sentiments should not occur in matrilineal societies, where mothers are presumably no less indulgent to their children. Evans-Pritchard (1929) and Homans (1951) both attempt to deal with this by assuming that the matrilineal case involves the imposition of specific external factors upon a general social situation.

But even in patrilineal systems, and this is our second criticism, the extension of sentiment hypotheses leaves much unaccounted for. Is the custom of 'ritual stealing' found among the LoDagaa and the Tallensi as well as the BaThonga, the Fijians, and the Tonga, properly interpreted as an indication of indulgence on the part of the mother's brother? The element of violence observed in Fiji (Hocart 1915) and among the BaThonga as well as by myself suggests that the term 'privileged aggression' is as appropriate a description as Radcliffe-Brown's 'privileged familiarity'. This privileged familiarity he later speaks of as a joking relationship. But if one turns to the Tallensi (Fortes 1949), behaviour towards the mother's full brother certainly has a strong element of respect. This is indicated by the fact that he is sometimes spoken of as 'like a father' and at others as 'like a mother', a formulation quite in accord with his position as a male member of the mother's agnatic descent group of senior generation to ego.

Fortes' material on the Tallensi makes it clear that the mother's role too is less simple than the hypothesis admits. On the extension argument, the maternal spirits should be more favourably disposed than the paternal ones. Yet among the Tallensi, the mother's spirit is stated to be the most capricious of all (Radcliffe-Brown 1952: 27; Fortes 1949: 235).

It is true that an attempt can be made to meet such empirical discrepancies by the assumption that what in fact is being 'extended' is an 'ambivalent' attitude towards the mother, who is at the same time provider and authority figure, and this may have some relevance in considering ancestor worship. But no simple hypothesis of extension can account for the variations in behaviour towards the 'mother's brother' and 'sister's son' depending upon the social (here, genealogical) distance between the two. On this point, the LoDagaa material will show that we cannot view the relationships either in matrilineal or patrilineal societies as being solely determined by the structure of the domestic group (to give Radcliffe-Brown's hypothesis a somewhat more sociological twist) and from there 'extended' outwards. This is to make the same mistake as to see 'incest' in a purely domestic setting (see Chapter 2). We must take into account both the more inclusive system of descent groups and associated institutions such as norms of residence, inheritance, and succession.

This leads to the third and major criticism. For the hypothesis not only assumes that sentiments are generated in the domestic family and then extended outwards, but also that the child's behaviour towards his mother's brother is an extension of sentiments spontaneously aroused in the child as a direct response to the mother's indulgence. Thus attention is concentrated on the filial generation. The customary forms of behaviour in fact imply an additional assumption, that in a patrilineal society a man extends his indulgence from his sister to her children. But in fact Radcliffe-Brown tended to adopt the standpoint of the junior partner in the relationship, as his selection of customs characterizing the relationship (1952: 16) and his final explanation (29) both demonstrate. One aspect of this tendency is the emphasis on the privilege-rights of the sister's son, little consideration being given to the question of any reciprocal demand-rights on the part of the mother's brother.

Such an approach not only gives a one-sided view of the relationship, it also leads to explanations of standardized actions in genetic terms. Hocart (1937) has criticized the related problem of the 'extensionist' view of kinship terminology, but he does so from a phylogenetic standpoint, maintaining that it is wrong to think of 'classificatory' systems as evolving from 'descriptive' ones. The extension of sentiment hypothesis however is based upon what Malinowski called 'sociological ontogenesis'. The fault of such a method is that it explains an institution such as 'ritual stealing' by reference to a hypothetical mechanism whereby the norms of society are transmitted to a new entrant. This type of 'explanation' may have a genetic validity; it does not have a sociological one. A discussion of the process of identification ('extension') does not explain why certain identifications are made in one society and not in another.

The confusion was not peculiar to Radcliffe-Brown. Malinowski went to even greater lengths with his 'biographical method' concentrating on the 'initial situation'. As Evans-Pritchard put it at the time (1929), kinship behaviour is thought of as built up by 'an extension of intra-family sentiments'. In a general discussion of Malinowski's theories of kinship, Fortes has shown to what extent the rejection of the 'mock-algebra' of Rivers and his school, together with commitment to the 'biographical method', hindered his analysis of kinship (1957).

It would have been unnecessary to attempt a refutation of the earlier hypothesis if it had been completely superseded. But Radcliffe-Brown never altogether rejected the extentionist argument despite his later contributions to kinship theory. Furthermore, this hypothesis has had considerable influence, and has formed the theoretical basis of an analysis of cross-cousin marriage by Homans and Schneider (1955). By adopting it these authors inevitably tend to examine the social structure from the family outwards, and in particular from the point of view of the junior generation. Thus matrilateral cross-cousin marriage in patrilineal societies is explained in terms of the generalization of the male ego's sentiment of liking from his mother to his mother's brother to his mother's brother's daughter. Following the patterns of research in temporary, minimally structured small groups, the authors attempt to explain institutionalized arrangements by reference to ego's sentiments. In so doing, they neglect not only the existence of a cultural tradition, but also the standpoint of the senior generation and their hand in promoting these marriages.

The difficulties arising from such an approach are not entirely obviated by a recognition of the limitations of the 'biographical method'. The dangers are more subtle for they are built into a number of the basic terms of social anthropology, which therefore predispose the user towards an analysis of kinship from the standpoint either of the domestic family or the filial generation. This seems implicit in concepts such as 'extension' and phrases such as 'matrilateral relationships', 'matrilateral cross-cousin marriage', or 'complementary filiation'.

To take the concept of 'extension', this is clearly indispensable if one starts from the Malinowskian point of view that kinship and clanship are recreated at each generation. But when one examines these customs between kinsmen as part of the body of standardized norms transmitted from generation to generation, it is surely irrelevant. Yet anthropologists often speak of the 'extension of kinship terms', or 'extended kinship', as if the analysis of kinship should invariably take as its baseline, not merely the elementary family, but the junior generation at that. This is particularly the case with kinship terms. Their application within the elementary family is given a primacy which, on further examination, turns out to be a primacy only from the point of view of the new entrant into society. It is true that in most cases the child first learns to apply kinship terms within the elementary family. But this fact does not mean that an analysis of the operation of kinship terminology and behaviour in a particular social system must take this learning situation as the primary point of reference of any attempt to explain these standardized procedures. Indeed such an assumption may well be confusing. As will appear from my own data, the primary referent may equally well be regarded as the common element in a range of accepted usages of a given kinship term, and therefore most apparent in membership of the most inclusive category to which the term refers, rather than the most specific.

While terms like 'matrilateral' and 'filiation' do not necessarily imply the domestic family as the point of departure, they do encourage an examination of social relationships from the standpoint of the junior partner. In the following section, therefore, I have suggested some alternatives. For concepts like these predispose the user towards hypotheses of the kind embodied in much of Malinowski's thinking on kinship, as well as in Radcliffe-Brown's essay on the mother's brother. These theories fitted well with Malinowski's discovery of the 'universality of the family' and with much contemporary psychological work which placed great importance on learning processes and the experiences of early childhood. But for the sociologists, this concentration upon the filial generation of the domestic family had a number of severe limitations, in particular the tendency to reduce analysis to ontogenetic terms.

(ii) Evans-Pritchard

In a brief contribution to *Man* written some years later, Evans-Pritchard (1929; and his reply to Hogbin, 1932) perceives some of the difficulties of the early hypothesis of Radcliffe-Brown and supplements it by the suggestion that the analysis of the mother's brother-sister's son relationship cannot be satisfactorily undertaken without considering the interaction between the members of the senior generation, a man, his wife, and her brother. For it is not only directly that the child learns but also by observing the behaviour of these persons one to another. And where the relationship between the parents and the mother's brother differs, this 'clash of sentiments' produces in the child an ambivalent attitude towards him. In patrilineal societies, this is expressed in 'ritual stealing', but in matrilineal societies the greater tension between a man and his wife's brother (here he instanced the transfer of property characterizing the relationship in the Trobriands) resulted in increased hostility between sister's son and mother's brother, which takes different forms of expression.

Evans-Pritchard's paper contains a number of interesting suggestions, such as the necessity for considering the changes which take place in relationships as a result of the movement of actors through the life cycle. More specifically concerned with our criticism of Radcliffe-Brown's earlier hypothesis is his emphasis on the interrelationships of the senior generation, and the brief consideration given to the influence of institutions such as inheritance and residence upon kinship relations. In stressing the senior generation he anticipated to some extent the analysis of Lévi-Strauss, while the discussion of ambivalence is taken up in the later theories of Radcliffe-Brown and his pupil, Sol Tax. But at that time he was firmly committed to the view that kinship behaviour was an extension of intra-familial attitudes; the strong emphasis on the standpoint of the growing child again goes with a tendency to explain institutions in terms of learning processes. As a result he did not develop the full implications of his insights.

(iii) Lévi-Strauss

Where Radcliffe-Brown had emphasized the filial, Lévi-Strauss stresses the affinal. While the former dwelt on the filial end of this inter-generational relationship between close kin, the latter quite transfers the focus of attention to the intragenerational relationships of the senior actors, in particular those between members of different kin-groups ('families') rather than those between close kin.

Lévi-Strauss' discussion of the mother's brother-sister's son relationship occurs in the course of a paper attempting to show the implications of linguistics for anthropology (1945). Starting explicitly from Radcliffe-Brown's first essay he praises the discovery that the father and mother's brother form 'two pairs of antitheses' which vary with the system of descent (*filiation*); where the relationship between the mother's brother and sister's son is strict (=negative), the relationship between father and son is one of familiarity (=positive), and vice versa. He criticizes Radcliffe-Brown for failing to realize that the 'avunculate' is not present in all societies with descent systems, a comment which appears somewhat misplaced in view of the fact that Radcliffe-Brown is not dealing in terms of any such isolate. But his major criticism is that the avuncular relationship consists not of two but of four elements; 'it supposes a brother, a sister, a brother-in-law, and a nephew'. In fact, of course, Radcliffe-Brown specifies not two but four actors, namely, ego, his father, his mother, her brother, and, if we take into account his total argument, a fifth, the father's sister. The same four actors appear in

45

both instances, but it is their relational roles which are differently specified.

Lévi-Strauss' comment reflects a certain failure to be clear about whether the units of analysis (the elements of the basic structure) are actors or roles,[3] a point which is later brought out by the fact that he speaks of the four elements as 'brother, sister, father, son' (48) instead of brother, sister, brother-in-law, and nephew. But what is more significant here is Lévi-Strauss' choice of roles. Characteristically this selection emphasizes the interrelationships of the senior generation and thus gives a primacy to affinity, a standpoint quite in keeping with his general view that 'the relationship between "brothers-in-law" is the necessary axis around which the kinship structure is built' (48). Indeed *intragenerational* relationships dominate the scene to such an extent that in the analysis of an *intergenerational* relationship, one between members of the parental and filial generations, he is led to ask the rhetorical question, 'why should the child issuing from the marriage in the elementary structure intervene?'—the elementary structure here being reduced to the senior generation. To this he gives the reply that 'the child is indispensable in validating the dynamic and teleological character of the initial step, which establishes kinship on the basis of and through marriage' (1963 : 47).

The assumption that 'kinship is built through marriage' dominates much of the writings of Lévi-Strauss, and it carries the corollary that the relationships between kin groups are primarily affinal. Here he seems to fall into a chicken-and-egg fallacy in some ways akin to Malinowski's 'sociological ontogenesis', which reduced extra-familial institutions to intra-familial ones. But in this case intergenerational relationships are reduced to intragenerational ones. Of course every filial relationship is dependent upon a marriage; but the opposite is equally true. It is clear that, both from the actor's and from the observer's point of view, relationships of affinity and kinship, relationships within and between generations, coexist within the social system at any one moment in time. The allocation of primacy to one set as against the other would seem to be a misapplication of developmental analysis (see Goody 1958). It leads to even affinal relationships being considered largely in intragenerational terms; the brother-in-law relationship is seen as the basis of all kinship; while 'incest' is exclusively treated as the brother-sister taboo. On the level of descent groups, the emphasis on the 'game' of exchanging women (1956: 282) neglects the contemporaneous existence within the social system of the ties of extra-clan kinship.

These theoretical weaknesses also appear in certain publications written under the influence of Lévi-Strauss' work. In his analysis of Dravidian kinship terms, Dumont claims that the relationship of a man with his mother's brother should be regarded as one of 'alliance' (affinity between persons of the same sex) rather than 'kinship' (residually defined), an interpretation which reflects his Lévi-Straussian view that 'marriage is in a sense the whole of society' (1953: 39). As Radcliffe-Brown points out in a characteristically incisive reply (1953), Dravidian systems, like Australian and some Melanesian systems, have no distinct affinal terminology, since by the incorporation of a rule of kin marriage, affinity is built into the kinship system. In such societies, a cross-cousin marriage rule means that there is no mother's-brother relationship which is not at the same time an 'affinal', or potentially affinal, relationship, either for the man under a matrilateral rule or for the woman under a patrilateral one.

Such systems must be treated differently from the ones with which we are concerned, a fact which Dumont recognizes in his reply to Radcliffe-Brown. Although there is perhaps a grain of truth in his suggestion that Radcliffe-Brown plays down their affinal component, his own attempt to categorize the relationship with mother's brother as one of 'alliance' *rather* than 'kin' derives from the much more one-sided approach of Lévi-Strauss. In dealing with these societies is there any need to regard the concepts of affinity and kinship as necessarily exclusive?

I have so far been concerned with Lévi-Strauss' criticism of Radcliffe-Brown and certain general theoretical implications which it reveals. His positive suggestion is this. Just as the relationships of a male ego with his father and his mother's brother form a pair of antitheses, so do relations with his wife and sister; where one is positive, the other is negative. The author briefly examines a number of societies to support this view. Unlike Evans-Pritchard, he proposes no necessary relationship between these antithetical pairs. Indeed he even abandons the accepted correlation of behaviour to father and mother's brother with systems of descent, on the basis of the somewhat sketchy data on the 'patrilineal' Kutubu supplied by F. E. Williams after a visit of four months' duration.

I would myself regard the Kutubu material as too slight to call for a rejection of the suggested correlation with descent, even though I believe this requires some refinement. Lévi-Strauss, however, is not concerned to link variations in kinship behaviour to other institutions, but only to demonstrate the existence of the two antithetical pairs. The material and method by which the second pair of antitheses are established also seem open to alternative conclusions, for the positive and negative categories of brother-sister, husband-wife relationships are ill-defined. But, given their establishment, what does this add up to? Lévi-Strauss concludes that we have a structure

> based on four terms (brother, sister, father and son) united among themselves by two pairs of correlative antitheses so that, in each of two generations in question, there is always one positive and one negative relationship. What then is this structure and what can be its cause? The answer is as follows: this structure is the simplest kinship structure which is conceivable and which could exist. It is properly speaking the rudiments of kinship.

This somewhat flat conclusion is in keeping with the inspiration from some linguistic sources; when a C(onsonant) V(owel), VC relationship has been shown to exist within two or more distinct sets of terms, one rests content with the demonstration of symmetry; the discussion is ended. But is it? The study of social institutions cannot afford to accept such restrictive practices, which fail to allow for the interaction of kinship and affinity with other institutions. While Evans-Pritchard's suggestion for other possible kinship correlations, with the father-mother's brother 'antithesis' is well worth pursuing, Lévi-Strauss does not seem in this paper to have advanced the study of these institutions.

(iv) Tax and Radcliffe-Brown's Later Hypothesis

More directly in line with Evans-Pritchard's paper of 1929 was the development largely sponsored by Radcliffe-Brown himself but not published by him until 1940. Radcliffe-Brown by now accepted that the mother's brother role was not simply indulgent, but 'ambivalent' in the same way as other joking relationships. Applying Radcliffe-Brown's 'principles', Tax (1937) notes that by the 'sex principle' the brother respects his sister and hence her child, while by the 'generation principle' the child respects its parents and therefore their siblings. This situation is settled in matrilineal societies by female dominance which sets the mother's brother above the child, while in patrilineal societies, no such solution is possible and the ambivalence results in a joking relationship (27). The difficulty about this type of explanation is that by manipulation of the 'principles' other results can be obtained. Why for example should the 'sex principle' be operative in the relationships between brother and sister rather than the 'equivalence of siblings' as Radcliffe-Brown had originally maintained? Moreover, once having introduced a supplementary explanatory principle of 'female dominance', the way is open to the introduction of other such external factors, such as the structure of unilineal descent groups, mode of transmitting property, etc. This in fact is what Radcliffe-Brown himself does in his second contribution to the discussion. In his paper 'On Joking Relationships' (1940), he attempts to show that such relationships occur when there is both conjunction and disjunction, and he goes on to explain how the mother's brother-sister's son relationship fits in with this:

> A person's most important duties and rights attach him to his paternal relatives, living and dead. It is to his patrilineal lineage or clan that he belongs. For the members of his mother's lineage he is an outsider, though one for whom they have a very special and tender interest . . . here again there is . . . both attachment . . . and separation.

In this succinct statement of the relationship of the mother's brother and sister's son in a patrilineal society, we have reached a point from which our analysis can begin.

II

TERMS EMPLOYED

In the following sections, we shall be dealing with the complications of extra-clan kinship in societies with descent groups based on both methods of reckoning descent. It is therefore especially important to be precise in our terminological usage. In particular I am concerned to distinguish between patrilateral and matrilateral relationships, and patrilineal and matrilineal relationships. By patrilineal and matrilineal relationships, I mean those which occur between two persons by virtue of their membership of the same descent group. By descent group I mean a segment (Nadel 1951) whose membership is determined unilineally, and whose members regard themselves as of common descent. Descent, as I here use the term, is unilineal by definition and 'applies only to the mode of determining membership of a social group' (Rivers 1914; II, 90; see also Firth, 1956: 17). I speak of matrilineal descent when eligibility for both males and females is acquired through females, and patrilineal when it is obtained through males. Although the transmission of offices and property is also described by means of the same pair of terms, the usage carries somewhat different implications because rights of inheritance and succession, unlike the membership of kin-groups, are usually sex-linked and therefore apply to males or females only. This distinction is central to my analysis.

I speak then of any relationship as matrilineal or patrilineal when the actors are both members of the same descent group; whereas relationships traced through the sibling *residual* to the reckoning of descent are matrilateral in a patrilineal system and patrilateral in a matrilineal system. It is the first degree of matrilateral ties with which Radcliffe-Brown is concerned, namely the mother's brother-sister's son relationship in a patrilineal society.[4] At the second ascending generation matrilateral relationships dichotomize into relationships with members of the father's mother's patrilineal group and those with members of the mother's mother's patrilineal group. These are the second degree of matrilateral ties and to distinguish them we may use the somewhat clumsy terms patri-matrilateral and matri-matrilateral. The recognition of these relationships traced through the residual sibling and arising from what Fortes (1953) has called 'complementary filiation' may be carried back yet farther in some societies, to the third and fourth generation. For the LoDagaa, only the matrilateral relationships of the first and second degree are important and of these the relationships with the father's mother's patrilineal group are more important than those with the mother's mother's, despite the fact that the same kinship terms are employed in each case. This feature of matrilateral relationships must be associated with the system of descent groups. The father's mother's group is attached to ego's patriclan by one female link, the mother's mother's by two. In terms of the structure of patrilineal groups the latter is more distant. In this paper I will only be concerned with matrilateral relationships of the first degree, and I mention this point only by way of elucidating the concepts I employ.

I have here made use of the term matrilateral, which in a previous section I criticized as possibly leading to the analysis of the relationship purely from the standpoint of the junior generation, for a relationship traced through the mother. It must be remembered that we are dealing with relational roles and that any matrilateral relationship, though from the junior partner's standpoint traced through the mother, is at the same time a sororilateral relationship, in that from the senior partner's standpoint it is traced through a sister. Equally any patrilateral relationship in a matrilineal context is at the same time a fratrilateral relationship, because in this case it is the male members of the group who are residual to the reckoning of descent. In order to emphasize the relational aspect and to avoid the use of a double set of terms, I propose to speak of the relationships traced through the residual sibling as uxorilateral (through women) in a patrilineal context and virilateral (through men) in a matrilineal one. Terms such as matrilateral which imply a positional reference point I shall use to indicate only one aspect of the relationship, the relationship as viewed from one actor's point of view.

III

THE LODAGAA

(i) The Formal Differentiation of Roles

My own fieldwork data is derived from two communities in the north-west of northern Ghana, which I refer to separately as the LoWiili and the LoDagaba, and collectively as the LoDagaa.[5] They are sedentary hoe farmers, cultivating guinea-corn, millet, maize, and some root crops. From the point of view of their economy, and in many other ways, they are very similar to the Tallensi. However, both LoDagaa communities, in addition to a system of named, dispersed patriclans with localized clan sectors distributed over widely separated parishes, also have named non-localized matriclans. A clan sector is the subdivision of a clan localized within a particular parish or settlement. Among the LoWiili it is segmented into a limited number of patrilineages of shallow depth. The central difference between the two communities is this: among the LoWiili, all property is vested in the patriclan, and the matriclan plays relatively little part in social life. Among the LoDagaba, property is divided into two categories, which may be referred to as immovable and movable, the former being vested in the patriclan and the latter in the matriclan. This corresponds broadly to the distinction between 'capital' and 'income'. Immovable property consists of the main productive resources, land, the tools with which it is exploited, and the houses built on it. Movable property consists of the ends of production rather than the means, namely, the harvested crops, money, and cattle. Reproductive resources, rights over women, fall into an intermediate position, being vested in matriclansmen who are also members of the same patriclan.

In these systems of dual clanship the same classificatory kinship terms apply within both the patrilineal and matrilineal descent groups. The term for 'mother's brother' is *madeb* and literally means 'mother male'. It is applied to male members not only of the mother's patriclan but also to male members of her (and therefore ego's own) matriclan. Indeed, among the LoWiili we may distinguish four analytically separable types of relationship which are designated by the term *madeb*. They are:

> *madeb* 1. The mother's full brothers, the eldest being somewhat differentiated from the others.
> *madeb* 2. Male members of the same patrilineage and same generation as *madeb* 1.
> *madeb* 3. Male members of the mother's patriclan, irrespective of generation.
> *madeb* 4. Male members of ego's matriclan of the same generation as mother.

The reciprocal, *arbile*, can be broken down in a similar way.

> *arbile* 1. Male and female children of ego's full sisters.
> *arbile* 2. Children of the female members of the same patrilineage and of the same generation as ego.

arbile 3. Children of all female members of ego's patriclan.
arbile 4. (plural only) Members of an adjacent patrilineage or clan sector of a different patriclan whose founding ancestor is said to be the son of a female member of ego's patriclan.
arbile 5. Male and female members of ego's matriclan of junior generation.

Three comments on the above table are required as a preliminary to further discussion. In the first place, difference in number of the subdivisions attributed to the role categories *madeb* and *arbile* is deceptive.[6] The additional role within the *arbile* category is *arbile* 4. A clan sector may sometimes speak of another clan sector as 'our sister's sons' in a particular context. Clearly not everyone in these groups can be related to each other as sister's son and mother's brother except under a system of obligatory cross-cousin marriage. No such rule exists among the LoWiili. I have heard this usage only from senior members of the clan sector of the first arrivals in a particular area referring to clan sectors descended from persons visualized as later migrants. These subsequent movements are seen as occurring within the framework of sororilateral relationships. A sister's son comes to live with his mother's brother and begs land from him to farm and build his house. Thus the spatial position of two adjacent lineages, and their ritual relationships to the Earth (for the custodianship of the local Earth shrine is vested in the clan sector thought of as descended from the first settler) are conceptualized in terms of the acquisition of land by a sister's son from a mother's brother. The use of the kinship term, 'sister's son', is thought of by the actors as derived from this initial event, although the observer may regard it as referring to the contemporary scene. Logically it should be balanced by a similar usage of *madeb*, and indeed such a usage, always implied, may well exist. But although the descent groups of the later arrivals might agree that their founding ancestor was related to the clans of the first comers through a female, they would be most unlikely themselves to refer to that group in general as 'our mother's brothers'. For this would indicate a generation difference and therefore inequality. And apart from the matter of ritual rights and duties, certainly as much a responsibility as a privilege, the segments of LoDagaa society display the essential characteristic of a typical acephalous system, namely that they are structurally equal (Goody 1957). The question of matrilateral cross-cousin marriage apart, this fact is in itself incompatible with a consistent application of the terms *madeb* and *arbile* between lineages or clan sectors among the LoDagaa.

The second preliminary comment concerns the sexual imbalance in the use of the kinship terms *madeb* and *arbile*. The former designates males only, the latter males and females. Throughout this analysis I have concentrated on the position of the sister's son and neglected that of the sister's daughter. For the introduction of differentiation by sex renders the relationship qualitatively different. Because property is usually sex-linked in African societies, and because most of that which is not so linked is none the less transmitted between members of the same sex, the relationships between members of opposite sex are rarely of the holder-heir variety. The BaThonga customs obtaining between sister's sons and mother's brothers are mostly connected in some way with property. Females are by definition unconcerned with such property and consequently the standardized aspects of their relationships with their mother's brothers differ considerably from those of their male siblings. Among the LoWiili, for example, they do not 'snatch' in the same way. Because of these differences, I shall confine my attention to the relationship between mother's brother and sister's son, but the explanation offered attempts to account for these sex differences in a way the extension hypothesis fails to do.

My third preliminary comment concerns the nature of the mother's brother-sister's son relationships in dual descent systems. Within the system of patrilineal descent groups these are uxorilateral (matrilateral) relationships. Within the system of matrilineal descent groups they are matrilineal ones. The classificatory terms are applied with reference to both systems of descent groups. This is so among both the LoWiili and the LoDagaba. The boundaries of these groups differ slightly in the two communities, but in principle the terminological usages are the same. This is certainly not true of behaviour. Because the matrilineal descent groups of the LoDagaba are property holding, the relationship between close matrilineal kin is complicated by the presence of a holder-heir component. Among the LoWiili this is thrown entirely on patrilineal kin. As far as this relationship is concerned, the LoWiili represent a variant of the typical patrilineal pattern discussed by Radcliffe-Brown, whereas the LoDagaba approximate to the matrilineal type. In dealing with the LoWiili, therefore, the matrilineal as distinct from the uxorilateral aspects of the relationship are relatively unimportant, and it will be upon the latter that I shall concentrate. In any case, as far as terminology is concerned, *yeb* (brother) is a more frequent usage for *madeb* 4 and *arbile* 5; for generation differences are rarely relevant within the matriclan when the relationships between matri-kinsfolk are not overlaid by a holder-heir component.

Having made these preliminary comments, I want to expand two main points made in discussing Radcliffe-Brown's original hypothesis in the light of my own data. Firstly, I pointed out that this relationship cannot be satisfactorily analysed from the point of view of one actor only. This is to some extent demonstrated by the fact that the two terms are not mirror opposites one of another. As I have mentioned, *madeb* is used by a person of either sex to address or refer to a male, while *arbile* is used by a male to address or refer to a person of either sex. Moreover, the classificatory usages of the terms are quite distinct. From ego's point of view his 'mother's brothers' (*madeb* 2) are all to be found in one lineage. In fact they *are* the male core of the lineage group, for it is virtually only in the mother's brothers' compound itself that generation differences are recognized; outside this group, the principle of the unity of the patriclan is operative in kinship terminology. Ego's relationship with *madeb* 2 is therefore a relationship between an individual and a segment of a descent group.

On the other hand ego's relationship with *arbile* 2 is a relationship with a category of kin dispersed in many patriclans, all of whom have certain rights and duties towards him. The classificatory usage of the term (*arbile* 2 and 3) is determined not by the descent group of the person addressed, as with *madeb* 2, but in both cases (2 and 3) with reference to the speaker's own descent group, that is, the mother's brother's group. It is true that a clan sector may sometimes speak of another such group as 'our sister's sons' (*arbile* 4) but the genealogical reference here is primarily to the founding ancestor of the second group, the spatial position of which may be conceptualized in terms of the acquisition of land from a mother's brother. In all other contexts the classificatory usage of *madeb* 2 and 3 refers to membership of a descent group and of *arbile* 2 and 3 to membership of a category of dispersed kin. This is bound to be the case unless there is a rule of prescribed marriage. Otherwise, as far as the system of patrilineal groups is concerned, a man's 'mother's brothers' are located in one descent group, his 'sister's sons' in many. Moreover, a man's descent group has a classificatory relationship with its 'sister's sons', which it does not normally have with its 'mother's brothers'. As has often been pointed out, matrilateral ties usually tend to *differentiate* the members of a patrilineal descent group, providing distinguishing reference points for the children of different mothers in a polygynous household.

Radcliffe-Brown's list of practices which typify the mother's brother-sister's son relationship among the BaThonga mentions only the rights of a sister's son vis-à-vis his maternal uncle. There is little indication of any concomitant duties, an omission which I have suggested may possibly stem from the adoption of the genetic approach. In the LoDagaa case the rights have corresponding duties. As among the BaThonga and the Tallensi, a LoWiili may snatch a portion of a sacrifice offered by his 'mother's brother'. When a patrilineage jointly performs a grave sacrifice to its ancestors, the 'sister's sons' of all its members are entitled as a body to snatch (*ara*) the front leg of the slaughtered animal. Indeed this is probably the derivation of the kinship term, *arbile*. But this privilege has a concomitant duty. The 'sister's sons' cut the throat of the first offering made on such an occasion, for they are able to appease the ancestors of their maternal lineage on behalf of those who have sinned. The snatching of the meat is in part the privilege of those who can 'throw ashes' and 'make hot things cold'.

In other words, the *madeb-arbile* relationship must be seen as a whole and not solely from the standpoint of the junior generation. But—and this was the point made earlier in criticizing Radcliffe-Brown's original hypothesis—even accepting this standpoint, the extensionist argument fails to take account of the differences in behaviour within the 'mother's brother-sister's son' relationship, depending upon the social distance between the two actors involved. The use of a single kinship term indicates a complete uniformity neither of sentiment nor of overt behaviour.

I have already mentioned the three analytic subdivisions of the category *madeb* which fall within the system of patrilineal descent groups. Among the LoWiili, whom I shall first discuss, they are similar in many respects to the three subdivisions which Fortes notes among the Tallensi.

The relationship with mother's full brothers (*madeb* 1) is characterized by a certain degree of respect. Indeed such relatives demand respect of the same order as that required by parents and members of the patriclan of the next senior generation. It is certainly not a joking relationship in any ordinary sense of the term.

The relationship with members of the mother's patrilineage of same generation (*madeb* 2) is not dissimilar. The sister's son is himself almost a member of this group, and I have often heard him spoken of as *ti yirsob*, a member of our 'house' or patrilineage. Indeed, so close is this sister's son (*arbile* 2) considered to be that the snatching by him of a portion of the sacrifice destined for the 'sister's sons' is regarded as incompatible with these ties. 'With such a person, we share. He cannot seize from us. When we cry, he cries.'

When one of these 'mother's brothers' dies, a man may marry his widow without any payment of the brideprice, if he succeeds in attracting her. But the offspring belong to the dead man's patriclan, not to that of the new husband.

It is only with members of his mother's patriclan outside of her patrilineage (*madeb* 3) that a man carries on anything that can be described as a joking relationship. It is from such relatives that a man will enforce by snatching his claim to the left front leg of the sacrificial animal. It is from them too that, when he reaches puberty, he asks for arrows to fill his first quiver.

A similar, though not identical, pattern of relationships emerges among the LoDagaba, who inherit movable property through females. The terminology is similar but the norms very different. Unlike patrilineal societies, the first sub-category of the mother's brother-sister's son relationship is complicated by the presence of a holder-heir component. It is here that the greatest differences exist.

Madeb 2 includes all the mother's patriclansmen, generation differences rarely being recognized outside the members of her own dwelling group. Among the LoDagaba, there are no distinct patrilineages forming definite segments of wider units. The local sector of the patriclan corresponds in certain respects to the patrilineage of the LoWiili. The reciprocal tasks carried out between patrilineages of the same patriclan sector among the LoWiili are here carried out by the local sectors of linked patriclans. The relationship with the 'mother's brothers' of one's mother's patriclan is free from the particular tensions which characterize the specifically matrilineal relationship with *madeb* 1. But the friendliness which is often apparent in no way resembles familiarity and 'joking' is out of the question. Again, one shares rather than snatches.

Madeb 3 includes members of the mother's linked patriclan. Linked patriclans are united by a vague tradition of common origin and separated on the question of exogamy. Structurally the linked patriclan of the LoDagaba corresponds among the LoWiili to the other constituent patrilineage of the same patriclan sector. It is from the members of this group that one can snatch and with them that one can joke.

The examination of the LoWiili and LoDagaba emphasizes that the roles subsumed under the term *madeb*, 'male mother', and *arbile* can best be considered not as one but several. The critical points defining the different relationships with the kinsmen so designated are provided by the boundaries of certain significant social groups whose principle of recruitment is that of unilineal descent. This reinforces the evidence provided by the Tallensi situation. No hypothesis of an 'extension of sentiment' can account for these variations in attitude within the category 'mother's brothers'. It is a problem which has to be viewed from the point of view of the mother's membership of a descent group as well as from the standpoint of the sister's son.

(ii) Differences Between the 'Patrilineal' and the 'Matrilineal' Case
Although terminological usage and the pattern of role differentiation are broadly similar in the two communities, the mother's brother-sister's son relationship differs greatly. Among the LoWiili the relationship is similar to that obtaining among patrilineal societies such as the Tallensi and the BaThonga; among the LoDagaba it resembles that reported for matrilineal societies like the Ashanti and the Trobriands.

The matrilineal case is typified by the Ashanti proverb recorded by Rattray that 'a sister's son is his mother's brother's enemy, waiting for him to die so that he may inherit' (Fortes 1950: 272; 1929: 20). Fortes comments upon this that 'the critical element in the relation of mother's brother and sister's son is the latter's status as the former's prospective heir' (1950: 270). The patrilineal case, as typified by the BaThonga and the Tallensi, is quite different. The mother's brother is not a senior member of ego's descent group, and not therefore in a position to exercise jural authority over him on that account. His home is a place which as a youth one visits from time to time, that always constitutes a possible haven if trouble develops with one's own agnates. He is in other words one's nearest kinsman outside the clan, apart of course from the mother herself. There is undoubtedly less tension in the relationship in patrilineal than in matrilineal societies, and this appears to be balanced (in a general way) by the extra weight put upon the father-son relationship in the former.

The same differences are found among the two LoDagaa communities. For example, Delafosse, the first European observer to visit the Birifor, a neighbouring tribe to the LoDagaba and one whose social structure is very similar, was told that a 'neveu et héritier' would kill his mother's brother 'pour s'emparer de l'héritage' (1908: 158). Yet there are no apparent differences in the relationship between mothers and their children, as we would expect if the extension of sentiments hypothesis were correct. LoDagaba mothers are not noticeably less indulgent to their children than the LoWiili.

Nor can the differences be simply associated with the presence or absence of certain types of descent groups, for both societies have dual clanship, descent groups based upon both patrilineal and matrilineal reckoning. Moreover, residence and therefore domestic authority are the same in both cases. If then neither linearity nor yet the locus of domestic authority (Homans and Schneider 1955) provide the relevant variable, what does?

A clue to the answer is given by the quotations referring to the situation among the Ashanti and the Birifor. In both cases the hostility between the mother's brother and the sister's son is ascribed to the system of inheritance. In both cases the mother's brother-sister's son relationship is that of holder and heir. It is true that, unlike these societies, the LoDagaba have a double, not a single, system of inheritance of male property, land and other immovables being vested in the patriclan. But, in a system of agriculture where shifting cultivation appears to give a greater return and where sufficient land is available at not too great a distance, the category of property over which divergent interests appear most likely to arise is not land but wealth, and this is vested in the matriclan. The holder-heir tensions therefore fall mainly upon uterine kin.

Not only are these correlations apparent among the LoDagaa, they are consciously attributed by the actors themselves to the influence of uterine inheritance (*gbandiru*).

(iii) The 'Matrilineal' Case of the LoDagaba

Documentation for the 'patrilineal' type has been provided in my earlier study of the LoWiili (Goody 1956a). Both for general purposes of comparison and for the elucidation of the problem of the mother's brother in descent systems, I shall now do the same for the 'matrilineal' case of the LoDagaba.

The first point that struck me, on moving from the LoWiili, was the much greater 'interaction', in terms of a simple sociometric count, between *madeb* 1 and *arbile* 1. But the relationship is undoubtedly more full of tension as well. The case of Timbume is illustrative of this. His father died when he was still an adolescent and although his mother remained in the house he himself went to live with her full brother in the same village. He did not stay there long before running away to a Mission some forty miles distant. I would point out here that residence with the mother's brother is no more common in the community in which wealth is inherited matrilineally than among the LoWiili where it is not (Goody 1958).

From the mission Timbume went to the South and took a job as a steward. He first returned to his village for any length of time with me. His father had been a very energetic farmer and had been well off in local terms. All his wealth had been taken by his uterine kin. Timbume, it is true, had a claim on the land which his father had farmed and the bush areas belonging to his patriclan sector. But land in itself was not an object of great value. It was not in short supply near Tom and in any case he had alternative sources of supply within the village. Timbume was the recognized heir to his mother's full brother. His mother and her elder brother were both dead when we came to

Tom and, apart from a cripple, he was the next in line to inherit (Fig. 1).

Although Timbume had classificatory 'fathers' within his own patriclan sector, his interaction with his mother's full brother, Naale, was both greater and more intense. Indeed he spent much more time generally with members of his mother's patriclan sector than with his own agnates. Yet the relationship with Naale was far from being a

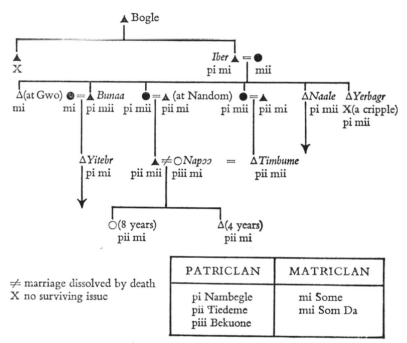

FIGURE I. Genealogy of Bogle's Descendants.

relaxed one. The year previous to our stay he had come on a visit and had given Naale a smock. Now he was asked for one of those he was using and he eventually allowed Naale to take this away without remonstrating. A little later he was asked for money to buy seed yams. To some extent Timbume was in a special position in respect of these monetary demands because he did not himself farm and it was therefore impossible for him to take a farming party to his uncle's farm, as was the normal practice. But he was not unique in having such demands made upon him. Indeed the exactions of one's mother's brother were a frequent subject of conversation among the young men. For although they did not argue this in front of their uncles, they often expressed their resentment in private. Yitebr, the son of Naale's elder full brother, now dead, had the same complaint. His mother's full brother lived in the near-by settlement of Gwo and when Yitebr came back from working in Kumasi he had gone there to pay his respects. He cycled over on the bicycle he had bought out of his wages. But his uncle had taken a fancy to the machine and Yitebr found he had to leave it with him.

Yitebr did not complain of the loss of the bicycle. He complained of the fact that his mother's brother had made no reciprocal prestation. Indeed, because his uncle had made no such transfer, he now only took two or three people to farm for him instead of a large farming party. Timbume felt the same way about Naale. They were both conscious of their position as heirs but they nevertheless expected return prestations within the lifetime of their uncles. 'Dead people's things (*kũ bume*) are not good', Yitebr explained. This statement carried ritual connotations, for inherited wealth has to be ritually treated. It is 'hot' and must be made 'cool' by a joking partner before the heir can touch it. But his words had a more immediately practical significance. For it might happen, as he explained to me, that the sister's son died first, in which case he would enjoy nothing of his uncle's goods. Or alternatively his uncle might dissipate the wealth he had acquired, on drink, gambling, or food.

In the end Timbume received a cow but Yitebr did not. Naale did not actually hand a cow over to Timbume but he called him to his compound one day and pointed one out. For a while Timbume was delighted and considered himself ahead on the prestations. Soon however, the difficulties inherent in the situation reasserted themselves. Timbume felt that, as with the rest of the property not specifically assigned to him, Naale might use it before it ever reached him. He would have liked to have gained physical possession of the animal so that he could hand it over to a 'friend' (implicitly, not a matrikinsman) to look after for him.

The fact that both mother's brother and sister's son belong to the same wealth-holding corporation means that the wealth which each individually possesses at any one time is in some sense subject to joint rights. Yet a change in possession within the matriclan creates a tension situation which can only be relieved by a reciprocal prestation. I say relieved rather than released because the structure of the situation is such that tension must inevitably be present between the holder and the heir. Such tension was quite explicit in the case of Yitebr and Timbume. It is equally explicit on the part of the mother's brother. I was visiting one day the house occupied by Landis, a man in his thirties, and found him being harangued by his mother's full brother, Dakpaala. Apparently Dakpaala had seen a small calabash of milk on the roof top and had spoken of his thirst. Landis said he had bought it from a Fulani herdsman to mix with his porridge, for himself and his children. There was too little to share all around. Dakpaala did not press his request for the milk but he became angry and abused Landis' clan sector in general. Two days later they met again by chance at my own compound and Dakpaala continued to express his disgust at the conduct of Landis' patriclan in various matters, though this time more quietly. Landis said little in reply. Like Timbume and Yitebr he could not express his feelings in the presence of his mother's brother. The latter had too much authority over him, ritual and otherwise.

Landis provided me with another illustration of the conflicts which arise, this time from the father's point of view. We were discussing the pros and cons of sending children to school and Landis spoke of the advantages of becoming a clerk, and particularly of the wage he could command. I asked him why he did not put any of his own children in school and he replied, 'What should I gain from that? If they stay with me we farm together and fill the granary. If they become clerks, only their mother's brother will gain.' Land and the actual produce of the land are vested in the patrilineal descent groups, but wealth belongs to the matriclan and comes under the control of the mother's brother. Among the LoWiili, as in patrilineal societies generally, father and son belong to the same wealth-holding corporation; among the LoDagaba they belong to different wealth-holding groups. Thus Landis did not wish to invest money in his children's education partly because they could not farm if they attended school. This objection, however, could have been overcome, had it not been that he visualized the interest from any investment he might make as accruing to the benefit of his brother-in-law, the children's mother's brother, rather than to himself.

In discussing the mother's brother-sister's son relationship among the LoWiili, I spoke of the institution of the *naab gwöl*, or Cow of Breeding (Goody 1956a). A mother's brother may 'lend' his sister's son a chicken to look after. When the chicken has grown to a hen and itself produced chicks, the sister's son will be given one of them. Sometimes the uncle will 'lend' a cow, and in some cases the sister's son is given half the calves but the cow and the other calves continue to belong to the mother's brother as long as he lives and to his heirs when he is dead. The cow I mentioned above as having been given to Timbume is different from this: it is an *arbile naab*, a Nephew's Cow, not a Cow of Breeding.

A Nephew's Cow belongs to the sister's son himself, and so do all the offspring. The only obligation resting on the recipient is the duty of providing one cow to be slaughtered at the funeral of his mother's brother. This cow (*kowel naab*, the Cow of the Dispersal of the Funeral) is killed in the dead man's name by his matriclan.

A Cow of Breeding is sometimes given by a LoDagaba uncle as among the LoWiili, but it happens much less frequently. A mother's full brother (*madeb* 1) gives his sister's son (*arbile* 1) a cow as his own; he does not merely lend him one to look after for him. Only a *madeb* 2 or 3 would do this, and then only a member of a different matriclan. It would be difficult, if not impossible, for a member of ego's own matriclan, and certainly his full mother's brother, to lend him anything in this way. In the eyes of the world at large such a transaction would inevitably be regarded as a transmission of corporate property *inter vivos*, a handing over, a change of possession, a *traditio*, of some object over which the parties had similar if not equivalent claims. Reciprocal prestations might be thought desirable, but no claim to the return of the objects themselves could ever be enforced.

The general point I wish to make here is this. In both societies the system of double clanship provides matrilineal and patrilineal reference groups for each kinship category. Ego's relationship with his mother's brother has both matrilineal and matrilateral components. In each society the institutions are differently weighted. It is not a question of totally different institutions but rather of differences of emphasis, a fact which adds considerably to the complexity of the analysis. The existence of corporate (in the sense of property-holding) matrilineal descent groups does not altogether eliminate the institution of the Cow of Breeding in favour of the Nephew's Cow. It does, however, emphasize the patrilineal character of that institution.

The same I think is true of the custom of 'snatching' which is so prominent a feature of the mother's brother-sister's son relationship among the BaThonga, the Tallensi, and the LoWiili. This is the feature which Radcliffe-Brown rightly singles out for discussion. Among the LoDagaba, 'snatching' by the sister's sons is not nearly so common as among the LoWiili. Indeed one is not permitted to snatch from one's mother's patriclan at all, but only from the clan which is linked to it by a vague tradition of common origin. As an institution 'snatching' exists in theory. But in practice it very rarely occurs. Among the LoWiili, on the other hand, the snatching of objects belonging to one's mother's patrilineal group occurs on many cere-monial occasions. Usually it consists of taking the left front leg of a sacrificial animal, often known as the 'sisters' sons' leg'. This is the case where a patrilineal group is offering a sacrifice, or where an individual is performing a sacrifice resulting from the obligations of patrilineal descent. Where a sacrifice is offered in a matrilineal context, the same leg is known as the 'joking partners' leg' and is allocated to the matri-clan standing in joking partnership to the matriclan involved. In both cases other legs are usually reserved for the 'fathers', 'brothers', and 'sons' of the individual or group concerned, although in the first instance these terms are interpreted within a framework of patrilineal descent groups and in the second they refer to the membership of matriclans. But there is a certain amount of variability due to the coexistence of these two main modes of disposing of the sacrificial meat. Both these modes of sacrifice exist in the two societies, but there is a greater emphasis on the matrilineal type in the society where property is inherited matrilineally and on the patrilineal type where property is inherited patrilineally. This difference follows not from a vague commitment to different 'value system's but because the objects of sacrifice, namely livestock, are vested in different descent corporations in the two communities.

The main type of matrilineal sacrifice occurs at funerals, the main type of patrilineal sacrifice is that to the ancestors. In saying that the LoDagaba place greater emphasis on the former and the LoWiili on the latter, I do not necessarily mean that this statement should be interpreted numerically. It would be very difficult to support such an assertion adequately. What I do mean is that in terms both of the provision and of the distribution of the sacrifice, no matter what type of sacrifice it may theoretically be, the actual methods will be strongly influenced by the prevailing mode, not of descent for that is constant, but of property transmission. To support this statement in detail would require a lengthy analysis. But I have already shown elsewhere how, for the LoWiili, the provision and distribution of the main animal killed at funerals, namely the Roof Cow or alternatively the Cow of the Dispersal of the Funeral, though made in a matriclan context, is effectively restricted to the patriclan of the dead man (Goody 1962). A very similar process occurs among the LoDagaba in respect of sacrifices to the ancestors.

In the study mentioned above, I compare funeral ceremonies and ancestor worship in the two communities, and link differences in these ritual institutions to the differences in the system of property relations. In both communities, ancestor worship is patrilineal, in that an ancestor shrine will only be created for a dead man if he leaves behind him an offspring who can carry out the ritual performances required. When the shrine has been created, it is aggregated to the other ancestor shrines kept in the dead man's compound. It therefore falls under the custodianship of his close patrilineal kin. In both communities only an agnate can actually address and sacrifice to the shrine. But, although the procedure of the sacrifice is the same, the provision and distribution of the animal vary. I attended six ancestral sacrifices among the LoWiili; in each case the donor was an agnate of the recipient. In four of the five LoDagaba cases I attended he was a uterine kinsman, though in two of these he was also an agnate. The prevailing kinship relationship of donor and recipient coincides with that of the holder and the heir. As donor, the heir is as it were returning in sacrifice part of what he received at the death of the holder. The recipient of the sacrifice, though not necessarily the same person as the individual from whom the wealth was received, nevertheless belongs to the same matriclan, the same wealth-holding unit.

66

In both cases these relationships vary with the property-holding corporations. They reflect the joint interest in wealth, a category which includes the objects of sacrifice, of uterine kinsfolk among the Lo-Dagaba and of patrilineal kinsfolk among the LoWiili. Broadly speaking, a diviner will only call upon a man to sacrifice to a uterine relative in the first and an agnate in the second community. The incidence of sacrifice reflects not only the differences in property relations, it also indicates the tensions which are implicit in the two systems. For the LoDagaa do not normally sacrifice to the ancestors to obtain their blessing on some future occasion, but rather to get them to moderate the anger which is harming their descendants in the here-now. There are certain annual offerings of a type associated with Rogation and Thanksgiving Ceremonies, the regular festivals of the productive cycle. But these irregular sacrifices are occasioned by the wrath which the ancestors visit upon their descendants as a result of a failure to fulfil certain of the recognized obligations that exist between the dead and the living. Among the LoDagaba these obligations are seen to exist mainly between uterine kinsmen, among the LoWiili between those related agnatically. In the former case, it is the anger of a uterine ancestor that is feared, in the latter case the spirit of a dead agnate.

Among the LoDagaba, therefore, a sister's son (*arbile* 1) is sometimes responsible for offering a sacrifice to his deceased kinsman. Whereas among the LoWiili it is the 'sister's sons' (*arbile* 3) who are entitled to the left front leg or *aro bɔɔ*, the Leg of Snatching. The snatching of part of the sacrifice is a corollary of their role as peacemakers for their mother's patriclan; as the nearest extra-clan kin they are in the best position to appeal to the matrilateral ancestors to put aside their wrath and to accept the sacrifice which is being offered them. I should add that, among the LoDagaba, the left front leg is also known as the *aro* or *arbile*'s leg. The children of 'sisters' can still theoretically fulfil this role; by 'sisters' here is meant the children of female members of the linked patriclan, for the elders would never permit children of the women of their own patriclan to do so. 'With them we share (*puon*); we all eat together (*ti zaa longna di*).' However, at no sacrifice that I attended did anyone snatch the *aro* leg, nor indeed did I see it given to the 'sister's sons' to divide among themselves. On one occasion I was told that no 'sister's sons' were present, so their portion had been included in the shares allocated to other categories. Upon another occasion, a cow provided by a sister's son out of the ones he inherited was sacrificed to the uncle, and the leg was indeed claimed by a man whose mother came from the linked patriclan of the recipient. But in fact he claimed it as a joking partner of the dead man (a member of the patriclan standing in a joking partnership to the deceased's clan), saying as he did so, 'I am throwing ashes' (*n loba tampello*), that is, making hot things cold. Leg and skin together were cut off for him to take away. Claims of those standing only in a 'sister's son' relationship were rejected. The snatching (*aro*) leg had become in effect a joking partner's (*lonluore*) leg, and the pattern of an ancestor sacrifice had been assimilated to that of the matrilineal funeral offering, even down to cutting off the leg together with skin, which a joking partner then takes to sew into a quiver. In other words, the important feature of the mother's brother-sister's son relationship in patrilineal societies, 'ritual stealing', is so played down among the LoDagaba that it is virtually non-existent, even in situations such as ancestral sacrifices, where patrilineal groups are of considerable significance. These variations are associated with other specific differences in the role of *arbile* and *madeb*. It is clearly difficult to operate a system in which certain categories of sister's sons (*arbile* 1 and 5) provide the sacrifice and share with the recipient (because of joint membership of a descent group) while other categories of sister's sons (*arbile* 3, and possibly 2) are in a position to snatch some of the meat because they are peripherally attached to another series of descent groups. In discussing the LoWiili, we have already noted that the variations within a role category (i.e. *arbile*, *madeb*) may be considerable, but the possibility suggested above would mean much more than this: it would involve a direct conflict of roles within a designated role category.

The relative absence of 'snatching' among the LoDagaba is clearly compatible with the difference in the attributes of the relational roles, *madeb* 1 and *arbile* 1. The categories 'mother's brothers' and 'sister's sons' represent persons with whom one shares, however unwillingly, rather than snatches. This sharing is not the same as the 'sharing' which the LoWiili sometimes say occurs between a man and his mother's patrilineage. The latter depends upon a particular occasion and a particular quality of interpersonal relationship; the former belongs to the jural order, in that it is obligatory and enforceable.

Rights in Women

Property was not the only cause of conflict between Timbume and his mother's brother. A certain uterine 'brother', his mother's full sister's son, had died some while back and left a widow with two children. The widow 'belonged' to Som Da (Timbume's matriclan) and also to his matrilineage. He was the heir to all the property and could therefore marry the widow without giving any bridewealth, other than a small amount of a ritual nature. Timbume went to consult his mother's brother, Naale, about this and Naale in turn consulted his 'friend' Dakpaala. It took several weeks before the widow and her children eventually came to live with Timbume. Even relatively straightforward negotiations between affines can drag on for a long time. Nor is any negotiation as straightforward as it at first appears. In the first place, the widow's paternal uncle (her own father was dead) wanted her to marry elsewhere. In the second, Naale had made attempts to get the woman for himself. Timbume heard this from Dakpaala, who expressed his strong disapproval. 'A mother's brother of the deceased cannot possibly inherit while a "brother" remains.' I do not think that, at the present time, Naale could ever have made good his claim. But my point here is that the conception of the widow as a Som Da spouse, the 'wife' of a matriclan, inevitably arouses the possibility of conflict among the members of the matriclan, anyhow among those who are close genealogically to the dead man, over the transmission of rights in her. This is rarely the case among the LoWiili, for there the transmission *causa mortis* of rights in a woman is recognized solely as a patrilineal matter. Moreover transmission between adjacent generations within the patriclan is forbidden. So that the holder-heir tensions over the transmission of sexual rights are of an exclusively intragenerational character, involving only agnatic 'brothers'.

Debt

A concept central to the differences in this relationship between these two communities is that of debt (*san*). On one occasion Naale gave Timbume some kola nuts to sell. It is not uncommon for men or women to buy some kola nuts in one of the six-day markets and bring them back to the village to sell to their neighbours. In this case Timbume was expected to sell the kola and hand the proceeds to his uncle, who would reap all the profit from this transaction. This method of investing capital in trade resembles that employed on a much more extensive scale by the paramount chief of Ashanti. But the LoDagaa case represents the employment of kinship authority to acquire wealth, while, in the Ashanti example, it is political authority which is so used.

Timbume was somewhat tardy about selling the kola, or rather about handing over the proceeds. Naale did not himself remind him of this, but asked his friend Dakpaala to do so. 'It isn't a debt', Timbume explained, 'but if I don't pay he will fight (*zebr*) with me. It can't be a debt, for it is my mother's things I am taking (*n ma bume n dena*)'. An alternative phrase expressing the same idea is *m ma biro n 'yeni*, 'it's my mother's milk I'm sucking'. I have heard the same remark made by a LoDagaba in the context of patrilineal property to explain the taking over of an area of land, cultivated or uncultivated, by a full sister's son who had been living with his mother's brother when the last of these agnates died. It is also used to describe the acquisition of land by a sister's son from a living mother's brother. Land is owned by patrilineal groups, but, say the LoDagaba, a person and his mother's 'house-people' (*yidem*, in this context, patriclan sector) have joint rights over uncultivated land (*long so a wie*). The meaning of this phrase is that should the 'house' become extinct, then a sororilateral kinsman becomes the next of kin; he has a residual claim to the property of his mother's patrilineage. Moreover, even at other times this residual claim cannot altogether be denied. If the son of a female member of the patriclan sector asks for land, the request must be seriously considered unless land is in short supply. Indeed, if land is vacant, it will be exceedingly difficult to refuse the request, for the nephew may just take up his hoe and farm, saying, 'It is my mother's milk I suck'. In other words, he will 'snatch' the land.

The taking of the property of the mother's brother is seen as mediated by the mother both when the property is vested in patrilineal groups, as is the case with the land, and when it is vested in matrilineal groups, as is the case with wealth (or movable property). The difference is this. Except of course in the event of the death of all its members, land can in theory be reclaimed by the patriclan sector, although in practice it rarely is. Whereas wealth cannot; there can be no debt between *madeb* 1 and *arbile* 1. The difference between the LoWiili and the LoDagaba in this respect is that among the former you cannot be in debt to your father, whereas among the latter you cannot (as far as wealth is concerned) be in debt to your mother's brother. The difference turns on the fact that among the LoDagaba the matriclan (the group to which both mother's brothers and sister's sons belong) is a property-holding corporation, while among the LoWiili it is not. This means that among the LoDagaba there can be no persistent debts between matriclan members because on one level they are thought of as holding joint rights in the group's property.

Witchcraft
To this fact are related a number of other differences, of which I want to refer briefly only to the institutions of witchcraft and slavery.

The concept of debt is related to the attacks of witches in the following manner. Among the LoDagaba it is said that if a witch attends a coven and feeds on the human flesh provided by witches of other matriclans, he or she will eventually be called upon to provide a victim for the feast. The debt incurred must eventually be repaid. To bring the soul of a person of another matriclan would be to incur another debt to the matriclan of the victim, just as to kill a member of a descent group by other means is visualized in terms of debt. Witches of the victim's group would object to an outsider attacking one of their members, for these are their prey. So the witch is forced to take the soul of a member of his own matriclan, for this one can do without incurring a debt, just as one can take his wealth. As a consequence, it is the witches of one's own matriclan who have especially to be feared. This was how the LoDagaba viewed the connection between witchcraft and matriclanship. But among the LoWiili on the other hand there was no such connection; uterine kinsmen could be in debt one to another and witchcraft was not confined within the matriclan. As in the case of the matrilineal Ashanti and the Agni to the south, the range of a witch's activities among the LoDagaba are broadly defined by the boundaries of the wealth-holding corporation. Although accusations are also made between spouses, it is those standing in an actual or

71

potential holder or heir relationship to an individual who are considered most likely to bewitch him.

Slavery

The concept of debt is also associated with the institution of slavery. To sell a fellow member of the ritual area or parish into slavery was an offence against the Earth in both communities (Goody 1957). Or rather it was and is an offence for the alienated individual to return to live there without performing certain sacrifices at the Earth shrine. His birthright has been sold. Nevertheless in times of hunger individuals were sold into slavery by their relatives, and indeed the act was often a welcome one, for, by reducing the number depending on an exiguous food supply, it relieved the suffering of both the seller and the sold. Among the LoWiili, *patria potestas* obtained; a man had the power of selling an agnatic descendant, a son or, better still, a dead brother's son. Among the LoDagaba *avunculi potestas* obtains. A father has no such power and, were he to act in the same way, he would incur a debt with his wife's matriclan. The power over life and death, to sell or to slay, is vested in the hands of the maternal uncle.

The occasion of a severe famine in the LoDagaba community of Tom, some time at the beginning of this century, provides a concrete instance of this power. At this time even the growing crops had to be guarded against marauders. One day a man sent all his cattle to market to be sold so that he could buy food (*bunderi*, a category that excludes meat). But a neighbour who belonged to the patriclan of the man's heir, a full sister's son, noticed this happening and seized the cattle as they were being driven through the bush. He took them and handed them over to the sister's son, saying that if the holder sold these, then the next time he needed money for food he would seize his heir and sell him. To prevent this they took charge of his funds until the famine had passed.

In such ways as this members of a matriclan become involved in each other's debts. This responsibility is recognized by the outside world. If a matriclansman falls into debt, then the creditor may attempt to seize (*faa*) some of the possessions of another member. The latter will resist the seizure, but once it has occured he will not usually retaliate. Instead he will put pressure on his matriclansman to pay him what was formerly owed to the seizor. This pressure varies according to whether the debtor is of the same generation or of a junior one. If he is of a junior generation, and it is the mother's brother who has been forced to pay the debt, the latter's reaction may be one of physical violence, particularly if the debt has been incurred by theft from a neighbour. If a youth turned out to be a continual thief, the right of the mother's brother to kill him was formerly recognized, though it was probably more usual for the individual to be sold into slavery.

Nowadays of course slavery no longer exists. But former slaves are still alive and reference to the institution is still made as an index of social relations. Despite changes in institutions, the mother's brother-sister's son relationship among the LoDagaba remains in most respects the same as it was before the advent of the Europeans at the start of the century. What this account has emphasized is the very different character of this relationship from the LoWiili one, and the fact that these differences turn on variations, not in the presence or absence of certain descent groups as such, but on the question of whether or not such descent groups are corporate in the sense of property-holding corporations. Property relations rather than descent groups or residence constitute the crucial variable here, although it should be added that they are not in most societies independent one of another.

I want to emphasize here that, although strictly speaking the holder-heir relationship concerns only a limited category of matrilineally defined mother's brothers and sister's sons, the question of the redistribution of property in fact concerns every member of the sibling group. Even if a man has an elder sibling who will inherit before him, he nevertheless stands to gain eventually by his uncle's death. There seems to me little doubt that the tensions are most acute between the eldest sister's son and the last surviving male member of the mother's sibling group. The relationships between Naale and Timbume on the one hand, and Yitebr and his uncle on the other, were both of this kind. Nevertheless the same complaints are heard from the lips of younger brothers. For these are still regarded by their mother's brothers as potential heirs and have therefore to perform certain duties for them. If they fail to bring parties to farm for their uncles, then the uncles will not supply them with the bridewealth for a second wife. It is the father's duty to provide for the first wife a man marries and his mother's brother's for the second. But only if he has received farming services will either feel bound to meet this obligation.

Moreover, there is nothing to indicate that a younger brother was less likely to be sold into slavery than an elder, or to have demands made upon his resources. In other words, the holder-heir situation, in the strict sense of the relationship between the actual holder and the next heir, must be viewed in the context of the fact that inheritance occurs within the framework of a unilineal descent group and is not merely the concern of two persons. From one point of view, and this is overtly expressed by the actors themselves, property is vested in the group as a whole. But administrative power over the fund is held by members of the senior generation, and it is they also who have control over the disposal of the human personnel. It is because the LoDagaba matriclan is a property-holding corporation that the members of the sibling group find themselves in opposition to those fellow members of the matriclan whom they regard as mothers' brothers. Of course some opposition exists even within the non-corporate LoWiili matriclan and is a function of the very differentiation of the group into senior and junior members. But the existence of property relations quite changes the nature of this opposition and gives rise to a situation of potential conflict.

I do not wish to suggest that among the LoDagaba *arbile* 1 and 5 and *madeb* 1 and 4 are always in a state of open hostility. This is certainly not so. Although the mother's brother is the property holder, he is not the main authority figure in the domestic group. Domestic authority is essentially linked to residence. Despite the mother's brother's power over life and death, the father is in fact the person who is responsible for his son's upbringing. For the domestic group is agnatically based; marriage is virilocal and, even in the event of divorce, the proper place for sons is at their father's side. So the conflicts inherent in the socialization process are in fact separated from those arising out of the holder-heir situation. Potestality and domestic authority are vested in different persons.[7] This is also the case in matrilineal societies with virilocal residence, whereas in patrilineal societies both are normally thrown upon the father-son relationship.

The existence of this split tends to permit a more overt form of holder-heir conflict than is perhaps the case where this relationship is coincidental with domestic authority. For if these coincide, whether in patrilineal or matrilineal societies, both relationships are confined within the dwelling group. I would maintain that the sanctions against the expression of the tensions arising from these two situations, which in some form are constant features of all societies, must be greater where such expression might lead to a disruption of the basic living-together units.

It cannot be assumed, therefore, that the strength of the hostile element in the mother's brother-sister's son relationship among the LoDagaba can be definitively gauged from the actor's own statements of the situation alone. Opposition between holder and heir is certainly more openly discussed among the LoDagaba than among the LoWiili, but this is partly to be accounted for in terms of the structure of dwelling groups rather than the strength of the hostility generated. At this point, however, the question cannot be fruitfully pursued by the techniques ordinarily available to the social anthropologist, and I shall return to the opening problem, which can.

IV

LATERAL RELATIONSHIPS IN PATRILINEAL CONTEXTS

I have already suggested that a satisfactory analysis of the customs noted by Radcliffe-Brown must begin from his later remark that, although the sister's son in a patrilineal system is an 'outsider', he is the object of 'tender interest' on the part of his mother's clan and that this convergence of conjunction and disjunction gives rise to a joking relationship. Let us consider this statement in relation to our comparison of the mother's brother-sister's son relationship among the two Lo-Dagaa communities. The crucial variable associated with the differences in the relationship was membership of a corporate descent group, corporate in the sense of property-holding. Whereas, in a matrilineal context, the mother's brother and sister's son are members of the same corporation, in a patrilineal context they are members of different ones. By unilineal reckoning one sex is excluded from transmitting rights to group membership, property, and office and in patrilineal systems this residual sibling is the sister. But patrilineal descent, inheritance and succession are each somewhat different in their impact on the problem

75

of the residual sibling and will therefore be separately considered. They are also to some degree independent variables.

As far as patrilineal descent is concerned, though a woman is born a member of the descent group, she cannot transmit her membership. Moreover, her membership rights themselves are restricted; partly as a result of virilocal marriage, her role is inevitably that of a jural minor. Although virilocal marriage may reduce a woman's participation in the activities of her patrilineal descent group, it does not change her membership of it—at least not in societies of the Tallensi-LoDagaa kind. Among the LoDagaa, a woman continues to refer to the wives of her agnatic brothers as 'our wives'; she participates in the ceremonies of her husband's group as a 'wife' rather than as a 'sister', and when death finally comes and her last funeral ceremony is performed, her ancestor shrine is carried back to the byre of her father's house.

I emphasize these points to differentiate the systems I am dealing with from those in which marriage is said to involve a change in member-ship of the descent groups. There are two possibilities here, complete incorporation into the husband's descent group, or dual allegiance, the result of both of which would be what Murdock calls 'compromise kin groups' (Murdock 1949: 67–8). Perhaps a third alternative is the 'unisexual kin-group' implied by Lévi-Strauss' view of marriage in which women are 'treated as a commodity submitted to transactions between male operators' (1956: 284); here the units of analysis tend to be groups of males, as in the case of Leach's 'local descent group' (1951: 24). Space forbids a discussion either of the empirical material relating to the incorporation and exclusion of women, or of the usefulness of the Lévi-Strauss approach as an analytic tool. But assuming the existence of such systems, it is necessary to note that, for them, the problem of the residual sibling would have different structural implications.

The problem of the residual sibling differs somewhat in the field of inheritance from that of descent. 'Patrilineal' inheritance likewise debars the sister from transmitting the property visualized as associated with the descent group, but in certain respects she suffers greater dis-abilities here than over group membership. For not only is she unable to *transmit* rights in the patrimony to her children, she cannot normally *exercise* those rights. Another factor thus enters into the situation. In most African societies, whatever the system of descent, rights in the basic productive resources are vested in men, a situation related to the different roles of the sexes in the productive and reproductive processes. Even categories of property which are not tied exclusively to one sex (i.e. *sex-linked*) are usually transmitted only between members of the same sex, male to male, female to female. Unlike the eligibility for membership of a descent group, which is transmitted to members of both sexes, property tends to be transmitted only between members of the same sex (*homogeneous transmission*). For if a person's property were to be transmitted to members of both sexes, it would become rapidly dispersed (*diverging transmission*). Whereas death disposes automatically of the problem of the residual sibling's membership of a descent group, his or her property remains and has either to be destroyed or transferred to another person. Consequently the basic property of any descent group, its patrimony, must be transmitted 'homogeneously' if it is to be limited to members of that group.

Despite the male-to-male inheritance of the patrimony in societies of the Tallensi type, a woman has nevertheless a submerged claim on the property of her patrilineal descent group. Among the LoDagaa, I encountered occasional instances of women who either as widows or as divorcées had returned to their natal homes and were allotted land on which to farm.

There is in a sense a basic contradiction between the principle of unilineal descent and the unity of the sibling group. For unilineal descent splits the sibling group into the sibling relevant for the reckoning of descent and the residual sibling who cannot transmit membership to his or her offspring. In societies with patrilineal descent this situation is aggravated by the disabilities placed upon females, especially under a system of 'homogeneous' transmission of property.

This conflict between the principle of unilineal descent and that of the equivalence of siblings is not merely an invention of the anthropologist. It is often recognized, in one form or another, by the actors themselves. Among the Tallensi and LoDagaa, a woman calls the wife of any of her 'brothers' by the term 'wife', that is, by the same term that her brother uses. A joking relationship exists between the two women in question. The explanation put forward is 'if I'd been a male, wouldn't she then have been my "wife"?' A similar phrasing is used to account for certain features of the uxorilateral relationships. It is not uncommon to find explanations initiated by the remark 'if my mother had been a man'. The rights and obligations of a person vis-à-vis both the members of his mother's patriclan and the offspring of his clans-women must be related to the qualified rights and obligations a woman possesses in her patrilineal descent group, to the rights she would have possessed had she been a man, and to the rights her offspring would have possessed had she not been the residual sibling.

The inherent contradiction is illustrated by a comparison of the position of a legitimate and illegitimate child among the LoWiili, the community inheriting patrilineally. A child born of an unmarried sister becomes a member of his mother's patriclan and can inherit property. Whereas the very act of legitimizing the child—by the marriage of his mother to an 'outsider'—excludes him both from the descent group itself and from a full claim upon its property.

But if he has no full claim, the legitimate sister's son has nevertheless a shadowy claim upon the group by virtue of his mother's position. In some societies this claim may be fully realized upon incorporation into the mother's patriclan, either if its numerical strength is weak, or if a man becomes the heir by virtue of the absence of close agnates of his mother's brother. And apart from such cases of the realization of a potential claim under special circumstances, the claim a man has on his mother's group, and the claim that group has on him, may be enacted in standardized behaviour between the mother's brother and the sister's son.

This is particularly clear in the context of property rights. In snatching objects from the mother's brother, the sister's son asserts the residual claim of the offspring of the non-descent sibling. In addition, he is in some respects acting on his mother's behalf, asserting her submerged rights in a manner that only a male can. The residual nature of the claim is demonstrated by the standardized form of aggressive behaviour. Like certain forms of joking, snatching is an act of privileged aggression rather than of privileged familiarity. By snatching a leg of the sacrifice he asserts a claim in the face of the opposition of the descent group itself, which cannot freely admit an outsider's right to its resources.

Among the LoWiili the snatching of part of the sacrifice has another aspect, connected not so much with the sister's son's exclusion from property rights as with his exclusion from group membership. Mother's brother and sister's son, each is the other's closest kinsman outside the descent group. Mention has already been made of the services a mother's brother can perform in acting as a haven in times of trouble. The nephew stands in a similar structural position and can assist his maternal 'uncles' when they are in difficulties. If a particularly serious sin has been committed against the ancestors by a living member of the lineage, the LoWiili offer a preliminary sacrifice, a peace offering, which indicates whether or not the ancestors are prepared to accept the expiatory offering itself. In a patrilineal context, the nearest kinsman not directly involved in the anger of the ancestors is the male offspring of a female member of a lineage, a sister's son. He it is whom the LoWiili select to perform this duty, and the seizure of the left front leg of the sacrifice is, on one level, a reciprocal payment for such a service. Indeed, the very presence of a sister's son may be considered as a ritual service, for if anything goes wrong, he is available to 'make hot things cool' by the ritual act of throwing ashes—ashes representing the cooling of the fire, the calm after the release of tension. Here, then, the custom has an additional aspect, the claim upon the flesh of the sacrificial animal, having as a concomitant duty the performance of certain ritual services for the individual or group concerned.

The widespread custom of the inheritance of a widow by the sister's son, found in such emphatically patrilineal societies as the Nuer and the Tallensi, fits logically into this framework. Fortes puts this very clearly when he writes, 'a "sister's son's" leviratic rights go back to the notion that his "mother" might have been a man and a "brother" of the dead man. He is exercising the rights that might have been his "mother's"; hence this, too, is a recognition of the equivalence of siblings' (1949: 275). The same custom exists among the LoWiili, although the dead man's lineage do not invariably acknowledge such claims. Moreover, it is linked to the terminological usage whereby a woman refers to her brother's spouse as 'my wife'. It is the person addressed as 'wife' by his mother over whom the sister's son has a claim on the death of the husband, his mother's brother. Rights over women are a type of male 'property'; her male offspring exercises residual rights. It should be noted that, even in Radcliffe-Brown's later analysis, there is no logical place for this custom. In 1941 he wrote that

79

this practice is 'found in African societies that are markedly patrilineal in their institutions. There does not seem to be any theoretical explanation that will apply to all the known instances of this custom' (1952: 81).

Other institutions which can be similarly explained are those which centre upon the claim a man may have to a bridewealth contribution from his mother's brother (e.g. among the Gusii, Mayer 1949), or the claim of the mother's brother upon the bridewealth received for his sister's daughter (e.g. among the Lakher, Leach 1957). Mayer speaks of the *emesuto* heifer contributed by the uncle who used his mother's brideprice to marry himself a wife as being 'specifically a return out of the bridewealth' (1949: 7). Equally the claim on a sister's daughter's bridewealth may be seen as a delayed payment rather than a subsequent repayment. But the very existence of such claims in respect of the *children* of the residual sibling illustrates once again the contradiction between the unity of the sibling group and virilineal (male-to-male) inheritance.

Assuming these conclusions to be correct, they will nevertheless apply only to societies with patrilineal descent groups and the transmission of property between male agnates. Excluded from consideration are those societies based either upon 'one-sex kin groups' or upon 'compromise kin groups', whether constituted by incorporation or by dual allegiance, as well as those systems of 'concubitant cousinhood' (Thomson 1908: 195) where the maternal uncle is at the same time the father-in-law. It is also essential to set aside the widespread system where patrilineal descent groups are found in conjunction with 'diverging transmission' of property, either *causa mortis* (through inheritance), or *intra vivos*, by such institutions as the dower proper. Societies of this type, which I intend to discuss in a subsequent work, are found in Oceania, Asia, the Near East, and in the Mediterranean world. They display important structural differences from those of the African type, especially in the sphere of marriage, marriage prestations, and the ease of change to other modes of reckoning descent (Goodenough 1955). It is clear that, in such systems, though the sister's children are excluded from membership of her patrilineal group, they are not excluded from the inheritance of property, which in default of specific mechanisms such as cross-cousin marriage is dispersed in both lines. The sister's son, though an 'outsider' in descent group terms, enjoys the property of both parents. Hence we might expect to find the customs associated with the role of extra-clan kin, but not those such as ritual stealing which have been linked with submerged property rights.

Empirically, however, the facts are otherwise. For one notable instance of ritual stealing occurs in a patrilineal system with the diverging transmission of property, namely Tonga. Fiji was somewhat similar, for while inheritance was normally between male agnates, the daughters of chiefs apparently received a landed dower (Roth 1953: 73).[8] I suggest that two factors are associated with the presence of ritual stealing in these societies. The first is agnatic succession to office. Unlike the LoDagaa, in Tonga and Fiji there are important offices to be transmitted from generation to generation. Offices, unlike property, are usually indivisible and pass from individual to individual. Moreover, though in these societies property may pass to both sexes, office is overwhelmingly transmitted agnatically through males (Gifford 1929: 153; Roth 1953: 73). This suggestion appears to be confirmed by the fact that ritual stealing (*vasu*) in Fiji is discussed by the main authorities in the context of chieftainship alone (Hocart 1915, 1923; Thomson 1908: 75), while one authority defines *vasu* as 'the relationship between a chief and his sister's son, under which the son had enormous privileges' (Roth 1953: 75). Of Tonga, Gifford writes that anciently the custom was not extensively practised among commoners. He adds that 'the institution of *fahu* is established in the lower strata of society as well as in the higher, but it reaches its most extravagant developments among the higher chiefs' (1929: 24). I suggest that one aspect of the *vasu* relationship is the exclusion of the sister's children from succession, in flagrant contradiction to their claims on property.

The second aspect of the privileged aggression of the sister's son in such systems is to be associated with the fact that though the woman and her offspring of both sexes may have a claim to certain property, it is nevertheless a considerably weaker claim than 'if she had been a man'. The institution of virilocal marriage makes this particularly true of immovable property such as land. Her claim, if no longer 'submerged', is at least 'subdominant' in comparison with that of her brothers. It is this subdominant claim which is asserted by the offspring in the form of 'ritual stealing'.[9]

V

LATERAL RELATIONSHIPS IN MATRILINEAL CONTEXTS

If this explanation of the relationship between mother's brother and sister's son in patrilineal contexts in terms of the membership of unilineal groups and the mode of property distribution is correct, it ought to be capable of application to virilateral relationships in matrilineal contexts, especially that between father and son. Is there any standardized behaviour here which is comparable to the 'snatching' in patrilineal societies?

It has been impossible within the compass of this paper to compare the 'father-son' relationships in these two communities, but I have in passing made various references to them. There was the LoDagaba father who argued that it was not worth his while sending his children to school because the wages they subsequently earned would only accrue to their mother's brother. He himself would have no full claim on the wealth which they accumulated independently. The corollary of this situation from the child's point of view is that the son has no full claim upon the property belonging to his father's group, just as the sister's son has no full claim upon his uncle's property when this is vested in a patrilineal group. On the other hand, just as the sister's son has a residual claim through the submerged rights of his mother in her patrilineal group, so the son has a residual claim to the matrilineal property of his father. The son has no full claim in a matrilineal system because the father is the residual sibling for the purpose of transmitting the property and membership of the matriclan. But the situations are not precisely symmetrical because, in most matrilineal systems, it is men not women who hold the significant rights in the group's property. Thus, in the LoDagaba matriclans, it is the males who control the group's property, whereas the women, though they act as agents for the purposes of transmission, do not in fact hold these rights. In a patrilineal society, a man's claim through the residual parent is, as it were, weaker than in a matrilineal society, because it is made through the member of the sibling group who is the jural minor, whose claim upon the property is 'submerged'. I suggest this is the reason why 'snatching' is apparently not characteristic of matrilineal systems. The residual rights of the 'sons' are granted fuller recognition than in the parallel case of a patrilineal society, for it is the residual sibling who actually enjoys the use of the property. His position is recognized in the institution of gifts *inter vivos*, a feature which has often been reported for matrilineal societies. Instead of the children of the residual sibling having to affirm their claim by 'snatching', they find that it is in fact acknowledged by the father and accepted, if at times unwillingly, by the members of his descent group as a legitimate institution. The property does not have to be snatched, it is given.

Gifts *inter vivos* among the Ashanti and, in certain contexts, among the LoDagaba are then comparable to the customs noted by Radcliffe-Brown among the patrilineal peoples of South Africa and subsequently reported for other patrilineal systems. Both are acknowledgments of claims through the residual sibling. By means of gifts *inter vivos* most LoDagaba fathers pass on a certain amount of their wealth to their sons; they recognize the residual claim of their sons on the property which is vested in their unilineal descent group. And this residual claim may be made on classificatory 'fathers' as well as on male parents.

A few days after Naale had taken a smock from him, Timbume, his sister's son, was visited by Yitebr, who asked for and was given a shirt. Yitebr was the son of Naale's elder brother and therefore Timbume was his patrilateral cross-cousin, his father's sister's child. Yitebr's own father was dead; his property had been inherited by Naale and would eventually go to Timbume. Timbume would then take over not only the property but also the responsibilities. For instance, he would be responsible for providing the bridewealth for the first wife of any of the dead man's sons if the father had not already discharged the obligation. On Naale's death, Timbume would become in some ways a proxy-father to Yitebr. Indeed Yitebr, when he wished to emphasize Timbume's responsibilities towards him, referred to him as 'my father' (*n sāā*). All members of his father's matriclan, which was called Som Da, could in fact be addressed in this way. Yitebr made, and Timbume acceded to, the request for the shirt because the former was a 'child' of the latter. Yitebr was a 'child' of the Som Da matriclan, but had the residual claim been made on these grounds alone, it is doubtful whether it would have been successful. What ensured success was Timbume's position as the prospective heir of Yitebr's father's full brother, the person who would act as his proxy-father in matrilineal contexts. Even while Naale was alive, the rights and duties of proxy-fatherhood were recognized. Yitebr's residual claim on the property of his 'father' was counterbalanced by the duty to obey the father's command. 'However far Timbume sent me', he said, 'I would go.'

In matrilineal groups, then, the offspring of the residual sibling are the sons of the male members. If the group is property-holding, they have no full claims on that property. But they have a residual claim through their fathers, who in fact control the property of their matri-clan. In patrilineal societies, the residual claim of the sister's sons is mediated by the female members of the groups who themselves have only submerged rights. Their claim often requires an aggressive affirmation. In matrilineal societies, the residual claim operates directly between males and consequently receives more open acknowledgment. This acknowledgment often takes the material form of gifts *inter vivos* between fathers and sons.

Conclusion

The first sections of this chapter reviewed earlier discussions concerning the relationship between the mother's brother and the sister's son. Radcliffe-Brown's early extension of sentiment hypothesis was found unsatisfactory for the explanation of the snatching of property by the sister's son in patrilineal societies, and objections were also raised to the ideas of those who, like Lévi-Strauss, assign a sort of structural primacy to affinal relations as against relationships of filiation.

The analysis of the fieldwork material began from the proposition that the relationships of a man with his father will be more full of tension in a patrilineal system than in a matrilineal one, the relationship with the mother's brother, less so. An examination of the two Lo-Dagaa communities in northern Ghana, the LoWiili and the LoDagaba, pointed to the desirability of refining these variables. Both had systems of double clanship but, in the second community, the matrilineal groups were property-holding. There was thus a shift in the holder-heir situation as between the two; in this respect the LoWiili approximated to the patrilineal type, the LoDagaba to the matrilineal.

This shift in the holder-heir situation was associated with a number of other differences. Although the kinship terminology and even the formal subdivision of the designated role categories were found to be similar in the two communities, nevertheless kinship behaviour varied considerably. Similar institutions exist in both societies, but the differences in the incidence of the holder-heir situation and in the corporateness of the descent groups gave them a different emphasis in each case.

These differences centred on the fact that, among the LoDagaba, there could be no debt between the mother's brother and the sister's son belonging to the same matriclan, because each held joint rights in the same fund. However, the necessity of allocating the administration of the fund to the senior generation creates a situation of potential conflict within the relationship. In many cases the relationship was dominated by tensions over property and rights in women. The institutions of slavery and witchcraft provided further evidence that differences in property relationships were related to differences in the character of the basic kinship relations. Thus in the dual clanship systems of the Lo-Wiili and the LoDagaba, there was seen to be a major difference between the matrilineal and uxorilateral aspects of the 'mother's brother-sister's son' relationship depending upon the location of holder and heir.

In the customs which Radcliffe-Brown took as his starting point for a discussion of the mother's brother-sister's son relationship, property also played a large part, the sister's son 'snatching' from members of his mother's patriclan. The alternative explanation put forward in this paper centred on a recognition of the contradiction between the unity of the sibling group and the disunity created by the operation of the rules of inheritance, succession and descent. In most societies women are jural minors, a fact connected with their reproductive functions. In patrilineal systems in Africa they are debarred not only from holding full rights in the major resources of the descent group, but also from acting as agents through which such rights are transmitted. However, although a woman is a jural minor and her children (even her sons) are excluded from enjoying the membership or property of her descent corporation, these sons nevertheless have certain residual rights which are expressed in customary behaviour towards the male members of her clan, his 'mother's brothers'. In terms of property, these residual rights are expressed in 'ritual stealing'; while in terms of group membership various acts, such as assistance on ritual occasions, the allocation of bridewealth received, and the contributions to bridewealth given, demonstrate the residual rights of a man in his mother's patriclan and, on the other hand, of the patriclan in their sister's children. The position of the offspring of the residual sibling is somewhat different in matrilineal contexts, but the transmission of property *inter vivos* between father and son is in a sense the counterpart of 'ritual stealing'.

Postscript

Since this chapter was written, further contributions to the discussion have been made. Dumont (1957) expands the thesis presented in his earlier article that in South India 'the role of the maternal uncle is of an affinal nature' (33), one of 'alliance' as opposed to 'kin'.

Beattie (1958) attempts to apply this point to systems without a built-in marriage rule and appears to fall into the chicken-and-egg fallacy when he writes of the mother's brother-sister's son relationship: 'Its nature can . . . only be understood when it is seen in the context of affinity, that is, as owing at least part of its character to the fact that the parties to it are members of two different groups, *originally* linked in the unequal *buko* (in-law) relationship' (21, my italics). In his paper Beattie in fact puts forward an explanation not dissimilar to Radcliffe-Brown's second hypothesis (1940), that is, in terms of 'complementary filiation', but he accepts a hangover from the ontogenetic assumption, implicit in much of the writing of Lévi-Strauss, Dumont, and others, that in inter-group relations marriage has some kind of structural primacy over ties of extra-clan kinship. A similar theme is manifest in Leach's discussion of bridewealth and marriage stability, particularly the statement that Fortes 'while recognizing that ties of affinity have comparable importance to ties of descent, disguises the former under his expression "complementary filiation" ' (1957: 54). Leach, who has signified his approval of Dumont's analysis of the maternal uncle in South India (Leach 1958), does not appear to allow for the necessary coexistence of affinal ties and extra-clan kinship in exogamous systems. Indeed, an examination of his diagrams (figs. 1 and 2) and of the accompanying discussion, indicates how distracting a 'model' can be; for all the relationships between members of different descent groups are shown and analysed as if they were of the affinal kind. It is hardly correct to analyse the relationship between descent groups as dependent upon affinal links alone, when those coexist with ties of extra-clan kinship which are not dependent upon the fragility of particular marriages.

Winter's excellent analysis of extra-clan kinship among the Bwamba (1956) demonstrates that such ties have the 'greatest importance for the large-scale organization of society' (190). He also stresses the point to which I have myself drawn attention, namely the differences in the classificatory aspects of the 'mother's brother' and the 'sister's son', and neatly relates this to the types of standardized acts associated with each role. His discussion is admirably free from ontogenetical reductionism of either the Lévi-Strauss or the Malinowski variety.

NOTES

1. Earlier versions of this paper have been read at seminars at Cambridge and Manchester (1953); I am most grateful to members of these groups for their comments, particularly to Meyer Fortes, my wife, Esther Newcomb Goody, and Max Gluckman.

2. In his appreciation of Radcliffe-Brown's achievement, Fortes over-emphasizes, I believe, the 'sociological' as against the 'psychological' or biographical aspects of the early work. Indeed his characterization of the final theory as an application of 'behaviour originating in the relationship of one member of a group to the other members' (1955: 20) and his own analysis of the 'extension of parental roles' (1949: 280) indicate a tendency to adopt the standpoint of the junior generation as the analytical baseline. On the other hand, Fortes was well aware of the other side of the picture and it is a suggestion made in his study of Tallensi kinship that this paper takes up.

3. This is related to a certain confusion between the analysis of ego-orientated kinship maps and the structure of unilineal descent groups which has characterized even the best of recent studies of cross-cousin marriage carried out under the shadow of Lévi-Strauss' *Les Structures elémentaires de la parenté* (1949); but this is a point which requires elaboration in a different context.

4. Although matrilateral relationships comprehend those with the mother's father, the mother's brother's son and the mother's brother, to mention only the male roles, I am primarily concerned with the last of these.

5. For a general account, see Goody 1956a, 1957, and 1958.

6. Nadel (1957) equates role as an analytic concept with role as an actor concept. His units of analysis are by definition the units employed by the actors themselves. For reasons which are explicit in the text, I prefer to distinguish between role as an analytic concept and role category as an actor concept.

7. The term potestality I take from Homans & Schneider (1955), where it is used with reference to the 'locus of jural authority'. By jural authority, they mean 'legitimate or constituted authority' which exists when 'according to the stated norms of his group' a person 'has the right to give them orders and they have the duty to obey' (21). The LoDagaba situation points to the desirability of

refining the concept. There both father and mother's brother have jural authority in Radcliffe-Brown's sense (1950: 11), in that it is capable of definition in terms of rights and duties. I therefore distinguish between domestic authority, which is in most cases vested in the main socializing agent, and potestality, by which I mean the ultimate powers, of a non-political order, over the disposal of a human being, here represented by the power of life and death and the power to sell into slavery. Whereas the domestic authority varies with the residence pattern, potestality appears in general to be linked to the holder-heir situation.

8. Thompson (1908: 372) describes the landed dower without any suggestion that it was limited to the daughters of chiefs.

9. Quain stated about the 'matrilineal' part of Fiji in which he worked that 'the term *vasu*, much discussed in the literature, is interpreted in Nakoroka to mean specifically the right to belong to the land of the mother' (1948: 182n.). This has particular interest in view of the association suggested between ritual stealing (Fiji, *vasu*; Tonga, *fahu*) and the exclusion from rights of succession and of inheritance.

REFERENCES

Beattie, J. H. M., 1958, 'Nyoro Marriage and Affinity', *Africa*, **28**, 1–22.

Delafosse, M., 1908, *Les Frontières de la Côte d'Ivoire, de la Côte d'Or et du Soudan*, Paris.

Dumont, L., 1953, 'The Dravidian Kinship Terminology as an Expression of Marriage', *Man*, 1953, 54 and 224.

Dumont, L., 1957, *Hierarchy and Marriage Alliance in South Indian Kinship*. Occasional Paper of the R. Anthrop. Inst., no. 12.

Evans-Pritchard, E. E., 1929, 'The Study of Kinship in Primitive Societies', *Man*, 1929, 148, and 1932, 7.

Firth, R., 1956, Introduction, *Two Studies of Kinship in London* (ed. Raymond Firth). London School of Economics, Monographs on Social Anthropology, no. 15, London.

Fortes, M., 1949, *The Web of Kinship among the Tallensi*, London.

Fortes, M., 1950, 'Kinship and Marriage among the Ashanti', in *African Systems of Kinship and Marriage* (eds. A. R. Radcliffe-Brown and D. Forde), London.

Fortes, M., 1955, Radcliffe-Brown's Contribution to the 'Study of Social Organization', *Brit. J. Sociology*, **6**, 16–30.

Fortes, M., 1957, 'Malinowski and the Study of Kinship', in *Man and Culture* (ed. Firth, R.), London.

Gifford, E. W., 1929, *Tongan Society*, Bernice P. Bishop Museum Bull., no. 61, Hawaii.

Goodenough, W. H., 1955, 'A Problem in Malayo-Polynesian Social Organization', *Amer. Anthrop.*, **57**, 71–83.

Goody, J., 1956a, *The Social Organization of the LoWiili*, Colonial Research Studies, no. 19, London.

Goody, J., 1956b, 'A Comparative Approach to Incest and Adultery', *Brit. J. Sociology*, **8**, 286–305, reprinted as chapter 2.

Goody, J., 1957, 'Fields of Social Control among the LoDagaba', *J. R. Anthrop. Inst.*, **87**, 75–104.

The Mother's Brother and the Sister's Son in West Africa

Goody, J., 1958, 'The Fission of Domestic Groups among the LoDagaba', in *The Developmental Cycle of Domestic Groups* (ed. J. Goody), Cambridge Papers in Social Anthropology, no. 1.

Goody, J., 1962, *Death, Property and the Ancestors*, Stanford.

Hocart, A. M., 1915, 'Chieftainship and the Sister's Son in the Pacific', *Amer. Anthrop.*, **17**, 631–46.

Hocart, A. M., 1923, 'The Uterine Nephew', *Man*, 1923, 4. (Reprinted in *The Life-Giving Myth*, London, 1952.)

Hocart, A. M., 1937, 'Kinship Systems', *Anthropos*, **32**, 345–51. (Reprinted in *The Life-Giving Myth*, London, 1952.)

Hogbin, H. I., 1930, 'The Study of Kinship in Primitive Societies', *Man*, 1930, 89.

Homans, G. C., 1951, *The Human Group*, London.

Homans, G. C. and Schneider, D. M., 1955, *Marriage, Authority and Final Causes*, Glencoe, Illinois.

Leach, E. R., 1951, 'The Structural Implications of Matrilateral Cross-Cousin Marriage', *J. R. Anthrop. Inst.*, **81**, 23–55.

Leach, E. R., 1957, 'Aspects of Bridewealth and Marriage Stability among the Kachin and Lakher', *Man*, 1957, 59.

Leach, E. R., 1958, 'Review of Dumont, L. Hierarchy and Marriage Alliance in South Indian Kinship', *Brit. J. Sociology*, **9**, 191–2.

Lévi-Strauss, C., 1945, 'L'Analyse structurale en linguistique et en anthropologie', *Word*, **1**, 33–53. (Reprinted in *Structural Anthropology*, New York, 1963.)

Lévi-Strauss, C., 1949, *Les Structures élémentaires de la parenté*, Paris.

Lévi-Strauss, C., 1956, 'The Family', in *Man, Culture and Society* (ed. H. L. Schapiro), New York.

Mayer, P., 1949, *The Lineage Principle in Gusii Society*, International African Inst., Memorandum no. 24.

Murdock, G., 1949, *Social Structure*, New York.

Nadel, S. F., 1951, *The Foundations of Social Anthropology*, London.

Nadel, S. F., 1957, *The Theory of Social Structure*, London.

Quain, B., 1948, *Fijian Village*, Chicago.

Radcliffe-Brown, A. R., 1924, 'The Mother's Brother in South Africa', *S. Afr. J. Sci.*, **21**, 542–55. (Reprinted in *Structure and Function in Primitive Societies: Essays and Addresses by A. R. Radcliffe-Brown*, London, 1952.)

Radcliffe-Brown, A. R., 1940, 'On Joking Relationships', *Africa*, **13**, 195–210. (Reprinted in *Structure and Function in Primitive Societies: Essays and Addresses by A. R. Radcliffe-Brown*, London, 1952.)

Radcliffe-Brown, A. R., 1950, Introduction to *African Systems of Kinship and Marriage* (eds. A. R. Radcliffe-Brown and D. Forde), London.

Radcliffe-Brown, A. R., 1952, see above, 1940.

Radcliffe-Brown, A. R., 1953, 'The Dravidian Kinship Terminology', *Man*, 1953, 169.

Rattray, R. S., 1929, *Ashanti Law and Constitution*, Oxford.

Rivers, W. H. R., 1901, 'On the Functions of the Maternal Uncle in Torres Straits', *Rep. Brit. Ass.*, 800.

Rivers, W. H. R., 1914, *The History of Melanesian Society*, Cambridge.

Roth, G. K., 1953, *Fijian Way of Life*, Melbourne.

Tax, S., 1937, 'Some Problems of Social Organization', in *Social Anthropology of the North American Tribes* (ed. F. Eggan), Chicago.
Thompson, B., 1908, *The Fijians*, London.
Winter, E. H., 1956, *Bwamba*, Cambridge.

CHAPTER FOUR

The Classification of Double Descent Systems

Introduction

One of the commonest methods of classifying human societies is by their systems of descent, of which four varieties are usually distinguished: bilateral, patrilineal, matrilineal, and double descent. However, such a classification has different meanings for different social scientists. The phrase 'patrilineal descent' may refer to one or more among the following: the inheritance of property, succession to office, eligibility for membership in unilineal groups, or the degree of emphasis given to ties traced with or through the father. The major difficulties about any usage involving more than one of these criteria are that, in the first place, no two are invariably found in association and, in the second, the terms carry different meanings in respect of these four features. Hence confusion can, and does, easily ensue.

Rivers confined the term 'descent' to the single feature of eligibility for membership in kingroups, and, further, restricted his definition to unilineal kingroups (1924: 86). Thus his characterization of a society as having 'patrilineal descent' referred to the presence of unilineal descent groups (UDGs), eligibility to which was through males; likewise, his use of the phrase 'matrilineal descent' indicated the presence of UDGs, eligibility to which was through females.

If we accept Rivers' definition, then the concept of 'bilateral descent' becomes self-contradictory. Indeed, an examination of the so-called 'bilateral' societies reveals little that is common to them apart from an absence of UDGs.

In such societies, certain of the functions elsewhere carried out by persons as members of the UDGs—blood vengeance, for example— may be performed by persons standing in specified degrees of kinship;

in certain circumstances these ranges of kin may constitute 'kindreds', but such groupings always have overlapping memberships and cannot by themselves form mutually exclusive segments of the society in the manner of UDGs. These kindreds are of two main kinds: the personal kindred (Leach 1950) and the descending kindred. Eligibility to a personal kindred is determined by reckoning degrees of kinship—ascending, descending, and lateral—from a specific individual through both males and females; it is therefore 'ego-oriented', differing for each person. The descending kindred consists of the descendants of a single individual, or of a marital pair, through both males and females, over a specified number of generations. The range of the former corresponds to what in English usage would be one's *relatives*; the latter, to one's *descendants*. The former has been referred to by Phillpotts (1913) as the 'fluctuating kindred'; the latter, by Goodenough (1955) as the 'unrestricted nonunilinear descent group', and by Firth (1957) as the 'completely bilinear group'.

In many 'bilateral' societies, especially in the Pacific area, a social group of considerable importance is a more restricted form of the descending kindred. Membership is restricted by the introduction of additional, non-kinship criteria, such as locality. For example, a person may be entitled to belong to the kingroup of his father or his mother, but is only reckoned to be a member if he is residing with him or her. This social group is referred to by Goodenough as a 'restricted nonunilinear descent group', and by Firth as a 'ramage'. It should be emphasized that while the ramage is usually a kingroup in the sense that all members are related consanguineally, or affinally, membership is not determined by such criteria alone.

Societies may be classified, then, according to the presence or absence of UDGs. The residual category we will refer to by the customary though ambiguous term 'bilateral', while the former category is subdivided into those societies with patrilineal UDGs, those with matrilineal UDGs, and those with both, that is, double descent systems.

The distribution of these systems has been discussed by Murdock (1949 and 1957). In the earlier of his two analyses he tallied the distribution of 'Rules of Descent' for a world sample of 250 peoples (1949: 194); his figures are reproduced here as Table 3.

TABLE III

THE DISTRIBUTION OF 'RULES OF DESCENT' (MURDOCK 1949)

Rule of Descent	Africa	Eurasia	North America	Oceania	South America	Total
Bilateral	4	8	36	13	14	75
Matrilineal	11	2	20	15	3	51
Patrilineal	45	23	13	21	4	106
Double	5	1	1	11	0	18
Total	65	34	70	60	21	250

In his later analysis (1957), Murdock defined the geographical areas somewhat differently, and included 565 peoples in his sample. Subsequently the more extensive Ethnographic Atlas (1967) included 863 societies, the distribution of which is given in Table 4.[1]

TABLE IV

THE DISTRIBUTION OF UDGs (ETHNOGRAPHIC ATLAS 1967)

	Africa	Circum-Med.	East Eurasia	Insular Pacific	North America	South America	Total
UDGs absent ('Bilateral')	13	30	17	43	143	65	311
Matrilineal UDGs only	37	7	8	28	34	7	121
Patrilineal UDGs only	176	57	68	43	42	15	401
Both ('Double')	12	2	1	12	0	—	27
Insufficient information	0	0	0	1	0	2	3
Total	238	96	94	127	219	89	863

When these later figures are expressed in percentages, the results are as in Table 5. The figures in the bottom row of Table 5 indicate the percentages of systems in the total sample which occur in each of the

93

continental areas, e.g. 28 per cent of the sample are located in Africa. The percentages in the four upper rows indicate the distribution of all societies with a given type of descent system among the continental areas. A comparison of any of the latter figures with the figure in the last row of the same column will show whether any particular type of system is over- or under-represented relative to the proportion of societies from that continent. For example, although 28 per cent of the societies in the sample are drawn from Africa, only 4 per cent of all those in which UDGs are absent are found on this continent.

TABLE V

THE PERCENTAGE DISTRIBUTION OF UDGs BY CONTINENTAL AREA

	Africa	*Circum-Med.*	*East Eurasia*	*Insular Pacific*	*North America*	*South America*	*Total*
UDGs absent ('Bilateral')	4	10	5	14	46	21	99 (311)
Matrilineal UDGs only	30	6	7	24	28	6	101 (120)
Patrilineal UDGs only	44	14	17	11	10	4	100 (401)
Both ('Double')	44	7	4	44	—	—	99 (27)
% of total sample	28 (238)	12 (96)	11 (94)	15 (126)	25 (219)	10 (87)	101 (860)

A number of dimensions other than linearity, patrilineal or matrilineal, are relevant to the classification of UDGs. Some of these, earlier discussed by Fried (1957) in connection with *corporate* UDGs, are, apart from corporateness itself, the presence or absence of stratification, ranking, and demonstrated descent. This last refers to the customary distinction between clan and lineage: a lineage is a genealogically defined group, while the members of a clan, though recognizing their common descent in general terms, do not reckon this by means of specific links between named ancestors. With regard to ranking, Fried refers to the existence of offices, restricted social position, eligibility to which is based upon criteria 'other than sex, age, and ephemeral

94

personal attributes' (1957: 23). By 'stratification' he refers to differential access of adults to 'strategic resources', those necessary to maintain subsistence. Customary usage gives these terms a somewhat wider reference; the criteria of eligibility are not seen as intrinsic to the definition of rank nor one specific base a prerequisite of stratification. In order to prevent the exclusion of alternative possibilities and hypotheses, it would seem advisable to preserve these wider usages, and at the same time distinguish between the types of ranking and stratification according to the various criteria employed in different societies. To some degree or other, then, all UDGs are internally ranked (though not necessarily rank ordered), if only by generation. Not all, however, are stratified externally one against another; that is, there is not necessarily any hierarchy of groups in terms of access to relatively exclusive rights, either in respect of persons or of property. To take one example, that of restricted social positions: stratification, as applied to UDGs, means that membership entails differential access to offices whose jurisdiction extends beyond the confines of any one of these units. Thus the lineages of an Ashanti division are stratified (Rattray 1929), in that chiefship is vested in one particular UDG, while representatives of the remaining groups act as council members. The differential access may be to positions other than those usually thought of as 'political', as among the Anuak of the Eastern Sudan, where the chiefships are largely ritual in character (Evans-Pritchard 1940).

Other dimensions employed to categorize UDGs, such as numerical strength and the extent of restrictions upon in-marriage (exogamy), cannot be discussed here. However, one that is of central concern to this paper is that of corporation.

The concept of the corporate group has been variously employed in the literature of comparative sociology. It has served to translate Weber's *Verband*, which is defined as a social relationship where 'order is enforced by the action of specific individuals whose regular function this is, of a chief or "head" (*Leiter*) and usually also an administrative staff' (1947: 145–6). Maine, on the other hand, thought of a corporation in terms of the ownership and transmission of property. Radcliffe-Brown in his earlier writings (1935, reprinted 1952) followed Maine. However, his use of the Australian horde as a type-case, and his acceptance of Durkheim's emphasis on the importance of assemblies in the

95

maintenance of group solidarity, led him to introduce the criterion of physical proximity. Thus, his last definition of a corporate group, which includes elements from Maine, Durkheim, and Weber, ran as follows (1950: 41):

> A group may be spoken of as 'corporate' when it possesses any one of a certain number of characters: if its members, or its adult male members, or a considerable proportion of them, come together occasionally to carry out some collective action—for example, the performance of rites; if it has a chief or council who are regarded as acting as the representatives of the group as a whole; if it possesses or controls property which is collective, as when a clan or lineage is a land-owning group.

It seems preferable here, both to avoid confusion and to encourage analysis in terms of further variables, to give independent designations to these three characters. In the first case, we may speak of assembling or convening groups. In this connection, it should be added that the term 'corporate' has also been used to describe the degree of localization of a group, i.e. whether it is compact, dispersed or non-localized. In a compact group (Radcliffe-Brown 1950:41), such as the Tale patriclan, the main body of the members not dispersed through marriage live contiguously in one locality. In a dispersed UDG, such as the Ashanti matriclan, the localized segments are separated one from another, often by segments of other UDGs. In a non-localized UDG, such as the Yakö matriclan, none of the segments has a territorial framework. In each of these cases, the group may 'come together occasionally to carry out some collective action', either in plenary session or by means of representatives. Consequently, the degree of localization should be considered separately from the question of assembling.

With regard to the second of Radcliffe-Brown's 'characters', where groups have a hierarchical system of authority or representation converging upon one man or a few individuals, I would speak of these as 'pyramidal', following the usage of Fortes and Evans-Pritchard (1940). It is for the third feature that I would reserve the term 'corporate', to distinguish those UDGs in which rights in material objects are vested, or, more precisely, within which property is inherited.

The main part of this chapter is concerned with double descent systems, the classification of which raises basic problems concerned with the definition of descent and the minimum criteria for social groups. With regard to the first of these points, it seems preferable to confine the term 'descent' to some one of the four criteria enumerated at the outset, and I suggest, following Rivers, that this should be eligibility for membership in kin groups. With regard to the second, the attempt to develop criteria to identify the presence of social groups, I employ as indices of degree of group identification, or 'consciousness of unity', the existence of a relevant technical term in the native language (e.g. *clan*) or a specific name (e.g. 'MacDonald').

Against the background of these introductory remarks, we can now proceed with the discussion of the classification of double descent systems.

Discussion of Double Descent

The assumption of early anthropological writers that societies character-ized by unilineal descent groups were either 'patrilineal' or 'matrilineal' was disposed of with some difficulty, mainly through the efforts of Radcliffe-Brown.[2] In his essay on 'The Mother's Brother in South Africa' (1924, reprinted 1952), he called attention to the fact that these modes of reckoning descent may co-exist in the same social system. He mentioned specifically 'the tribes of Eastern Australia' (1952: 22), and the Ova-Herero of South Africa which, he writes, is 'subdivided into two sets of segments crossing one another' (1952: 23). He tentatively referred to this feature as 'bilateralism', and it was not until a subsequent article that he distinguished clearly between what we would now call 'bilateral kinship' and 'double descent'. This he did in a penetrating comment on Deacon's discovery of a section system in Ambrym, where he showed why it was that Rivers, when he had visited the island some years before, had failed to notice the existence of double descent. Rivers had apparently gone there expecting to find a matri-lineal dual division. 'His first enquiries showed him the existence of patrilineal local clans. He thereupon gave up looking for the matrilineal dual division, because, perhaps unconsciously, he assumed that the two forms of organization could not exist in the same people' (1929*a*: 50; Rivers 1915). Radcliffe-Brown's comment was confirmed when Eme-neau showed that Rivers had similarly failed to observe the presence of matrilineal descent groups among the dominantly patrilineal Todas

97

(Rivers 1906; Emeneau 1937).[3] I myself had an identical experience. The French ethnographer, Labouret, had described some of the 'Lobi' peoples of the Ghana-Ivory Coast border as matrilineal, a classification which seemed in some ways inconsistent with his account of their system of residence and inheritance (Labouret 1931). My own investigations in the area showed that, of these peoples, the Birifor at least were characterized by double descent (Goody 1956), thus partly confirming Radcliffe-Brown's prediction of thirty years ago: '. . . we have reason to suspect that similar double clan systems will be found when carefully looked for in many of the tribes of West Africa that lie between the Herero and the Ashanti' (1929*a*: 51).

Subsequently, double descent was recognized in many parts of the world. Radcliffe-Brown himself compared Ambrym to the Australian systems, as well as to the Herero, the 'Congo region' (tribe unnamed), and to the Ashanti (1929*b*: 199). Herskovits pointed out the wider extension of the Ashanti system, which he claimed was also found among the coastal peoples of Ghana, the Ga and the Fanti, as well as among one group of their New World descendants, the Bush Negroes of Dutch Guiana (1937). Forde's study of the Yakö provided the first detailed analysis of what he called a 'double unilateral' organization (1938, 1939, 1950). Some years later Nadel discovered the existence of double descent among the Nyaro and Tullushi in the Nuba Hills and possibly, he suggested, among the Kunama of Eritrea (1950). Murdock (1940) meanwhile called attention to the growing number of double descent systems, adding to the list the Nankanse of Ghana (Rattray 1932), the Venda (Stayt 1931), Manus (Mead 1934), Ontong Java (Hogbin 1931), and Pukapuka (Beaglehole and Beaglehole 1938).

This is a large and heterogeneous list. It includes the Ashanti, a people who place great emphasis on matrilineal UDGs. It also includes the Nankanse of northern Ghana, who appear to be very similar to the Tallensi, often taken as the epitome of an agnatic system. And there are others who fall somewhere between these two poles. As a means of approaching the central issues in the classification of double descent systems, with a view to improving upon the operational utility of the concept, I shall consider below the discussion which has developed around two cases from the list, the Australian and the Ashanti, each of which raises different points of theoretical interest.

The Australian Case

In his article on 'Double Descent', Murdock maintained that the difficulties concerning Australian marriage classes are 'easily resolved when it is recognized that the class area of Australia is actually characterized by double descent, by a combination of coexisting matrilineal and patrilineal modes of affiliation' (1940: 559). The author did not claim this as an original contribution but referred to Lawrence's 'penetrating analytical study', 'Alternating Generations in Australia' (1937).

However, long before this, in 1898, Durkheim had suggested that the system of 'four classes' resulted from a combination of matrilineal moieties and patrilineal local groups.[4] Durkheim based his argument upon the assumption that originally all Australian tribes were divided into two matrilineal moieties. In combination with virilocal marriage (and, implicitly, no child-return), this leads to a 'duality of the totemic group and the local group' (1898: 21) which gives rise to a four-class system separating the generations one from another. Eventually this duality causes the dispersed matrilineal clans to be displaced by local patrilineal ones. But in the transitional period we find traces of the coexistence of patrilineal and matrilineal 'filiation', such as 'bilateral' exogamy (1898: 26). |5 33⪶3

Radcliffe-Brown further developed this viewpoint, removing it from the realm of conjectural history. He maintained that, 'In Australian tribes with four sections or eight sub-sections every person belongs to one of a pair of matrilineal moieties and one of a pair of patrilineal moieties' (1929b: 199). In the earliest of his major papers on Australia (1913) he made no specific mention of double descent. But in the essay on 'The Mother's Brother in South Africa' (1924), he developed, implicitly rather than explicitly, the distinction between what Fortes calls 'complementary filiation' (ties with the unilineal descent group of the parent residual to the reckoning of descent) and the descent systems of Australia, where both matrilineal and patrilineal groups coexist in the same society. And in his comments upon Deacon's paper on Ambrym (1927), and in the ensuing discussion with Brenda Seligman, he emphasized a further contrast, that between bilateral kinship and double descent. There he distinguished two types of Australian marriage regulation, Type I with 'cross-cousin' marriage, and Type II with marriage to the Mother's Mother's Brother's Daughter's Daughter. Section systems are found with both types of marriage regulations, e.g. among the Kariera and the Aranda. The system of four sections, he maintained, is 'a systematization of Type I and may be best understood by regarding it as a double dual division of the tribe, a matrilineal and a patrilineal dichotomy combined together' (1927: 344).

This double moiety organization he considered similar to the Ashanti, Ova-Herero, and 'Congo' systems. Only of the Dieri did he specifically state that they have a 'double-clan system' (1927: 345);[5] later (1930), he listed other such tribes, mainly in Eastern Australia. Nevertheless all section and sub-section systems were treated as double moiety organizations. In a later summary of the position he wrote (1929b: 200):

> The four sections of Australian tribes are groups of persons who, by the classificatory system, stand in certain definite relations. Thus, in its simplest form, I and my 'brothers', 'father's fathers' and 'son's sons' form one group. Our fathers and sons form another, and so on. The sections are not descent groups in the ordinary sense, but the system does really include two sets of direct descent groups, often anonymous, namely, one pair of patrilineal moieties each containing two sections (AD, BC) and one pair of matrilineal moieties (AC, BD).
>
> Even if it were correct to speak of the sections as having 'bilateral descent', I do not think we should gain anything by the new term. But it is not correct. In most tribes irregular marriages take place, i.e., a man takes a woman outside the section within which he should marry if his marriage is regular. In such instances, in the majority of Australian tribes, the section membership of the child is determined through the mother alone.

Thus he not only recognized the Eastern tribes as having a double descent organization, but also appears to have included any section or sub-section system in the same category, speaking of two sets of 'descent groups' even though they are not named. Indeed, in his final statement on Australian systems he wrote (1951: 40):

> Although the social organization of Australian tribes is always based on patrilineal descent, there is always some recognition of matrilineal descent. For an individual, his most important senior relatives are his father and the father of his father, and his mother's brother and the mother's brother of his

mother's brother. The kinship system of an Australian tribe is usually one of double descent, patrilineal and matrinlineal. But in many tribes there is a more definite and organized recognition of matrilineal descent, sometimes by the existence of matrilineal clans or totemic divisions, sometimes by named matrilineal moieties, and in some tribes by the existence of eight 'classes' or 'sub-sections'.

This is essentially the position developed by Lawrence (1937) and later by Murdock (1940). Accepting Matthew's 'discovery' that all Australian marriage class systems were based upon the presence of matrilineal moieties (1900: 120)—Durkheim had earlier made the same point—and combining this with Radcliffe-Brown's claim that throughout the continent the local organization was one of exogamous patrilineal hordes, Lawrence found that all class systems are in fact characterized by double descent.

'Four divisions, called "sections" if they bear names, are formed because the patrilineal moieties and the matrilineal moieties bisect each other' (Lawrence 1937: 324). Indeed he went so far as to attribute even two class systems to the coexistence of local patriclans and matrimoieties, a seemingly unnecessary hypothesis. His conclusion was that 'three factors must coexist to provide the common denominator of all Australian class systems, viz.: (1) marriage by sister exchange; (2) matrilineal descent in exogamous moieties; and (3) patrilineal descent in exogamous patriclans' (1937: 334).[6]

In what sense is it profitable to speak about Australian societies as characterized by double descent? Let us first examine more closely what Radcliffe-Brown meant by referring to them in this way. The case which he quoted as being the most 'highly organized system of double descent' is that of the Dieri of South Australia, who have patriclans distinguished by totems known as *pintara*, and matriclans with totems known as *madu* (1951: 40). However, in other cases, and these are the more numerous, Radcliffe-Brown spoke of the matrilineal descent groups as being unnamed; in this usage he was followed by Lawrence. 'Anonymous' in this context could mean one of two things: the descent groups may be known by a technical term in the native language but have no names, or there may be lacking both terms and names. In this latter case, the questions then arise as to how these groups are recognized by the actors and how they are to be distinguished by the observers. When can we speak of a social system as being characterized by descent groups?

In perhaps the earliest, and certainly one of the clearest discussions of this subject, Rivers, as we have already said, defined 'descent' as (*a*) a criterion of eligibility for membership in a social group, (*b*) either through males or through females (i.e. unilineal).[7] This definition was adopted by Radcliffe-Brown, who wrote, 'Descent is necessarily unilateral whereas kinship is equally necessarily bilateral' (1930: 442). Whereas Radcliffe-Brown stressed the second aspect of the definition, Murdock emphasized the first when he wrote, 'Descent means, as Rivers pointed out, not relationship itself, but affiliation with a particular group of relatives' (1940: 556). For the purposes of this chapter, 'descent' refers to eligibility for membership in kin groups and is also restricted to eligibility by a unilineal criterion, since this is what is usually meant in the phrase 'double descent'. However, in employing the word 'descent', as an abbreviation for 'unilineal descent', I do not wish necessarily to exclude Firth's and Goodenough's usage of the term in connection with the ramage, as newly defined by the former (1957).

One additional aspect of 'descent' requires to be included in any definition. Among the Fanti, and, to a lesser extent, the Ashanti of Ghana, the personnel of military regiments (*asafo*) were recruited from the sons of existing members. In Britain too a tendency towards such patrifilial recruitment is present in a number of army regiments, in certain occupations such as that of docker, and in some of the more ancient collegiate institutions, though here this is never the exclusive method of replacement and usually functions primarily to maintain social position. Among the Fanti, on the other hand, this was the compulsory mode of recruitment to the *asafo* and, as such, would appear to fulfil the requirements of Rivers' definition of the term 'descent'.

Yet the Fanti regiments were morphologically different from, say, the Ashanti clans. For in the latter case the 'unilineal' principle is not merely a criterion of eligibility to the social group, but is also the means by which the personnel of the group reckon relationships among themselves. Each member of an Ashanti clan is related unilineally to every other member, not only to the single person whom he replaces socially. In the Fanti case, we may speak of patrifilial recruitment, in the Ashanti of unilineal descent.

Clearly, unilineal descent is potentially available in any society as a mode for the ordering of social relations; it is a selection from the totality of possible kinship ties which serves as a mode of organizing mutually exclusive social groups. Descent groups may perform a variety of functions, and their importance in different societies varies widely. This diversity makes the problem of their recognition a difficult one, and in view of the discussions that have developed as to whether or not a particular system is characterized by 'double descent', one must ask how, given the criteria I have suggested to define 'descent', the social scientist demonstrates the presence of such 'groups'.

This question immediately raises the whole sociological problem of what constitutes a social group. One criterion often used to distinguish *group* from other social units such as *plurel, class*, or *aggregation* is that the former is characterized by observable interaction among the members (Lundberg 1939: 340-1). However, this criterion, which forms the starting point of so much work on small groups in a laboratory setting, is not entirely satisfactory for the anthropologist. The type of group with which the latter is mainly concerned is that which, in Nadel's words, 'may be defined as a collection of individuals who stand in regular and relatively permanent *relationships*, that is, who act towards and in respect of each other, or towards and in respect of individuals outside the group, regularly in a specific, predictable, and expected fashion' (Nadel 1951: 146; my italics). Of course, as 'the relationships making up the group are . . . visible only in the institutionalized modes of coactivity,' 'relationships' and 'interaction' are not independent variables. But, in emphasizing the relational structure of the anthropologist's 'groups', one is pointing out that in the main he is dealing with 'institutionalized groups'.

These groups display 'institutionalized modes of coactivity' which 'appear as the *rights and obligations* vested in or incumbent upon the individuals in virtue of their group membership' (Nadel 1951: 146). To use Radcliffe-Brown's terminology, a group is therefore a 'jural' institution—'meaning by that relationships that can be defined in terms of rights and duties' (Radcliffe-Brown 1950: 11). To put it in a way which brings out the conceptual *rapprochement* to the work of Max

Weber and G. H. Mead, the action of group members has 'meaning' for the actors in that it follows, to a greater or lesser extent, from a conscious awareness of expected behaviour. A group may therefore be said to be 'conscious of itself in that each actor is aware that he "belongs" and that, in virtue of his belonging, he is entitled or required to act in a given way' (Nadel 1951: 147). This consciousness of unity may be concretized in various forms, but of particular importance is the existence of group terms and names which give tangible form even to the abstract 'awareness of "belonging"'.

Nadel himself gave an excellent demonstration of the importance of names in his account of the Nupe state (1942).[8] However, except in 'very large human aggregates', he did not regard the existence of a name as essential 'to make the group complete, that is, to entitle us to impute to the human aggregate in question the requisite consciousness of unity' (1951: 148). It is perhaps the case that in certain marginal situations the co-activities of the members may in themselves afford sufficient awareness of 'belonging' without requiring the existence of either a technical term or a specific name. However, empirically this is the limiting case. The difficulties in the way of laying down minimal criteria of a functional nature (i.e. the kind and degree of co-activity necessary to establish the existence of such a group) make it operationally desirable to demand the presence of at least a technical term, however ambiguous, as an index of the presence of an 'institutionalized social group'.

A descent group, then, is such an institutionalized social group, recognized by the presence of a technical term or a distinctive name, which is organized on the basis of unilineal consanguinity, actual or supposed. Double descent systems are those in which a person belongs to a pair of such groups, one based on the patrilineal, the other on the matrilineal, mode of reckoning.

It is clear that on this criterion we would have to reject a number of the Australian 'section' (or 'class') systems. We cannot accept Murdock's contention, based upon Lawrence's paper, 'that the class area of Australia is actually characterized by double descent, by a combination of coexisting matrilineal and patrilineal modes of affiliation' (1940: 559). From our point of view this conclusion needs to be supported by a demonstration of the presence of UDGs. This Murdock does not afford. He argues for the existence of double descent throughout the 'class area' (it certainly occurs in part of it) on the grounds that it is demanded by the 'class' system.

Radcliffe-Brown came to a conclusion similar to that of Lawrence and Murdock. Elsewhere he stated clearly enough that: 'By "descent" I understand membership of a closed group (social segment) determined at birth by the fact that a parent belongs to that group' (1929b: 199). But he did not always abide by the logical implications of this definition. For he too assumed that marriage 'sections' necessarily presuppose the existence of both patrilineal and matrilineal descent groups. Just as Lawrence was forced to speak of 'anonymous sections', so Radcliffe-Brown wrote of 'anonymous moieties', thus assuming the coexistence of matrilineal descent groups cross-cutting the omnipresent patrilineal ones throughout the 'section' area. In the absence of either a name or a term, how is one to know that such plurels are not simply constructs of the anthropologist's imagination and on quite another level of reality from the institutionalized descent group? Doubt is thrown on the assumptions of these writers by the Murngin material, which shows that it is quite possible for a section system to exist in the absence of matrilineal descent groups.[9]

Further light is shed on Radcliffe-Brown's position by an examination of his own comments on Murngin social organization (1951). He argued against the analysis put forward by Lawrence, Murdock, and Lévi-Strauss, which was in any case rejected by those social anthropologists who had actually worked in Arnhem Land (Warner 1937 and 1958; Berndt 1955). But during the course of the paper he repeated the interpretation of Murngin kinship terminology previously offered by Warner, utilizing the concept of 'lines of descent'. A 'line of descent' he defined as 'an arrangement of the relatives of an individual which can be shown on a chart of kinship terms' (1951: 43). The number of 'basic lines of descent' depends upon the number of kinship terms for relatives in the second ascending generation. Thus these 'lines' consist only of a series of terms laid out in generation order. One may draw a line: father, (ego), son, or, alternatively, mother's brother, (ego), sister's son. The first Radcliffe-Brown referred to as a line of patrilineal descent, the second as a line of matrilineal descent. This concept he then used to analyse the Murngin data: '... if we take the three patrilineal lines . . . and the three matrilineal lines . . . then, in combination, they include all the terms of kinship of either Yir-Yoront or Murngin' (1951: 49). Radcliffe-Brown was well aware that these descent lines are not unilineal descent groups. Indeed, it was for making this mistake that he criticized Murdock and other writers (1956: 364). However, the misunderstanding must be laid partly at his door. For although Radcliffe-Brown followed Rivers in limiting the term 'descent' to the unilineal reckoning of kinship as a criterion for membership in social groups, he then employed the word in a different sense, to indicate a 'line' of terms on a kinship diagram. There is of course some connection. The roles linked in a particular descent line may all fall within one unilineal descent group; in patrilineal systems, this is often the case with the 'patriline', father-(ego)-son. But equally there may be no overlap. One of the difficulties in the Lévi-Strauss-Murdock analysis is the assumption that, for example, all of ego's 'mother's brothers' will be found in one descent group, when it appears from Warner's study that they are neither in one local, nor in one unilineal, descent group. Leach's contribution to this discussion (1951) did a lot to clear away confusions caused by these authors, but it seems still to involve some such assumption. He maintained that Radcliffe-Brown 'failed to make clear just what is the degree of correspondence between these descent lines and the local descent groups which constitute actual Murngin society at any particular point in time' (1951: 33). There can be no single answer to this question because the so-called lines of descent may be variously related to the kin groups. The matrilineal lines clearly have no 'correspondence' at all to descent groups, as there are no matrilineal UDGs.

This discussion of Australian systems is an attempt at a preliminary clarification of the concept of double descent. Double descent is compatible with a 'section' system, but is no necessary counterpart. Radcliffe-Brown, Murdock and others could only take the view that it is a counterpart by positing the existence of 'anonymous descent groups'. To bring out further theoretical points I now turn to another case around which controversy has arisen, the Ashanti of Ghana.

The Ashanti Case
In his field monograph on the Fanti (1954), Christensen attempts to refute the thesis, attributed to Fortes, that the term 'double descent' is

inapplicable to the Ashanti, the northern neighbours of the Fanti, and a society with a very similar social structure. He tries to show that 'the paternal line' in these societies has been neglected because of the concern of earlier writers with the jural aspects of kinship. Had they fully recognized the importance of this 'line', he maintains, they would have agreed with Murdock that this society is really characterized by double descent.

Part of the evidence submitted by Christensen shows, not the strength of the patrilineal descent group, but rather the importance of the father role, which is a very different question. The difficulty appears to lie in a blurring of the concepts of filiation and descent.[10] However, there are other grounds for Christensen's statement. Unlike some of the Australian tribes quoted by Murdock, Lawrence, Radcliffe-Brown and others, the Ashanti do have descent groups, in the meaning we have given this term, based on both patrilineal and matrilineal modes of reckoning. Why, then, should this case have given rise to further controversy?

Radcliffe-Brown constantly used the Ashanti as a type case of double descent; in this he was followed by Herskovits (1937), Lawrence (1937), Murdock (1940, 1949) and Nadel (1950). On the other hand, in his introduction to *African Systems of Kinship and Marriage*, Radcliffe-Brown contrasted the Ashanti with 'double lineage systems', maintaining that the Ashanti have 'the nearest approach to pure mother-right' in Africa (1950: 79). This statement is in fact in line with Fortes' re-examination of their kinship system which appears in the same volume. Although Fortes did not specifically reject the classification of the Ashanti as a double descent system,[11] he maintained that one of the misinterpretations in previous work was the view, which he attributed to Murdock, that 'Ashanti kinship is characterized by the *equal* recognition of both matrilineal and patrilineal descent' (1950: 253; my italics).

But although Fortes did not specifically deny that the Ashanti have a double descent system, he did point out that the structure of their descent groups differs considerably from, say, that of the Yakö, discussed in the same volume (Forde 1950). The Ashanti *ntoro*, the patrilineal descent group, is not a 'corporate group'—'there is no corporate organization based upon the father's line, nor are jural or political rights (such as rights of inheritance) or duties derived from paternal descent' (1950: 267).

Fortes' analysis of the Ashanti, and Radcliffe-Brown's change of mind concerning their classification as a typical case of double descent, bear upon a theoretical point which has not received full attention in the literature. It is this. When we include within the category 'double descent' all those systems which have some kind of descent group, however minimal its functions, based upon both lines of descent, then the societies brought together under this head have little or nothing in common but this fact alone. Moreover, such a classification cuts right across existing typologies. The Ashanti, for example, are, according to Radcliffe-Brown, 'the nearest approach to pure mother-right' in Africa. Yet, from Murdock's standpoint, the Ashanti ought to be included in the same general category, not only as the Yakö, but also as the Tallensi of northern Ghana, who are usually considered a proto-typical patrilineal society. For the Tallensi have uterine descent groups which, though they have no name, nevertheless are known by a technical term *soog* (Fortes 1949: 40). Although the *soog* may be viewed as kinship effective only through personal contact, nevertheless a shadowy uterine descent group of four-generation depth emerges around exogamy, witchcraft, and blood-guilt. From a comparative point of view, the critical attribute is the rejection of the sexuality of the women as embodied in the rule of exogamy and the incest taboo.[12] However, here I am only concerned with establishing the inadequacy, for most purposes, of a classification which includes societies structurally so dissimilar as the Tallensi, the Ashanti and the Yakö. For although Murdock did not specifically include the Tallensi in his list, he did mention their neighbours, the Nankanse: 'Among the Nankanse of the Ashanti hinterland, Rattray reports exogamous, non-totemic, and non-localized matri-lineages (*soo*) as well as exogamous, totemic, localized and politically organized patri-sibs (*bute*)' (Murdock 1940: 558). The Nankanse *soo*, like the Tallensi *soog*, is characterized by the prohibition on sexual intercourse and the inheritance of the taint of witchcraft (Rattray 1932: 29). Rattray also mentioned similar groups among the nearby Kusase, as well as among other societies in northern Ghana—the 'Lobi', Vagala, and Tampolense—all of whom, he said, inherit matrilineally.

It was among some groups of the people called by Rattray the 'Lobi' (or Lober) that I myself carried out some studies. The second group I worked with, the LoDagaba, do inherit certain types of property matrilineally, but the first community, the LoWiili, while having named matriclans as well as patriclans, inherit all property patrilineally. In this they provided a patrilineal parallel to the Ashanti, for the matriclans were distinctly secondary to the main series of descent groups. The patrilineal *ntoro* of the Ashanti, like the matrilineal *belo* of the LoWiili, have a greater degree of organization than the Tallensi *soog*, for besides being known by the technical term they also have individual names. Small exogamous groups of a generation depth and span similar to that of the *soog* are linked together by more inclusive, named descent groups associated with particular sacred *loci*. The attribution of names indicates greater organization, the actors then viewing the groups as defined segments of a total system.[13]

Thus, although all these societies have institutions which meet the minimal definition of double descent, it would be misleading to confound the system found among the Tallensi, the Ashanti, and the LoWiili with that of the Yakö or LoDagaba type.[14] The Tallensi and the LoWiili are to be compared with patrilineal societies such as the Nuer which have no descent groups based on the uterine tie, and the Ashanti are most profitably considered together with matrilineal societies. The difference here relates to the question of the corporateness of the descent groups in question. As stated above, when I speak of a descent group as 'corporate', I refer specifically to property-holding and thus give the term a more restricted meaning than is customary in current comparative usage. By 'property-holding' I do not mean that the members of the group necessarily all hold similar rights in respect of the same objects but that these objects are transmitted within the group, either after death (inheritance) or before, and that this transmission is seen as related to group membership.[15] As I earlier remarked, while the existence of an 'estate' is often cited as one of the characteristic features of corporate groups, a number of other criteria have also been introduced into the discussion. This wider usage seems to me not only to depart from legal and economic practice but, more important, to render the term less valuable as an analytic concept.

The importance of distinguishing systems in which the property is divided between patrilineal and matrilineal groups emerges from Forde's analysis of the Yakö. The general point is well brought out by Fortes, when he writes (1953: 34):

> One of the most developed systems of this type (double unilineal) is that of the Yakö; and Forde's excellent analysis of how this works (Forde 1950) shows that it is much more than a device for classifying kin. It is a principle of social organization that enters into all social relations and is expressed in all important institutions. There is the division of property, for instance, into the kind that is tied to the patrilineal lineage and the kind that passes to matrilineal kin. The division is between fixed and, in theory, perpetual productive resources, in this case farm land, with which goes residence rights, on the one hand, and on the other, movable and consumable property like livestock and cash.

Fortes goes on to point out that there is a 'similar polarity' in religious cult, with the matrilineal group being 'ritually somewhat stronger'. I would put the position yet more definitely than this. In a previous chapter (3), I compared the mother's brother-sister's son relationship among the LoWiili and the LoDagaba, that is, in a patrilineal society with complementary (or secondary) descent groups and in a full double descent system. The crucial variable appeared to be property relationships. I was therefore led to regard the division of property not merely as an expression of a principle of social organization on the same level as the division in ritual cults, but rather as the fundamental feature around which other differences—for example, in nuclear kinship relations—revolve. It is the importance of property relationships, as illustrated here and in the analyses of Forde and Nadel, which suggests that it is profitable to distinguish a class of systems within the general category of what has been called double descent. I therefore suggest the phrase 'double descent' be reserved for full systems of the Yakö type in which both descent groups are corporate, that is, in which 'double clanship' is accompanied by 'double inheritance'. This is admittedly to limit the implications of the term 'descent' in this context. My excuse is that I am concerned with defining analytically useful categories, and this necessitates some clarification and restriction of existing usages. Systems like those found among the Tallensi and the Ashanti may, on the analogy of Fortes' 'complementary filiation', be referred to as unilineal systems with complementary (or secondary) UDGs. Here UDGs are based upon both lines, but only one set is corporate.

The classification I propose is summarized below. The specific terminology is somewhat clumsy and can doubtless be improved; it is the recognition of the distinctions which seem to me of use in comparative sociology.

I. *Unlineal systems with complementary (or secondary) descent groups*
   A. *Patrilineal* UDGs with
   (*i*) *Unnamed* complementary uterine UDGs (technical term only), e.g., Tallensi
   (*ii*) *Named* complementary uterine UDGs, e.g., LoWiili
   B. *Matrilineal* UDGs with
   (*i*) *Unnamed* complementary agnatic UDGs
   (*ii*) *Named* complementary agnatic UDGs, e.g., Ashanti
II. *Double descent systems* (where both groups are property-holding corporations, e.g., the Yakö and the LoDagaba)

The adoption of these distinctions naturally involves a reclassification of the societies which have been regarded as double descent systems, for a considerable proportion of those listed by Murdock (1940, 1949, 1957) have only complementary descent groups. Nevertheless, the number of double descent systems is much larger than has been supposed, particularly in Africa. In the Appendix to this paper I show the distribution of double descent systems and complementary descent systems in Africa, the only continent for which my information can claim any degree of completeness. In addition, I have reclassified those societies in other parts of the world which have been discussed as double descent systems.

Conclusion
In this paper an attempt has been made to refine the classification of 'double descent' systems, i.e. systems in which a person is at once a member both of a patrilineal and of a matrilineal descent group. For this purpose, a unilineal descent group is conceived as one which the actors themselves recognize by the use either of a technical term or of a specific name; thus many Australian systems with so-called 'anonymous' UDGs are excluded from the category.

Examination of the Ashanti case points up the necessity of making distinctions within the general class of societies with descent groups based upon both modes of reckoning unilineal descent. A crucial factor here seems to be the division of property between the two sets of groups. It is suggested that the phrase 'double descent system' be reserved for those societies in which both patriclans and matriclans are groups which are corporate, in the sense that property is inherited within them. The non-corporate descent groups I refer to, in this context, as complementary (or secondary) descent groups. This distinction is necessary partly because comparative work demands finer discriminations than former usage provides and partly because the presence of corporate descent groups has different implications for the social system from those arising out of the presence of weaker, secondary descent groups.

APPENDIX

TABLE VI

PROVISIONAL CLASSIFICATION OF DOUBLE AND SECONDARY (COMPLEMENTARY) DESCENT SYSTEMS

I. Unilineal systems with complementary (secondary) descent groups
    A. *Patrilineal systems with complementary uterine groups*
        (i) *Unnamed*
            Africa Tallensi (Fortes 1949); Nankanse (Rattray 1932: I, 233); Kusase (Rattray 1932: II, 375); Builsa (Rattray 1932: II, 399); Dagaba (Rattray 1932: II, 404); Kagoro (Smith 1953: 308); Bavenda (Stayt 1931: 185); Dera (Kanakuru) (Meek 1931); Kpe (Ardener 1956);[16]? Wolof (Ames 1959: 255); Iraqw (Winter, personal communication).
            Elsewhere Manus (Mead 1934).
        (ii) *Named*
            Africa LoWiili (Goody 1956); Arochuku (Jones, personal communication).
            Elsewhere Toda (Emeneau 1937); Yap (Schneider 1953); Wogeo (Hogbin 1938);? Ambrym (Deacon 1927); Australian 'double-clean systems' listed in Radcliffe-Brown 1930: Areas No. 5, 10 (Dieri), 13 (Tjapwurong), 14 (Wati-Wati), 15 (Bakandji), 16, 17 (Ngarigo), 21 (Kamilaroi), 25 (Kabi), 26?, 27, 28, 31?, 43 (Tiwi).
    B. *Matrilineal systems with complementary agnatic groups*
        (i) *Unnamed*
            Africa Wambugwe (Gray 1953);? Ila (Richards 1950: 244).

(ii) *Named*

Africa Ashanti (Fortes 1950); Fanti (Christensen 1954); Agni (Lystad 1959);? Abron (Tauxier 1921); Nyanja (Barnes, 1922: 147); Longuda (Meek 1931); Mwera (Ehrenfels 1959).

Elsewhere Bush Negroes of Suriname (Herskovits 1930):? Caraja of Brazil (Lipkind 1948).

II. Full double descent systems

Africa These may be divided into 6 groups:

(i) the Cross River group of south-eastern Nigeria, consisting of the Yakö and some adjacent peoples, the Ekumuru, Abayong, Agwa'a-guna, Enna, Abini, Agoi, Asiga, and the eastern Ibo groups of Ada and Abam (Ohaffia) (Forde 1950: 286; Forde and Jones 1950: 52); Afikpo Ibo (Ottenberg 1959).[17]

(ii) the northern Nigerian group, consisting of the Chamba Lekon and the Daka (Gandole and Lamja) (Meek 1931).

(iii) the Voltaic group, consisting of the LoWilisi (or 'true Lobi') and the adjacent Tegesye, Birifor, Dyan (Janni), Doghosie, Gan (or Gane), LoDagaba, Chakalle (Labouret 1931: 253; Rattray 1932; Westermann and Bryan 1952; Goody 1954).[18]

(iv) the Nuba group, consisting of the Nyaro, the Tullishi and possibly the Kunama of western Eritrea (Nadel 1950).[19]

(v) the East African group, consisting of the Nyika, Digo, Duruma and Rabai (Prins 1952: 63).

(vi) the Southwest African group consisting of the Herero (Gibson 1956), the Ovimbundu (McCulloch 1952), the Kwanyamba-Ambo and the Nyanekas (Estermann 1952).[20]

Elsewhere Ontong Java (Hogbin 1931);[21] Pukapuka (Beaglehole and Beaglehole 1938). *Information inadequate.* Vaitupu, Ellice Islands (Kennedy 1931: 258, 297).[22]

NOTES

1. Ethnographic Atlas, *Ethnography*, 1967, 6, 2.

2. I am indebted to M. Fortes and A. I. Richards for their comments upon this paper and to the late S. F. Nadel, the late A. R. Radcliffe-Brown, G. I. Jones, A. H. J. Prins and E. H. Winter for personal communications relating to its subject matter.

3. In his article on double descent (1940), Murdock mentioned the Toda case, apparently unaware of Radcliffe-Brown's similar comment on the Ambrym. But this is perhaps hardly surprising as he made no reference at all in this article to any of Radcliffe-Brown's comments on double descent. Indeed he stated, 'It is the purpose of this paper to call attention to a third primary type of affiliation, "double descent", which has been reported by recent ethnographers for a number of widely separated areas, but which has thus far escaped extended theoretical consideration' (1940: 555). In view of the fact that he referred to an article by Lawrence on 'Alternating Generations in Australia' (1937) which attempted to

re-examine Radcliffe-Brown's analysis of Australian social organization (Radcliffe-Brown 1930), and indeed edited the symposium where it appeared, I find this omission difficult to understand.

4. A decade earlier, Francis Galton, in a communication to the Anthropological Institute, suggested that Australian marriage systems could be more readily understood 'if we suppose a cross division' (1889: 71). But he realized that the 'testing question' is 'does such a cross division as that which I have supposed, really exist?' This is still the 'testing question'. But, as Galton pointed out, whether or not they exist, his theory has much to recommend it as a *memoria technica*. The analysis of Australian systems would be a simpler matter if other writers had maintained so clear a distinction between the concepts of the actors and the tools of the observer.

5. The Dieri (or Dyerie) were also chosen by Durkheim as an example of 'double exogamy' (1898: 26).

6. I should add that what Lawrence means by sister exchange is that when male members of a marriage class, 'A', marry female members of 'B' (i.e., Δ'A' = $\bigcirc$'B'), then, Δ'B' = $\bigcirc$'A'. However, the members of 'A' do not necessarily belong to the same UDG; they merely fall into one marriage class and, usually, one kinship category. It can therefore be misleading to express this marriage:

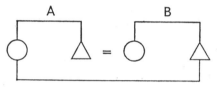

Indeed this error appears to lead to one of the major misunderstandings of Australian systems.

7. His exact words were: 'Whenever I use this term it will apply to membership of a group, and to this only . . . the use of the term is only of value when the group is unilateral' (1924: 86).

8. See also my account of the 'positional terminology' of the LoWiili (Goody 1956: 16–26).

9. Discussing explanations of cross-cousin marriage as resulting from cross-cutting pairs of exogamous descent groups, Lévi-Strauss is also led to complain of the invention of non-existent groups or classes: 'Dans la plupart des cas . . . c'est le sociologue qui, pour rendre compte d'une loi compliquée de répartition des conjoints possibles et des conjoints prohibés, invente une hypothétique division du groupe en classes unilatérales . . . ces travaux contreviennent à un principe bien connu des logiciens: à savoir que l'existence d'une classe définissable en extension ne peut jamais être postulée. On constate la présence d'une classe; on ne la déduit pas' (1949: 140–1).

10. This blurring has complications for cross-cultural analysis. For example, Zelditch, in Parsons and Bales (1955), includes the French Canadians, Germans, Irish, Polish and Spanish Americans among the 'patrilineal' cases, though the U.S. Middle Class are 'bilateral'. Mundugumor is classified as 'double descent'.

11. Christensen (1954: 4) maintains that he does, but I can find no statement to this effect.

The Classification of Double Descent Systems

12. 'Except in Ontong Java and Pukapuka, exogamy is everywhere associated with both patrilineal and matrilineal kin groups' (Murdock 1940: 561).

13. A further degree of organization is represented by segments which are not only named but are viewed as being of a specific number, like the twelve tribes of Israel. The latter I have called 'co-ordinated', as distinct from unco-ordinated, segments (Goody 1957).

14. I am grateful to H. Th. Fischer for having pointed to a lack of clarity in my using the term 'full double descent' as an alternative designation for the Yakö type of system.

15. In other words, members have with respect to one another what in Anglo-American law might be described as a contingent property interest of the nature of an expectancy, but somewhat more substantial, approaching in fact a future interest. I should add that it is not always easy from the reports of ethnographers to determine the extent of corporate interests in property. However, as the holder and heir may be held in themselves to constitute a corporate group in this respect, I have for present purposes taken the existence of inheritance or 'anticipatory inheritance' within such a group as sufficient to identify it as a property-holding corporation.

16. Murdock (1959: 277) suggests that the Koko, Dundu and Puku of the same area may be similar in this respect to the Kpe.

17. These are the double descent peoples of the Cross River area as given in the literature, but G. I. Jones, in a personal communication, suggests the following classification: Mbembe group (Ukelle, Okum, Intrigum, Osopong, Ofungbonga, Adun, Agbo and Igbo, including Asiga); Ekoi group (Nkim, Nkumm, Akajuk, Nnam, Nsele, Abanyum, Atam, Akparabong, Nde, Ofitop, Etung, Olulumo, Ikom); Agwa'aguna-Yakö group (Bahumunu or Ekumuru, Abayong, Agwa'a-guna, Abini, ? Ugben, ? Akpet, Yakö including Ekuri, Umor, Nko, Nkpani and Idomi villages, ? Agoi, Enna, Agballa and Umon ?); Cross River Ibo group (Akeze, Amaseri, Okpoha, Afikpo, Ada, Unwana, Abiriba, Abam, Ohaffia). It should be noted that among the Ohaffia Ibo and the Ada some land is inherited matrilineally.

18. In Labouret's account of the 'Lobi' peoples, which I here refer to by the names LoWilisi, Tegesye, Birifor, Dyan, Doghosie and Gan, he makes no mention of the existence of patrilineal descent groups, although double inheritance is the rule, and land and compounds are transmitted agnatically. However, the Birifor settlements I visited on the Upper Volta side of the border had the same patriclans as the LoDagaa in Ghana. It is on this basis that I make the assumption that all these tribes have full double descent systems; subsequent research may of course lead to a modification of this conclusion. I have explained the reasons for my assumptions about the other peoples listed here in the earlier publication mentioned. There may be other such systems to the south, among the Gbeinngn (or Gan) for example (Tauxier 1921: 375). They are described as 'teintés de matriarchalisme'. In the original paper I included the Tampolense, Vagala and Safalba of Gonja, but further research throws doubt upon this suggestion.

19. Nadel (1947: 31) mentions the Kamdang and Tima as inheriting houses and some land patrilineally and yet speaks of them as matrilineal; the former he refers to as a strictly unilateral matrilineal system (1950: 357). I would expect them both to be double descent systems.

115

20. Radcliffe-Brown wrote in a personal communication: 'North of the Herero and extending through Angola, beginning with Ova-kuanyama, there are a number of tribes all described as having matrilineal clans (*ikanda*). It is now more than a quarter of a century ago since I was making a systematic study of African tribes. I formed the strong suspicion that some of these tribes, besides their matrilineal clans, would be found on investigation to have patrilineal descent groups.' He went on to say that he could find no clear evidence in the existing ethnographical literature because of the prejudice that any particular society must be either patrilineal or matrilineal.

McCulloch (1952) analyses Childs' discussion of the Ovimbundu (1949) and concludes that this appears to be a system of double descent.

The word *ikanda* is cognate to the Mayombe *dikanda*, which Richards (1950) translates as 'major lineage'. The Mayombe are matrilineal. A feature of the distribution of double descent systems in Africa is that in general they fall between groups of patrilineal societies on the one hand and matrilineal societies on the other. This does not mean that they represent an unstable, halfway house between 'ideal' patrilineal and matrilineal types, as some ethnographers appear to suggest; in themselves, they are no more and no less transitional than any other system of descent groups.

21. Bulmer points out that the accounts of Ontong Java give neither name nor term for the matrilineal group. The same is true for the patrilineal groups of the Tullishi and the Chamba Lekon, and for both groups among the Daka. In each case double inheritance is reported.

22. The original article was followed by the comments of 14 scholars, together with a reply that attempted to clarify some of the difficulties my colleagues felt existed.

REFERENCES

Ames, D. W., 1959, 'Wolof co-operative work groups', in *Continuity and Change in African Cultures* (eds. W. R. Bascom and M. J. Herskovits), 224–37, Chicago.

Ardener, E., 1956, *Coastal Bantu of the Camerouns.* (Ethnographic Survey of Africa.) London.

Barnes, H. (Rev.), 1922, 'Marriage of cousins in Nyasaland', *Man*, **22**: 147–9.

Beaglehole, E., and Beaglehole, P., 1938, *Ethnology of Pukapuka.* (Bernice P. Bishop Museum, Bulletin no. 150.) Honolulu.

Berndt, R. M., 1955, ' "Murngin" (Wulamba) Social Organization', *American Anthropologist*, **57**: 84–106.

Childs, G. M., 1949, *Umbundu Kinship and Character*, London.

Christensen, J. B., 1954, *Double Descent Among the Fanti*, New Haven.

Deacon, B. A., 1927, 'The Regulation of Marriage in Ambrym', *Journal of the Royal Anthropological Institute*, **57**: 325–48.

Durkheim, E., 1898, 'La Prohibition de l'inceste et ses origines', *L'Année Sociologique*, **1**: 1–70.

Ehrenfels, U. R., 1959, 'Bilineal Clan Succession in East Africa', *Anthropos*, **54** 576–8.

The Classification of Double Descent Systems

Emeneau, M. B., 1937, 'Toda Marriage Regulations and Taboos', *American Anthropologist*, **39**: 103–12.

Estermann, C., 1952, 'Clans et alliances entre clans dans le sud-ouest de l'Angola', *Anthropos*, **47**: 587–606.

Evans-Pritchard, E. E., 1940, *The Political System of the Anuak of the Anglo-Egyptian Sudan*, London.

Firth, R., 1957, 'A Note on Descent Groups in Polynesia', *Man*, **57**: 4–8.

Forde, D., 1938, 'Fission and Accretion in the Patrilineal Clans of a Semi-Bantu Community in Southern Nigeria', *Journal of the Royal Anthropological Institute*, **68**: 311–38.

Forde, D., 1939, 'Kinship in Umor', *American Anthropologist*, **41**: 523–53.

Forde, D., 1950, 'Double Descent Among the Yakö', in *African Systems of Kinship and Marriage* (eds. A. R. Radcliffe-Brown and D. Forde), 285–332, London.

Forde, D., and Jones, G. I., 1950, *The Ibo and Ibibio-speaking peoples of South-Eastern Nigeria*. (Ethnographic Survey of Africa.) London.

Fortes, M., 1949, *The Web of Kinship Among the Tallensi*, London.

Fortes, M., 1950, 'Kinship and Marriage Among the Ashanti', in *African Systems of Kinship and Marriage* (eds. A. R. Radcliffe-Brown and D. Forde), 252–84, London.

Fortes, M., 1953, 'The Structure of Unilineal Descent Groups', *American Anthropologist*, **55**: 17–41.

Fortes, M., and Evans-Pritchard, E. E., 1940, *African Political Systems*, London.

Fried, M. H., 1957, 'The Classification of Corporate Unilineal Descent Groups', *Journal of the Royal Anthropological Institute*, **87**: 1–29.

Galton, F., 1889, 'Note on the Australian Marriage System', *J. Anthrop. Inst.*, **18**: 70–2.

Goodenough, W. H., 1955, 'A Problem in Malayo-Polynesian Social Organization', *American Anthropologist*, **57**: 71–83.

Goody, J. R., 1954, 'The Ethnography of the Northern Territories of the Gold Coast, West of the White Volta', London.

Goody, J. R., 1956, *The Social Organization of the LoWiili*, London (2nd ed. 1967).

Goody, J. R., 1957, 'Fields of Social Control Among the LoDagaba', *Journal of the Royal Anthropological Institute*, **87**: 75–104.

Goody, J. R., 1959, 'The Mother's Brother and the Sister's Son in West Africa', *Journal of the Royal Anthropological Institute*, **89**: 59–88 (chapter 3).

Gray, R. F., 1953, 'Positional Succession Among the Wambugwe', *Africa*, **23**: 233–43.

Herskovits, M. J., 1930, 'The Social Organization of the Bush Negroes of Suriname', *Proceedings of the 23rd International Congress of Americanists*, New York, 1928, 713–27.

Herskovits, M. J., 1937, 'The Ashanti Ntoro: a Re-examination', *Journal of the Royal Anthropological Institute*, **67**: 287–96.

Hogbin, H. I., 1931, 'The Social Organization of Ontong Java', *Oceania*, **1**: 399–425.

Hogbin, H. I., 1938, 'Social Reaction to Crime: Law and Morals in the Schouten Islands, New Guinea', *Journal of the Royal Anthropological Institute*, **68**: 223–62.

Kennedy, D. G., 1931, *Field Notes on the Culture of Vaitupu, Ellice Islands*. (Memoirs of the Polynesian Society, no. 9.) New Plymouth, New Zealand.

117

Labouret, H., 1931, *Les Tribus du Rameau Lobi*, Paris.

Lawrence, W. E., 1937, 'Alternating Generations in Australia', in *Studies in the Science of Society* (ed. G. P. Murdock), 319–54, New Haven.

Leach, E. R., 1950, *Social Science Research in Sarawak*. (Colonial Research Studies, no. 1.) London.

Leach, E. R., 1951, 'The Structural Implications of Matrilateral Cross-Cousin Marriage', *Journal of the Royal Anthropological Institute*, **81**: 23–55.

Lévi-Strauss, C., 1949, *Les Structures Élémentaires de la Parenté*, Paris.

Lipkind, W., 1948, 'The Caraja', in *Handbook of South American Indians* (ed. J. H. Steward), **3**: 179–91, Washington.

Lundberg, G. A., 1939, *Foundations of Sociology*, New York.

Lystad, R. A., 1959, 'Marriage and Kinship Among the Ashanti and the Agni: a Study of Differential Acculturation', in *Continuity and Change in African Cultures* (eds. W. R. Bascom and M. J. Herskovits), 187–204, Chicago.

McCulloch, M., 1952, *The Ovimbundu of Angola*. (Ethnographic Survey of Africa.) London.

Matthews, R. H., 1900, 'Marriage and Descent Among the Australian Aborigines', *Journal of the Royal Society of New South Wales*, **34**: 120–35.

Mead, M., 1934, *Kinship in the Admiralty Islands*. (Anthropological Papers of the American Museum of Natural History, 34, Pt. 2.) New York.

Meek, C. K., 1931, *Tribal Studies in Northern Nigeria*, 2 vols., London.

Murdock, G. P., 1940, 'Double Descent', *American Anthropologist*, **42**: 555–61.

Murdock, G. P., 1949, *Social Structure*, New York.

Murdock, G. P., 1957, 'World Ethnographic Sample', *American Anthropologist*, **59**: 664–87.

Murdock, G. P., 1959, *Africa*, New York.

Nadel, S. F., 1942, *Black Byzantium*, London.

Nadel, S. F., 1947, *The Nuba*, London.

Nadel, S. F., 1950, 'Dual Descent in the Nuba Hills', in *African Systems of Kinship and Marriage* (eds. A. R. Radcliffe-Brown and D. Forde), 333–59, London.

Nadel, S. F., 1951, *The Foundations of Social Anthropology*, London.

Ottenberg, P. V., 1959, 'The Changing Economic Position of Women among the Afiikpo Ibo', in *Continuity and Change in African Cultures* (eds. W. R. Bascom and M. J. Herskovits), 205–23, Chicago.

Parsons, T., and R. F. Bales, 1955, *Family, Socialization and Interaction Process*, Glencoe, Illinois.

Phillpotts, B. S., 1913, *Kindred and Clan*. (Cambridge Archaeological and Ethnological Series.) Cambridge.

Prins, A. H. J., 1952, *The Coastal Tribes of the North-eastern Bantu*. (Ethnographic Survey of Africa.) London.

Radcliffe-Brown, A. R., 1913, 'Three Tribes of Western Australia', *Journal of the Royal Anthropological Institute*, **43**: 143–94.

Radcliffe-Brown, A. R., 1924, 'The Mother's Brother in South Africa', *South African Journal of Science*, **21**: 542–55.

Radcliffe-Brown, A. R., 1927, 'The Regulation of Marriage in Ambrym', *Journal of the Royal Anthropological Institute*, **57**: 343–8.

Radcliffe-Brown, A. R., 1929a, 'A Further Note on Ambrym', *Man*, **29**: 50–3.

Radcliffe-Brown, A. R., 1929b, 'Bilateral Descent', *Man*, **29**: 199–200.

The Classification of Double Descent Systems

Radcliffe-Brown, A. R., 1930, 'The Social Organization of Australian Tribes', *Oceania*, 1: 34–63 (Part I), 206–46 (Part II).

Radcliffe-Brown, A. R., 1935, 'Patrilineal and Matrilineal Succession', *Iowa Law Review*, 20: 286–303.

Radcliffe-Brown, A. R., 1950, 'Introduction', in *African Systems of Kinship and Marriage* (eds. A. R. Radcliffe-Brown and D. Forde), 1–85, London.

Radcliffe-Brown, A. R., 1951, 'Murngin Social Organization', *American Anthropologist*, 53: 37–55.

Radcliffe-Brown, A. R., 1956, 'On Australian Local Organization', *American Anthropologist*, 58: 363–7.

Rattray, R. S., 1929, *Ashanti Law and Constitution*, Oxford.

Rattray, R. S., 1932, *Tribes of the Ashanti Hinterland*, 2 vols, Oxford.

Richards, A. I., 1950, 'Some Types of Family Structure Amongst the Central Bantu', in *African Systems of Kinship and Marriage* (eds. A. R. Radcliffe-Brown and D. Forde), 207–51, London.

Rivers, W. H. R., 1906, *The Todas*, London.

Rivers, W. H. R., 1915, 'Descent and Ceremonial in Ambrin', *Journal of the Royal Anthropological Institute*, 45: 229–33.

Rivers, W. H. R., 1924, *Social Organization*, London.

Seligman, B. Z., 1927, 'Bilateral Descent and the Formation of Marriage Classes', *Journal of the Royal Anthropological Institute*, 57: 349–79.

Schneider, D. M., 1953, 'Yap Kinship Terminology and Kin Groups', *American Anthropologist*, 55: 215–36.

Smith, M. G., 1953, 'Secondary Marriage in Northern Nigeria', *Africa*, 23: 298–323.

Stayt, H. A., 1931, *The Bavenda*, London.

Tauxier, L., 1921, *Le Noir de Bondoukou*, Paris.

Warner, W. L., 1937, *A Black Civilization*, New York (2nd ed., 1958).

Weber, M., 1947, *The Theory of Social and Economic Organization*; being Pt. I of *Wirtschaft und Gesellschaft*: trans. from the German by A. R. (i.e., M.) Henderson and T. Parsons; rev. and ed. with an introd. by T. Parsons, London.

Westermann, D., and M. Bryan, 1952, *Languages of West Africa*, London.

CHAPTER FIVE

Inheritance, Social Change and the Boundary Problem

SOCIAL anthropologists have in general been committed to the idea that they are examining 'societies', 'social structures' or 'cultures' which operate in some sense as functioning wholes, as 'systems', as 'boundary-maintaining units'. The gains of such an approach (and they are many) have received ample publicity; the costs, I think, have not. Yet it is significant that in discussing the 'contemporary' situation, fieldworkers tend to drop the wholistic approach and prefer to talk in terms of fields of social relationships.

This point was emphasized in Gluckman's critique of Malinowski (1947) where he calls for an analysis not in terms of the contact of unitary cultures or tribes, but of a total social field with its relationships of conflict and co-operation, a view earlier put forward by Fortes and Schapera (1936). To accept this statement does not preclude a recognition of the fact that the social field (particularly in the colonial context) is never evenly differentiated; major distinctions of language, colour, class, creed and custom are in themselves important factors in defining the social field and hence their use as a terminal point in an analysis is not altogether unjustified. But in this 'indigenous' situation with which I am dealing, the 'border' is not so sharply defined; differences in the social behaviour of neighbouring groups are matters of degree, not of kind. Consequently there are even greater costs in adopting a framework that is limited to a single culture or even to a single unit, a village or a state.

One cost of concentrating upon *a* village, *a* tribe, or *a* state, is that the analysis is oriented towards internal rather than external relationships. In particular, boundary problems between groups with differing patterns

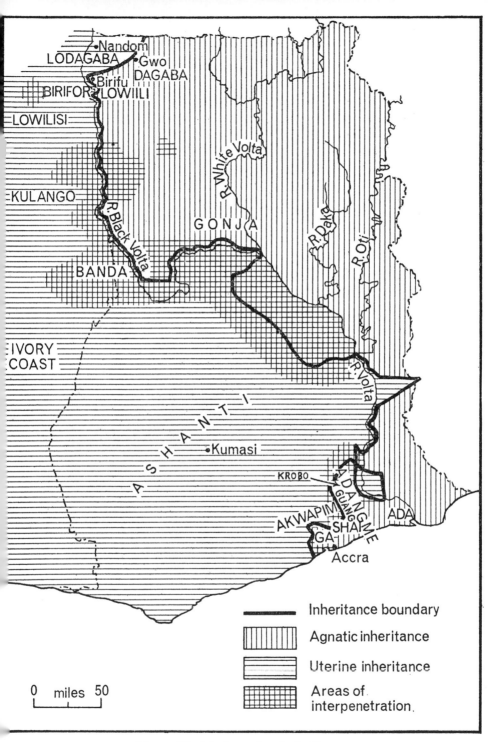

MAP 1. The inheritance frontier in Ghana.

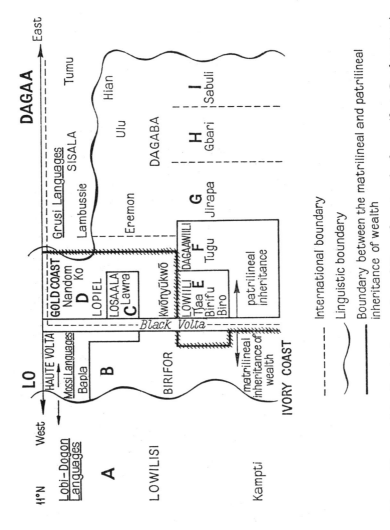

MAP 2. The use of the directional names Lo and Dagaa for external reference (from Goody 1962: 5).

of social action tend to get ignored. Yet the juxtaposition of such groups is clearly an important factor in leading to social change. This juxtaposition may occur vertically, as through conquest, or horizontally, though spatial proximity: both situations create a boundary problem though the implications are somewhat different when political control is involved.

In another chapter (6) I have discussed some aspects of the coming together of different cultural groups in northern Ghana, especially as this process is affected by their marriage policy. Here I consider another boundary situation that arises in many parts of the world when men practising one kind of social behaviour come into contact with those used to acting in very different ways. And such a situation is more frequent and of greater theoretical importance than is often realized. For fields of social relationships (as distinct from the more abstract cultures, structures, systems of the sociologist) have no *necessary* unity, no inevitable consistency about them, unless one takes as evidence of this unity and consistency the very fact that men are interacting with other men; and such a conclusion would be at once tautological and simple-minded. While social groups and customary patterns are always important parameters in the study of human action, fields of social relationships extend more widely across such boundaries. This fact is of considerable significance in the study of change, where the input from adjacent societies, positive in the form of property, women and religious cults, negative in the form of war, is a potential initiator of new modes of behaviour.

One of the most striking confrontations of this kind comes about when systems of patrilineal and matrilineal inheritance (and hence usually but not invariably succession and descent) are found side by side (or above and below), since they represent radically different modes of devolving property, modes that are inevitably in the forefront of men's minds because they deal with the recurrent distribution of scarce resources, of the means and ends of the productive processes.

The problem to which juxtaposition along this P/M boundary gives rise is this.[1] In the absence of any provision to the contrary, the members of neighbouring kin or local groups will inevitably intermarry. If the inter-marrying groups practise two different systems of inheritance, agnatic (or patrilineal) and uterine (or matrilineal), then the consequences for the distribution of property will be asymmetrical. Consider first the case of a 'patrilineal' man marrying a 'matrilineal' woman. For the purposes of this discussion I assume a unisexual system of inheritance, such as generally obtains in Africa.

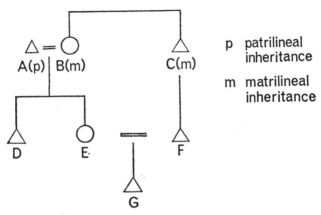

p   patrilineal
      inheritance

m   matrilineal
      inheritance

FIGURE 2. 'Patrilineal' man marries 'matrilineal' woman.

The male offspring of such a union (D) has two inheritance options open to him. He may inherit patrilineally from his father (with whom, under a system of virilocal marriage, he lives) or he can inherit matrilineally from his mother's brother (C). But if they have a choice in this matter, the mother's people are unlikely to allow their property to go to the sister's child unless they are confident that their wealth will remain a matrilineal possession and not simply be aggregated to the patrilineal patrimony. They may therefore insist that the heir, D, come to live with them, and accept full responsibility for looking after the orphans (F). Alternatively, they may adopt the 'circumventing mechanism' of getting the uncle's son to marry his FZD (Goody 1962: 349); the child of this union would thus be in a position to inherit the property of his maternal grandfather. Thirdly, supernatural sanctions may be so strong that even if the heir D does not reside with his maternal kin, he is nonetheless obliged to pass on matrilineally what he received matrilineally.

The alternative form of marriage between the groups is illustrated in Figure 3.

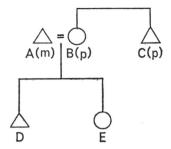

FIGURE 3. 'Matrilineal' man marries 'patrilineal' woman.

In this case, the male offspring of the union falls between two stools, for he can inherit neither from his father nor from his mother's brother. The father could perhaps ensure that his son obtained an inheritance only if he himself were to move to his wife's natal home, or alternatively if the boy were to attach himself to his maternal uncle. But in any case, the prospect is bleak.

In Ghana, there is a constant interaction between peoples inheriting patrilineally and matrilineally. Next to the great belt of matrilineal Akan in the forest zone are found the Ga-Adangme of Accra, the Guang, Krobo and Shai of the Akwapim hills, the Ada and Ewe of the mouth of the Volta, and a congeries of different peoples distributed up the Volta valley as far as the Banda hills. All of these latter practise a form of agnatic (or at least non-uterine) inheritance. And further north, on the western border of the country, the agnatic Dagaba and Wiili come up against the LoDagaba and LoBirifor who inherit movable property at least (and real property is usually of less value) down the uterine channel.

Some writers have recently tended to play down the difference between 'patrilineal' and 'matrilineal' systems. It is certainly true that descent groups may vary considerably in the functions they perform and in the degree to which membership is determined by unilineal reckoning alone, and in some cases the difference between systems of patrilineal and matrilineal descent groups may not be large. But the way in which property (relatively exclusive rights to scarce material goods, as distinct from group membership) is passed down by devolution from one generation to the next, either by inheritance or during the holder's lifetime, is of universal importance in farming societies and quite specific choices have to be made concerning the reallocation of these goods. You cannot prevaricate with inheritance the way you can with descent.

The P/M boundary situation occurs in the region to the north-west of Accra, especially on the Akwapim ridge. Here the belt of 'agnatic' peoples extending from Nigeria, Dahomey and Togo meets the matrilineal Akan. Nowadays the two groups are not only juxtaposed but interpenetrate to an increasing extent, since it is the inhabitants of the ridge who have migrated so energetically into Akan territory in the course of their exploitation of cash crops. 'From the time of *Kɔnɔ Sakité* (1867–92)', writes Huber 'it has become the passion of the Krobo to acquire new land for farming' (1963: 39); they moved in search of land to cultivate first the oil palm[2] and then cocoa.[3] As a result of this migration the settlements of people practising the two systems became more and more intermingled on the ground, though the incoming farmers usually retained a foothold in their hill villages and even when these were no longer inhabited, they returned to the site for funerals, for festivals and for the girls' puberty ceremonies.

Experience of another series of groups situated along an inheritance boundary (the peoples of northern Ghana that I collectively refer to as the LoDagaa) convinced me that the recognition of these differing modes of transmission is a major factor in the actor's view of his situation.[4] It appears to be so, too, in the Akwapim region, though writers have had little to say on this subject. The reason the issue is of practical concern has already been indicated. If a man belongs to a group that inherits agnatically and his son marries a 'matrilineal' girl, then the offspring of this union will be entitled to inherit both from the father and from the mother's brother. If he takes the second option, he is rejecting his father in a very fundamental way. If on the other hand the same man's daughter marries a 'matrilineal' husband, then the offspring have no-one from whom they can inherit property.

In any particular situation, the importance of this 'conflict of laws' will clearly depend upon the role played by inherited property. In West Africa, accumulated property (whether in cows, cowries or gold) has long been of great significance and its distribution is the subject of conscious thought and deliberate manipulation.

The considerations arising out of the contact between agnatic and uterine modes of inheritance are not given much explicit attention in the published literature on the Akwapim area. But there is some evidence that among agnatically inheriting peoples marriage policy is directed against unions of the property-losing kind. 'No Krobo man would (at least in the past) give his daughter in marriage to an uncircumcised which, in concreto, means to a member of the *Akan* tribe . . .' (Huber 1963: 96)[5] Among the Krobo, cross-cousin marriage (FZD) receives great stress. In addition a large number of marriages are within the same patrilineal 'house', though not normally between first cousins (Huber 1963: 97); one sample showed 36 per cent of such marriages, another 51.6 per cent. In his account of Larteh, Brokensha remarks upon the small number of marriages contracted with non-Larterians; 21 per cent of marriages were with cross-cousins (12 per cent FZD, 9 per cent MBD), a further 20 per cent within the same ward and a total of 88 per cent within Larteh, and half the rest from other Akwapim towns (1966: 219), mostly the 'patrilineal' ones. By close marriage, they avoid the matrilineal threat.

I raised this problem with Nana Bagyire VI, chief of the Guang town of Abiriw. He replied: 'If my daughter wanted to marry an Ashanti man I would try to dissuade her, since the child would be a "lost person", having no inheritance. Indeed my niece did marry an Ashanti and when he came to see me recently I told him that if he didn't look after her well, then the children would be for me' (J 3037). By this he meant that if his sister's daughter left her husband, then he would claim the children as attached members of his own kin group. Unlike the Krobo, they appear to have no specific ban on intermarriage, but it is nevertheless firmly discouraged, especially the marriage of a 'patrilineal' girl with a 'matrilineal' man. Moreover, the discouragement is phrased not only in terms of expediency but also of morality. Just as the Krobo are said to refuse to let their daughters marry uncircumcised men, so the Guang justify their attitude by referring to the Ashanti as 'bush people'; in this case specific reference was made to their earlier custom of human sacrifice.

The same situations that exist in Akwapim are also found on the western side of northern Ghana where there is a distinct boundary between peoples who inherit movable property matrilineally (immovables stay in the father's line) and those who inherit all property patrilineally. The Dagaba and Wiili (LoWiili and DagaaWiili) fall into the latter category, the LoDagaba (LoPiel and LoSaala) and the LoBirifor in the former; in the context of inheritance, the former are often referred to as Dagaa, the latter as Lobi (Lo).

Once again, it is not simply juxtaposition that occurs; there is also interpenetration as the result of the local migrations that have long been a feature of the whole area. The impetus behind such movements was the search for better land and the desire for greater security; poor tropical soils, a thinly spread population and the constant demand for slaves meant continual upheavals of a local kind. But when initial needs had been satisfied, the primary concern of the immigrants with regard to their hosts was to procure wives, for themselves or for their sons; and at the same time, of course, husbands for their daughters. To achieve this end they had either to adopt a policy of endogamy (unusual in Africa), or alternatively to permit marriage to girls from the host group. Intermarriage inevitably entailed an acceptance of the system of pre-stations and forms of marriage favoured by the locally dominant group. But of more far-reaching importance is the fact that the persons involved in such a marriage have different ideas about the role of their offspring. A 'matrilineal' mother will expect her son to inherit from her brother and she is sometimes in a position to encourage him to do precisely this, especially if her people are the locally dominant ones. When I asked some members of the Bekuone patriclan of Lyssa (Dagaba) how it came about that their clansmen in the Nandom (LoDagaba) area *dina gbang* (inherited movable property in the uterine line), the senior replied: 'What happens is that when we go to live there, we have to marry the daughters of the Lobi (*Lobr*). When the child grows up, his mother takes him to her father's house, keeps him there until her brother dies and then persuades him to keep the property.'[6]

The problem of adjustment arises in rather a different form when patrilineal and matrilineal groups live side by side, for it then becomes one of territorial boundaries rather than of social incorporation. And since in acephalous systems the groups concerned are politically equal (in a broad sense), the question of dominance does not arise.

From the standpoint of a matrilineally-inheriting (M) group, the disadvantage of taking a 'patrilineal' (P) wife is that the male offspring has no heritage—he can be only an 'attached' member wherever he goes, whether he returns to his mother's patriclan as a 'sister's son' or whether he stays with his father's matriclan as a 'son'. In a 'patrilineal' section of Kwõnyũkwõ (Kumansal), I was told that if one of their daughters married a 'matrilineal' man, the offspring could on no account come back to inherit; if he did he would die within three days. All a sister's son will receive is a cow to tend (*gwöl*) in return for which he will keep the increase. But the position of the 'lost person' is partially protected by a system of double inheritance which divides the property between the two lines; it does not seem accidental that, in Africa, these systems generally occur in the very borderland areas with which we are here concerned.

From the standpoint of a patrilineal group, the threat involved is yet greater because marriage to a matrilineal wife means that the male offspring can receive the same benefits at his mother's house as he can at his father's. And if the mother's brother has more cattle, or dies first; or if the mother returns to her natal home through divorce or widowhood, then the child may adopt the matrilineal rather than the patrilineal alternative.

The results of such a decision (whether made by the man himself or by his relatives) are of wide-ranging importance—and the LoDagaa are quite clear about the consequences. The settlement of Gwo near Nandom is inhabited by a number of lineages some of whom (e.g. the Bekuone) 'inherit in the house' (*dina yiru*, i.e. agnatically) and others (e.g. the Kusiele) who inherit in the uterine line (*dina gbang*). Intermarriage inevitably occurs both within and without the settlement, thus leading to a shift of the boundary. Indeed changes of this kind take place within one lineage. Dogber (a name meaning 'born away') was the grandfather of my assistant, Romulo Tadɔɔ, and a member of the Berewiele patriclan. His father had inherited patrilineally, but had married a Lo girl, a Bekuone from Tokũ. After a while, this woman left her husband's house, ran home and brought her child up with her own folk. Since Dogber had no property of his own, his mother's brother put up the cows he needed to get married; afterwards he continued to farm for his uncle, who managed to buy a cow with the proceeds and this in its turn produced many offspring. Eventually Dogber built his own compound and the uncle announced that because of all the help he had given he should inherit the cows. When the uncle died, his brothers opposed the claim of the sister's son, going before the 'chief' of the district to say that the Berewiele were Dagaba who inherited 'in the house'. But they knew that they were unable to insist, since the will of the ancestors had to be done or the consequences faced. The 'chief' allowed the inheritance to take place, but warned Dogber that henceforth this property must be passed on in the uterine line. So it was, and in his turn Dogber's son, Tadɔɔ, also inherited from the matrilineal side, for his father's property had already been collected by the matrikin (1238).

Commenting to me upon this case, one of Dogber's collateral descendants, a 'patrilineal' man, remarked 'If you inherit your mother's brother's property, you must leave your father's. You cannot inherit (= 'eat') in two places.'[7] Among the LoWiili, it is often maintained that 'things of the mother's stem are inherited in that line' (Goody 1962: 428). This maxim is recognized even in the patrilineal societies along the boundary; and the implications are that if you marry a matrilineal woman, your children may have to bear the consequences.

Of course, the consequences are often brought on by the acts of the offspring themselves. But it is not always easy to refuse the promise of riches when one's maternal uncle dies before one's father. Even about gifts there is a certain ambiguity. When I discussed this issue with the Earth Priest of Gwo, a member of the Haiyuri patriclan, he remarked that he had been given a cow (*naab gwöl*) to look after by his mother's brother, a widespread practice in the area—among the patrilineal Tallensi, a boy is first able to establish an independent fund by a gift of livestock from his mother's brother. But some time or other, the Earth Priest said, he would take the opportunity to return the cow (while keeping the increase) to his mother's people, possibly when they need one for a sacrifice or a funeral. Such a return would relieve the gift of any implications that it was *pre mortem* matrilineal inheritance.

However, there are situations where a man is under great pressure to raise capital, and in this case he may well turn to his mother's kin. The Dagaba of Lyssa and Tuoperi, who inherit in the agnatic line, give a bride-wealth composed exclusively of cowries (60,000 to 110,000), whereas the LoDagaa include cows as well. But when the chief of Tuoperi wanted to marry a Lo girl, her parents demanded cattle and he therefore turned to his mother's brother (a 'matrilineal' man) for help. The acceptance of this assistance creates a special kind of debt that tends to pull the debtor into the matrilineal system of the creditor. In this case it was instrumental in leading the chief of Tuoperi to give his allegiance to the LoDagaba (M) chief of Nandom rather than the Dagaba (P) chief of Lyssa, a decision that in turn influenced the arrangement of local government areas. And at his death, more far-reaching changes in social organization might well result.

One reason the chief had to meet the request of his in-laws was that he would not otherwise have been allowed to marry the girl. A chief is an attractive proposition as a son-in-law and is also in a position to exercise some force. But religious sanctions here give support to the weak (*pace* Marx, they do not always support the strong), for it is generally recognized that unless the proper payments are made, the girl's fertility may fail; 'we do not want her stem (*per*) to finish' (3030).

The radical consequences of the act of one individual in accepting matrilineal property are often discussed in border areas, and not simply in response to an observer's questions. Baaluon of Kwŏnyŭkwŏ explained to me how the Kusiele lineage in that settlement came to inherit in this way (some other lineages, e.g. the Puriyele, still inherit agnatically). 'Our grandfather took and so spoiled things, that's why we now inherit matrilineally (*Ti sāākum di song, bong zu ti dina gbandiru*)'. Baaluon's sons were dead set against the idea of his property, which was considerable, passing out of the house; but the father advised them to accept things as they stood. He explained how he himself had come to inherit in this way, implying not only that his matrikin would be entitled to claim his wealth on grounds of reciprocity, but also that such transactions were the concern of the dead as well as the living, for the ancestors continue to hold an interest in the distribution of the property they acquired from their own forbears (self-acquired property as distinct from ancestor-acquired is here, as elsewhere, subject to somewhat less stringent rules). He went on to tell the story of a man who had inherited from his maternal uncle, and when his own father died, had taken some seven of those cows in addition, though an elder warned against doing so. He used three of these, and died; the remainder were left untouched. 'All the other houses in our lineage (= 'room') flourish, but this one died out.'[8]

In earlier times, inheritance was not simply a question of property being transferred to the next of kin (Goody 1962: 345ff.). Property was held to be vested in the whole matriclan and it sometimes happened that more distant clansmen were able to establish successful claims. There were a variety of reasons for this; in the period for which I have evidence, that is, the early colonial period (1900–30), it would appear that men of influence, including government chiefs, might use their position to obtain part of the property of distant matrikin. As a consequence it could happen that, even in those areas where matriclans were present but not property holding (e.g. the LoWiili area), men might try and obtain a share of the estate of a fellow clansman in a nearby matrilineal settlement.

Claims of this kind were made at the death of Kumbiu, chief of Kwõnyũkwõ (M, LoDagaba), a village which lay immediately to the north-east of Birifu (P, LoWiili). Kumbiu's mother had come from the Ngmanbili section of Birifu. Naakpĩĩ from Chaa (Birifu) belonged to the same 'mother's stem' (*ma per*, i.e. matrilineage) and both were of the Some matriclan. When Kumbiu died in about 1922, Naakpĩĩ, supported by two other Some clansmen, went and collected 35 cattle, thus potentially opening up a series of further claims at their own death. In the end these efforts were not effective. Naakpĩĩ was forced to return the cattle by the chief of Birifu, Gandaa, who wanted to put a stop to uterine trends of this kind, especially as he fully intended his own, very considerable, property (derived from chiefship and from the export of shrines) to go to his own very numerous offspring. Discussion about this question was virtually taboo when I was in Birifu, and the inhabitants of Chaa displayed great reluctance to go into any details, partly because they were well aware what should have happened, and partly because they were worried about the supernatural consequences of what had been done (934).

The simplest way of preventing boundary problems of this kind is to prevent intermarriage. While the LoDagaa have no prohibitions of the Krobo kind, there is certainly much open discouragement. At Menuõ, a LoDagaba (M) village lying west of the Black Volta River, in what is now the Upper Volta, I was told 'We seek our wives from the LoSaala (M, a LoDagaba sub-group). We do not marry Dagaa (P) because, if they marry one of our women, they do not give us any of her daughter's bridewealth (*pɔɔ libie*) when she marries.'[9] Among the LoDagaba (M) a woman's kin retain a material interest in the marriage of her daughters; for part of the bridewealth received goes to the mother's brother. This does not happen with the Wiili (P) and the Dagaba (P). As a consequence, the 'matrilineal' peoples are not anxious to encourage their daughters to marry 'patrilineally', since not only may an outsider then come and inherit, with the consequent threat to reciprocity and to the social continuity of line or lineage, but they will also lose on the transactions that occur in the following generation.

One way of inhibiting such marriages is to place a higher price on the removal of their daughters, with the result that we find a situation where, contrary to most theoretical assumptions, bridewealth is higher in the more 'matrilineal' groups. This situation was recognized by the 'patrilineal' peoples. Indeed both the direct as well as the indirect bridewealth was greater for 'matrilineal' women. I knew only one LoWiili man in Birifu who had married a 'Lo' (LoBirifor) girl from across the river, although they were constantly attending each other's markets. He had had to give five cows, instead of the payment usually made in Birifu, that is, 20,000 cowries, plus two cows when children were born. His kin considered this a heavy burden, even though he would eventually be able to ask as much for any daughters as had been given for the mother.

For the LoBirifor themselves, anyhow in this area, the internal bridewealth is not so high as this payment would indicate. However a man carries out a great deal of farm service for his father-in-law, who uses his daughter as bait from an early age. Since matrilineal societies can in theory do without the husband/father role altogether (but not that of wife/mother), the brother is in a better position than in patrilineal societies to use his sister as a source of wealth and service. With outsiders the farm work is sometimes compounded into an additional payment as in the case above. But this is done only reluctantly; the 'matrilineal' LoDagaba of Menuõ referred to earlier told me that they were unwilling to marry LoBirifor (M) women at the nearby settlement of Singkaa, since they have to contract an early betrothal and the man has to farm five years for his in-laws, presenting them with a cow and a sheep each year. Thus these LoDagaba (M) found reasons for not marrying women from either of their neighbouring groups, the Dagaba (P) and the LoBirifor (M).

A similar situation appears to exist among the LoBirifor. My own data on their marriage is fragmentary and there are probably major differences within the peoples known by this name. The information I gathered from Nakpala (western Gonja) in 1966 provided evidence of larger payments than are mentioned either by Labouret in his ethnographic account (1931) or by my informants from the Bache area to the north (1950). I do not think that these differences are to be explained by inflation over the years, since this would have affected cows as much as women; but it is true that due to veterinary measures the supply of cattle is increasing faster than that of wives.

The large majority of LoBirifor girls are betrothed in their infancy to a suitor who pays the standard sum of twenty cowries and then begins to farm for his future in-laws (*kob zele*), bringing a party of helpers on two to three occasions every year until the bride is ready to come and live with him. Before she does so, both the father and the mother's brother of the girl have to give their consent. It is not until the girl has given birth to a child that the first bridewealth payment (*pɔɔ kyero libie*) is demanded, for only then will her kin know that she really wants her husband, that is, wants to stay.

Formerly this payment was made in cowries, but the shells are now scarce around Nakpala and reserved for funerals. As an alternative, a man may send a cow and perhaps £5 or £10; if the girl's father insists on cowries, he is in effect refusing permission for his daughter to marry, for he knows the suitor cannot find them. Once this payment has been made, the father informs the girl's mother's brother (*madeb*), who then asks for one to three cows in addition to those sent to the paternal relatives.

If at this stage the girl marries another man who has not farmed for her kin, the original betrothed has to be compensated by a payment of one or two cows for the labour he has put in. Moreover, the new husband will be asked for a further payment of anything up to 10 cattle, since he has in effect seized the girl by force (J. 4024).

High as these payments may seem, the demands of the LoWilisi (or 'true Lobi') further west are even higher: there are similar farming services, plus 15–20 head of cattle. Yet the LoWilisi are more 'matrilineal' than the LoBirifor, apparently having no patrilineal descent groups (like the LoDagaba, the LoBirifor have a fully-fledged double descent system). Indeed one of the reasons given by the LoBirifor for not taking LoWilisi women (though some of these live in a settlement hard by Nakpala) is that they have the terrible custom of marrying their paternal half-sisters—the other reason, of course, being that LoWilisi women require a much greater outlay.[10]

In this area, then, we find that bridewealth increases with dependence on matrilineal institutions. Indeed the difference in prestations becomes even more striking when one considers that except for the LoWiili the 'patrilineal' peoples also prohibit kin marriage, whereas among the 'matrilineal' groups some forms of kin marriage (e.g. FZD) are implied in the marriage transactions of the previous generation (Goody 1956: 48). In this area, the more 'matrilineal', the higher the overall cost of bride-removal.

I do not suggest that the explicit reason for these differences is to prevent 'patrilineal' men marrying 'matrilineal' girls and thus obtaining for their children a claim to their brother-in-law's property; I heard no comment to this effect. But it is certainly one factor in keeping down the number of marriages that occur between such groups. The low proportion of intergroup marriages in what seems to be a typical boundary situation can be seen from the figures in Table 7, which are derived from a recent survey among the LoWiili.

TABLE 7

MARRIAGES OF 76 LOWIILI MALES (BIRIFU 1966)

Within the parish (P)	to Dagaa (P)	to Lo (M)	to others
68	3	1	4

The four marriages under 'others' were west of the river, i.e. in the Lo direction, but they are all with a small group of LoWiili who have migrated to Zinkãã and who still seem to inherit agnatically. The one Lo marriage was to a MBD. 91 per cent of marriages were within the major ritual areas of Birifu, and nearly all of these to adjacent lineages living within a mile's radius.

The differences in bridewealth I have described occur along the range of groups who refer to each other by means of the two 'directional' terms, Lo and Dagaa (Goody 1956: 16ff.); the payments increase as one approaches the Lo or 'matrilineal' pole. In analysing this continuum, I earlier wrote as if the two poles, Lo and Dagaa, were always given equal value (1956). This is not altogether the case. The Lo are sometimes looked down upon by the Dagaa and other outsiders not only because of their matrilineal institutions (the prestigious Akan also have these) but because their women wear circular lip-plugs that distort the mouth, because they are unclothed, 'dirty' and 'bush'.

While these value judgements are certainly affected by the changing situation in the area (the Lo peoples have had less contact with the modern world), there is some evidence to suggest that similar attitudes were present, perhaps in less acute form, in earlier times. In the first place, distortion of the human features, though done for what the Lo consider aesthetic reasons (Labouret 1921; 1931), inevitably appears grotesque to those whose practices are different. Indeed the aversion that such customs arouse may have made LoWilisi women less attractive either as prey for slave-raiders or as brides for their neighbours. As in the case of the Krobo, bodily mutilations (or their absence) may have served to inhibit marriages across the P/M border (though the 'matrilineal' LoDagaba have the more restrained lip-ornament that is current in many parts of northern Ghana). For such deformations are the most permanent cards of identity an individual can take out and are often used to mark off the members of a religious sect or ruling estate, just as facial markings were used to distinguish one tribal group from another (Armitage 1924). While among the Ashanti, who forbid such mutilations and for whom the north was the source of foreign slaves (*odonko*), the main physical characteristic of such a person is summed up in the fact of his bearing tribal marks (Rattray 1929: 35). Neither the circumcised nor the scarified can hold chiefly office; whereas among their northern neighbours (and tributaries) the Gonja, the reverse is true.

The second and more fundamental piece of evidence I have presented in a discussion of the frequent appearance in 'matrilineal' groups of mechanisms which appear to circumvent the system of inheritance (1962: 354ff., 423ff.). The presence of these institutions suggests that matrilineal societies are themselves very conscious of the costs of the system they practise, and certainly, today, this is even more true of their 'patrilineal' neighbours who regard matrilineal inheritance with some contempt.

Lastly, there is another sense in which the matrilineal, Lo, or westerly direction is devalued compared with the patrilineal, Dagaa, or easterly direction. For a man is always buried facing the east, since (the LoDagaa say) it is the rising sun that tells him when to get up and go off to the farm. A woman is buried facing west, for when the sun sets her man will return from the fields to eat the food she has been preparing. In certain contexts, therefore, west is associated with night and woman, which are devalued in relation to day and man.

There is one striking way that direction (which carries cultural as well as physical meaning) is linked to ideas of pollution (dirt, L.D. *deyr*) and sickness. During the dry season, the unmarried girls and the young boys in Dagaa settlements carry out a cleansing ceremony, sweeping the rooms clear of dirt and dabbing large blotches of whitewash on the compound walls. When they have swept the dwellings, they take a housebat and an egg and cast them in a westerly or Lo direction, in an explicit attempt to banish dirt and sickness from their midst and to project it across the river. The trigger for this Vukāle ceremony (which is not known to the LoBirifor and others to the west) is its performance by the Dagaa peoples to the east; in other words there is a kind of ritual chain, though less formal than that described by Fortes for the Tallensi. When they know that the contamination has been cast in their direction, the LoWiili hasten to move it on yet further westwards. Thus dirt and disease are sent westwards to join night and deformity among the 'matrilineal' Lo.

I do not wish to over-stress the symbolic associations; war or pestilence could easily lead to a change in physical position which would destroy the present symmetry. In any case, this network of associations is strictly contextual; in warfare the Lo are regarded as displaying the male virtues to a high degree. And while groups in the LoDagaa continuum look down upon those in the Lo direction, they do not necessarily look up, or even across, to the Dagaa. The Wiili regard with great aversion the Dagaba custom of inheriting one's father's widows (marrying a 'mother'). This situation, I think, supports my point that these attitudes towards the customs of neighbouring peoples reinforce the barriers to marriage between adjacent groups practising different systems of inheritance. When people change to become Lo (*Lobr*), I was told by Dagaa, they then marry even within

137

the same patriclan (i.e. patriclans may split for marriage), an action that was connected with the adoption of matrilineal inheritance. In fact, matrilineal inheritance may encourage marriage to the FZD, where virilocal marriage is practised, since such a union may prevent the dispersion of property and act as a 'circumventing mechanism'. But the Dagaba (who prohibit all kin marriages and tend to have exogamous single-clan settlements) see this union as a particular example of the close (kinship) marriages of the Lo, as distinct from the distant (extra-kin) marriages of the Dagaa (3031).

In the chapter (8) on cross-cousin marriage in northern Ghana (J. and E. Goody 1966), it was pointed out that all societies in the region seem to regard close marriage with some ambivalence because of the problems involved in making near kin also act as affines. We argued there that in the societies we studied the prohibition upon cross-cousin marriage was part of a wider ban on kinship marriages and that, where cross-cousin marriage occurred, it did so because of specific rather than general advantages. One of these incentives, it would seem, is the existence of the P/M confrontation, which leads the actors to adopt a policy of in-marriage. It is perhaps not accidental that the distribution of close marriage in northern Ghana appears to be linked to proximity to the P/M borderline; more centrally placed patrilineal peoples like the Tallensi prefer to marry at a distance.

It is possible to gain some idea of the effects of these differing marriage patterns (close v. distant, in v. out, kin v. others) by examining the reports of the 1962 census. While the 'localities' of the census are by no means ideal for this purpose, there is considerably more marriage outside the locality in the 'patrilineal' societies. The trend accords with our prediction. In the Dagaba case, 40.5 per cent of adult women (not all of course wives) were born in the same 'locality' in which they are now living; among the neighbouring LoWiili and LoDagaba the figure is 62.1 per cent.[11] My own recent census shows that 91 per cent of LoWiili marriages occurred within the same ritual area. One factor in this different demographic pattern appears to be resistance to a change in the inheritance pattern through intermarriage along the P/M border.

It should be added that distant marriage of this kind is not to be confused with exogamy. A rule of exogamy imposes a general ban on marriage within a definite radius, defined in terms of kinship, locality or social group; it has a group reference.

But calculations of distant marriage take an individual's marriage as the point of departure. If two exogamous units reside in one locality, the prohibition applies only where a union has already taken place; it is not an outright ban on intermarriage, but only on 'repetitive marriage', and it is this fact that is reflected in the census figures.

Conclusions

Given relatively small 'cultural' groups and frequent movement, different systems of action necessarily come into contact and therefore undergo a process of mutual adjustment. The situation is no new one; virtually every settlement in northern Ghana produces a complex set of migration stories which are not mere legends. In this paper I have been concerned with the problems that arise from the juxtaposition rather than the interpenetration of culturally diverse peoples, and specifically with the juxtaposition of groups practising different systems of inheritance.

I have tried to analyse the spread of matrilineal inheritance in a border area and to look at those forms of behaviour which can be seen as inhibiting its extension. In so doing I have offered a partial explanation for the existence (in this area) of higher marriage payments among the 'matrilineal' peoples than among their 'patrilineal' neighbours. I have also emphasized that in certain contexts all these neighbouring peoples have to be viewed as falling within a single social field since they actively influence each other's behaviour.

Stretching from the very north of Ghana to the south, there exists a zone of contact between peoples practising uterine (matrilineal) and agnatic (patrilineal) inheritance. Intermarriage between these groups inevitably creates problems for the offspring. Where a 'patrilineal' man marries a 'matrilineal' woman (the P-M marriage), the male offspring is a 'double heir'. But in the opposite case (M-P marriage), he is a 'lost person'.

Marriages of both kinds sometimes occur, though the second even less frequently than the first. When a P/M union does take place, it opens up the possibility of change. Matrilineal societies display a number of acute problems in the sphere of inheritance, residence and descent, which might be thought to favour a change to patriliny. But in fact, they can readily incorporate neighbouring peoples wherever a system of free *conubium* exists. But since they are likely to lose property in the process, they do not encourage marriages across the border any more than their patrilineal neighbours who, while they gain an inheritance, stand to lose their identity. For the effects of a change in inheritance reach out into many corners of customary life (Goody 1962: 416ff.).

Change occurs, and in a direction that most writers have thought unlikely or impossible. The general assumption of Rattray (1932: ix), Baumann (1948: 45), Murdock (1959: 84ff.) and others about northern Ghana is that matrilineal systems everywhere preceded patrilineal ones. In another context Murdock puts forward the following propositions about such changes as having universal validity (though stating that 'exceptions are theoretically possible under extremely improbable combinations of circumstances'):

(1) Patrilineal societies cannot 'undergo direct transition to a matrilineal form of organization.'
(2) Where patrilineal and matrilineal peoples exist side by side, the first must have evolved from the second.
(3) With fully-fledged double descent systems, 'the matrilineal kin groups were the first to be evolved' (1949: 218).

Lévi-Strauss has claimed that if Murdock's contention were true, 'a vectorial factor would for the first time be introduced into social structure' (1953: 530). Vectorial factors can, I believe, be demonstrated elsewhere. But the material I have adduced from Ghana supports neither Murdock's general claims nor the more particular reconstructions of Rattray and Baumann. In the recent past, societies with matrilineal inheritance have been well capable of holding their own and indeed extending their influence by converting patrilineal groups through marriage or by conquering them in war—the matrilineal Ashanti were after all the most successful warriors in the area and extended the system northwards (Goody 1965). Conquest can be averted only by diplomatic or military means. But patrilineal societies can avoid the possibility of conversion through marriage by inhibiting unions without and by encouraging them within. In one sense these barriers may be 'deliberate'. For enough evidence has been produced to show that people are quite conscious of the contact situation and justify their marriage policy in homeostatic terms. But while the groups involved may wish to preserve their existing arrangements, some intermarriages do occur, with the result that offspring may become directly involved in their neighbour's affairs. Their subsequent actions may then give rise to social change in the shape of 'creeping matriliny'. For in this border situation there is a clear conflict between the interests of certain individuals placed in an interstitial position and those of the rest of the group, threatened by the anticipated consequences or by the desertion of their fellows. Under these conditions, whatever gains out-marriage may have, on a political or individual level it carries a possible cost in the loss of identity to line or lineage. An analytic frame that fails to allow for this type of conflict of interest and for the preventive measures associated with it has distinct limitations for the social scientist. A dominating interest in 'structure' can lead to a neglect of the dynamic forces that make for both continuity and change.

Postscript

I am indebted to Ivor Wilks, David Brokensha, G. K. Nukunya and others I have approached for their comments on this paper. As a result of their remarks I see the boundary problem in southern Ghana as yet more important than I had hitherto thought. Wilks points out that the boundary may lie within as well as between communities; this has long been a problem in Accra and Ada, where incoming Akan (M) lineages super-imposed themselves on the earlier Ga-Adangme (P) speakers. He has himself carefully analysed a series of dynastic marriages of Accra in the eighteenth century and describes an attempt at reconciling the interests of the local Ga (P) dynasty with immigrant Akwamu (M) rulers by means of a P-M marriage, the offspring of which would belong to both lineages (1959: 399). In Accra patrilineal and matrilineal lineages still reside side by side, though there is some compromise on the part of the older-established matrilineages which interestingly enough manifests itself in changes in the attitude to bodily mutilations. The Atifi section of Otublohum 'although in the midst of Accra, has not adopted the Accra custom of circumcision and still adheres to fairly well-defined principles of unilineal succession and inheritance. The Dadebana section, on the other hand, practises circumcision and admits a compromise between matrilineal and patrilineal principles . . . signs are not lacking of positive dissociative processes working to increase the distinctness of each section: Dadebana could be said to welcome, Atifi to resist, acculturation' (1959: 402). Wilks' essay is an example of how marriage arrangements were used positively to associate two unilineal dynastic segments in Accra; my essay has tried to demonstrate how marriage policy can be used negatively to avoid the problems of crossing the P/M boundary.

In areas like Accra, where groups inheriting patrilineally and matrilineally live side by side, intermarriages do occur and the problems of the 'double heir' and the 'lost person' make their appearance in the law courts. In his account of inheritance law in Ghana, Mr. Justice N. A. Ollenu writes of Edward Tetteh, 'one of those fortunate persons who could succeed on both his paternal and maternal sides, his mother's town Accra—Gamashie—being a maternal family community, while his father's own, Osu, is a paternal family community' (1966: 180). In giving decisions on such cases, modern and traditional judges are bound, Wilks suggests, to introduce considerations of equity, especially when the respective groups are resident in one township, under one political and legal authority. And such decisions, in their turn, are products and instigators of social change.

Resistance to this process is by non-marriage. Miss Schildkrout tells me that Mossi immigrants in Ashanti are very conscious of the possible results of marrying a local girl (the P-M marriage), and it is rare to find a union of this kind, which would lead to a complete discontinuity of cultural identity; the locally dominant people would certainly exercise the main pull over the children. Equally the Ashanti recognize that if they make a M-P marriage (as formerly with a northern slave), the children have no *abusua* and hence no heritage (Rattray 1923: 43).

It is for rather similar reasons that the Ewe (P) seem wary of marrying Akan (M) girls; in one of the few cases I heard of, the son of such a union ran off to take up an Ashanti chiefship to which he was entitled through his mother. It is perhaps no accident that of my 15 Ewe-speaking colleagues at Legon in 1967, none had Akan wives; 5 had married Ewe girls, 1 a Ga (P) and 6 Afro-Americans.

APPENDIX. A NOTE ON METHODOLOGY

I have adopted the convention of quoting from my own fieldnotes and giving the page reference; the notes are deposited with the West African Research Unit in the University of Cambridge.

I have done this for two reasons, the first personal, the second general. One commentator has found the detailed material I have presented on inheritance 'cloudy and contradictory' (Ethnographic Atlas, *Ethnography*, 4, 335), while another has attributed the differences between the LoDagaba and the LoWiili to 'curious discrepancies' in my fieldnotes (Leach 1961: 3). Both of these statements have been challenged (Goody 1967a; 1967b); and those interested can check the material from the notes. But a more general point is involved. It is, I suggest, desirable that all anthropologists should make their notes available for general (or at least reciprocal) inspection, since these documents are the only confirmation an investigator can offer for his conclusions.

There are a number of reasons why fieldnotes (often gathered at considerable social cost) should be preserved. In many cases they form the only existing records of daily life in a preliterate, or not fully literate, society, and as such will be of great value to future historians. Secondly, the standards of anthropological scholarship (which leave so much to be desired) can be raised by such a procedure; otherwise future workers have little check on the affirmations of their predecessors. And those statements themselves might be more carefully presented if the data on which they were based were subject to more general inspection: it is not the job of the social scientist to ignore discrepancies, cloudiness or contradiction.

I hope these remarks will encourage other fieldworkers (not only those who have criticized my own material) to make their notes equally available by depositing them in a public place; only if this is done can we discover the evidence for action statements, such as 'all X do Y', or for normative statements, such as 'among the X, the prescribed form of behaviour is Y'. Indeed until this is done, we should treat generalized ethnographic statements with some caution; at present we are in the curious position of being able to check the statements of the armchair anthropologists such as Sir James Frazer but unable to verify the assertions of the fieldworkers who followed and who have so heavily criticized his methods.

In this respect sociological research comes second to the best practice of modern folklorists; in his *Singer of Tales* (1960), a fascinating study of the relationship between Homer and the oral epic of modern Jugoslavia, A. B. Lord provides the reader with precise references to tapes and transcriptions. A similar procedure is followed by many ethnohistorians in Africa who refer to their fieldnotes in the same scrupulous manner as the graphohistorian does his documents. Not so the fieldworkers, some of whom are even reputed to have destroyed their notes once used, while others have been lost in one of the many accidents to which anthropologists are prone.

I would add a further point, at Brokensha's suggestion; that these notes should be deposited, sooner or later, in their country of origin. The details of local life recorded by the fieldworker soon become important as historical documents for that country, whatever their continuing value for sociological research. Moreover an essential aspect of the process of decolonizing anthropological (and sociological) thought is to make our documents available to the world at large, especially those parts of it upon which we have lavished our attention. Only such a process can test our objectivity and our hypotheses, can raise our standards of scholarship and of evidence to a generally acceptable level. And in so doing we may well find that, as far as anthropology is concerned, the *bricoleur* and the *homme de science* have changed continents.

NOTES

1. In this chapter I adopt the following conventions. I refer to the boundary between 'patrilineal' and 'matrilineal' systems of inheritance as the P/M boundary. When I want to indicate the nature of a marriage that takes place across this boundary I use P-M to signify 'patrilineal' man with 'matrilineal' woman, and M-P for the opposite. For the sake of clarity, I prefer to use the terms agnatic and uterine to refer to patrilineal and matrilineal inheritance, retaining the latter for eligibility to unilineal descent groups (UDGs). But as the usage is not generally accepted, I have stuck to the traditional terms in this chapter.

2. Huber quotes a report of the Basel Mission in 1874 about the Krobo. 'Their mind and interest are to get new land on which to plant palm trees, to have many children, and to get heaps of cowry shells (money)' (1963: 21).

3. See Polly Hill, *The Migrant Cocoa Farmers of Southern Ghana* (Cambridge, 1963).

4. David Brokensha writes 'When I was at Larteh I several times asked people about the subject and a general response was to hear laughter at the idea of a "pat" girl marrying a "mat" boy because of the bleak prospects, not only for inheriting property, but also of having a lineage group, rich uncle, or at least a big brother to whom the children would turn in times of trouble. Trouble would include illness, arrest, lorry accidents, unemployment, litigation and all the like troubles and desires of ordinary people.' In a further comment he writes 'my recollection is that where there was, for example, a Larteh (P)-Aburi (M) marriage (and I know of several), the wife was always from Aburi'; i.e. it was a P-M marriage.

5. The Ashanti increasingly practise circumcision. As in parts of East Africa embarrassment is felt by people who do not undergo this particular form of mutilation and there is strong pressure to conform.

6. J. Goody, 'LoDagaa fieldnotes', 1950–2: 3030 (see Appendix).

7. 'To eat in two places' (i.e. *zir ayi*) is the equivalent of the 'double-cross'. A young man I knew was called *Zirayi*, and his father told me that he had given him the name because he suspected the mother of having an affair; she was 'eating' (enjoying) in two places.

8. Goody, 'LoDagaa fieldnotes', 369. The elder in question was called Polle, who was, I think, the chief of Babile at the time.

9. J. Goody, VNB 1/72.

10. It is not that they were unable to afford such payments. I am reliably told of holdings of 200, and 400 cattle; even a poor man is said to have 15–20. It is rather the relative cost that is the deterrent. Moreover, now that men are called on to pay educational expenses and to sacrifice the labour of their sons, individuals are beginning to invest in children rather than wives.

11. The figures for the percentage of persons born in the locality in which they were enumerated appears in the tribal breakdown of the 1960 census (vol. V) as:

	Men	*Women*	*Difference*
Dagaba	63·0	49·1	13·9
Lobi	48·1	49·0	0·9

The Lobi referred to here are mostly LoBirifor who have been migrating from the Ivory Coast since 1917. The 'Dagaba', however, appear to include LoWiili and LoDagaba as well. The figures in this paper I obtained by taking a number of localities in the Lawra District I knew and working out the relevant percentages. These localities were:

Dagaba—Ulo (1 and 2), Ulkpon, Tuopaara, Chepuri, Gozuu, Ping.

LoWiili and LoDagaba—Mwangbil, Baapari, Birifo, Tanzeri, Chaa, Tome.

REFERENCES

Armitage, C. H., 1924, *The Tribal Markings and Marks of Adornment of the Natives of the Northern Territories of the Gold Coast*, London, Royal Anthrop. Inst.

Baumann, H., and Westermann, D., 1948, *Les Peuples et les Civilisations de l'Afrique*, Paris.

Brokensha, D. W., 1966, *Social Change at Larteh, Ghana*, Oxford.

Fortes, M., 1936, 'Culture Contact as a Dynamic Process. An Investigation in the Northern Territories of the Gold Coast', *Africa*, **9**, 24–55.

Gluckman, M., 1947, 'Malinowski's "Functional" Analysis of Social Change', *Africa*, **17**, 103–21.

Goody, J., 1956, *The Social Organization of the LoWiili*, London.

Goody, J., 1962, *Death, Property and the Ancestors*, Stanford, Stanford University Press.

Goody, J., 1965, Introduction to J. Goody and K. Arhin (eds.), *Ashanti and the Northwest*, Inst. of African Studies, Legon, Ghana.

Goody, J., 1967a, 'On the Accuracy of the Ethnographic Atlas', *Am. Anthrop.*, **69**, 366–7.

Goody, J., 1967b, Introduction to *The Social Organization of the LoWiili* (2nd ed.), London.

Goody, J., 1969, 'Marriage Policy and Incorporation in Northern Ghana', in R. Cohen and J. Middleton (eds.), *From Tribe to Nation in Africa*, San Francisco, Chandler Pub. Co.

Goody, J. and E., 1966, 'Cross-cousin Marriage in Northern Ghana', *Man* (N.S.), **1**, 343–55. Reprinted as chapter 8.

Hill, P., 1963, *Migrant Cocoa-farmers of Southern Ghana*, Cambridge.

Huber, H., 1963, *The Krobo: Traditional, Social and Religious Life of a West African People* (*Studia Instituti Anthropos*, **16**), St. Augustin near Bonn, Anthropos Inst.

Labouret, H., 1921, 'Mutilations labiales et dentaires parmi la population du Lobi', *L'Anthropologie*, **31**, 95–104.

Labouret, H., 1931, *Les Tribus du rameau Lobi*, Paris.

Leach, E. R., 1961, *Rethinking Anthropology*, London.

Lévi-Strauss, C., 1953, 'Social Structure', in A. L. Kroeber (ed.), *Anthropology Today*, Chicago.

Murdock, G. P., 1949, *Social Structure*, New York.

Murdock, G. P., 1959, *Africa: Its Peoples and their Culture History*, New York.

Murdock, G. P., 1966, 'The Ethnographic Atlas, 19th Instalment', *Ethnography*, **5**, 317 ff.

Ollenu, N. A., 1966, *The Law of Testate and Intestate Succession in Ghana*, London.

Rattray, R. S., 1923, *Ashanti*, London.

Rattray, R. S., 1929, *Ashanti Law and Constitution*, London.

Rattray, R. S., 1932, *The Tribes of the Ashanti Hinterland*, Oxford.

Schapera, I., 1935, 'Field Methods in the Study of Modern Culture Contacts', *Africa*, **8**, 315–28.

Wilks, I., 1959, 'Akwamu and Otublohum: An Eighteenth-century Akan Marriage Arrangement', *Africa*, **29**, 391–404.

CHAPTER SIX

Marriage Policy and Incorporation in Northern Ghana

Migration and Assimilation

THE problem of political incorporation arises when a central government is established over peoples of diverse culture, as in many colonial, pre-colonial and post-colonial states in Africa. Or when large-scale migration, forced or free, brings on the scene an alien population, as in the Americas. Or thirdly, by the process of internal differentiation that is continually taking place within all social groups.

The cultural differences to which these three processes give rise have a number of implications for the political system. Minority cultures, for example, are often foci of discontents against the regime and the pattern of ethnic differences is frequently reflected in political parties and in political decisions.

Since it is in most cases impossible to dissociate political and cultural factors, I shall examine the processes of assimilation as a whole, paying particular attention to marriage policy, which has a profound effect upon the integration of persons into a social system. Since processes of incorporation only operate over the long run and since they are so varied in kind, it will first be necessary to outline a general framework within which the more detailed study of some groups in northern Ghana can be considered.

Human communication itself involves some degree of incorporation, since attitudes often become modified in the very process of interaction. In this way the barriers and differences between persons and groups are continually being ironed out by social intercourse. Indeed, it has been claimed that one function of the taboo on sexual relations between brother and sister is to create alliances between the members of different kin groups and thus reduce their isolation. Where such kin groups form dwelling units, marriage usually involves a residential shift for one of the partners and hence the physical incorporation of an outsider into the domestic group of kinsfolk. And it is particularly the children of these unions that provide cross-cutting links between the groups to which the husband and wife belong.

This process of cultural assimilation is paralleled by one of internal differentiation. In complex societies some such differences inevitably result from the process of production and the division of labour which it entails. Others arise from the development of more elaborate forms of organization and some too from the varied access to cultural capital that literacy affords. Even in the simpler societies, diacritical features develop around the constituent groups and roles (e.g. totemic emblems and sumptuary laws), while other variations in behaviour arise from the same process of cultural drift that produces the dialects of a language.

The process of internal differentiation may of course lead to the splitting of groups; differences within a single polity then become differences between polities. This distinction is to some extent a relative one. Of course, even within a single system, economic and social differences may be so radical as to threaten the existing order; of such a kind are Marx's contradictions in a capitalist society. In distinguishing between internally and externally generated differences, I do not wish to mask these points. Nevertheless it does seem useful to set aside those kinds of cultural difference that arise directly out of the contact of peoples, either through temporary visits or more permanent migrations. If only because of the manner in which they originate, these differences tend to be more extensive in kind and to lack (initially at any rate) the element of consensus that marks the growth of difference within a single polity.

Migration has been defined as 'the physical transition of an individual or a group from one society to another' (Eisenstadt 1954: 1). This definition tends to assume what is now largely true, the division of the entire world into boundary-maintaining nation states, inclusive segments of the world's land and people. But to encompass earlier migrations, particularly those in stateless societies, we need to take account of the movement of peoples into empty and unclaimed lands, into the interstices between existing social groups. The resulting juxtaposition of ethnic groups requires the establishment of some kind of social relationships, of friendship, antagonism, or more usually a mixture of both. On the other hand, it does not raise the problem, in any radical way, of the incorporation, absorption or assimilation of the migrants in a single political system.

Following Eisenstadt (1954: 1) we may distinguish three main aspects of the migratory movement:

(i) initiating factors, including the motivation of the individuals concerned,
(ii) the nature of the migratory process itself,
(iii) the absorption of the immigrants.

It is the last of these upon which I wish to dwell, although it must be borne in mind that the way in which incorporation proceeds may be greatly influenced by other aspects of the migratory process, e.g. whether the dominant motive is to escape oppression or to find new farms, whether the move takes place individually or in groups, whether the sex ratio is in balance or imbalance. A factor of fundamental importance is clearly the social structures of the migrant and receiving groups.

Amongst acephalous peoples, immigration means rapid assimilation —there is no room for major cultural differences. In northern Ghana, a great deal of movement has taken place among stateless peoples (and still does), partly because of ecological factors such as the impoverishment of the soil, the incidence of disease[1] or the pressure of an increasing population; partly because of internal conflicts over inheritance, succession or status;[2] and partly too because of pressure from centralized states and their slave-raiding off-shoots.[3] Among the Isala the result is seen in the varied origin of the clans, Fulani, Mossi, Gonja, Mamprusi. But there, as in the case of the Tallensi or the LoDagaa, diverse elements are fused into a relatively homogeneous culture (Rattray 1932). Even Muslim traders got drawn into the acephalous melting pot and emerged, like the Mafobe Dagarti of Jirapa (Goody 1954: 32) or the Hen'vera clan of Isala (Rattray 1932: ii, 472), as pagan farmers, arranged in polysegmentary lineages.

Nowadays in these areas one finds stranger settlements, known by the Hausa term *zongo*, scattered along the main traffic routes. But in earlier times, before the establishment of European over-rule, it is doubtful how far small communities could have sustained an independent identity in acephalous societies; if they did, it was by creating a completely separate existence where relationships with the local population were confined to market activities. Indeed the new *zongos* that have formed near such communities are still characterized by juxtaposition rather than incorporation, except in the limited context of trading activities. Nowadays they also tend increasingly to attract government services and consequently act as a magnet for the educated elements in the local population.

It is not only Muslim groups that undergo downward assimilation into acephalous societies; at times a similar process takes place with segments of the dynasties of centralized states who start by dominating but are later absorbed into the local system, the social structure of both groups becoming modified in the process. In northern Ghana incorporation of this kind often occurs on the periphery of the savannah states whose fluid boundaries are sometimes the result of the ebb and flow of raiding, conquest and retreat, and sometimes of the resurgence of local forces, the strength of 'commoner opposition' to chiefly privilege. The process forms a recurrent feature of the politico-military history of northern Ghana, and is reported for the Tallensi, Nankanne Builsa, Kusase, and for some Wala groups.

Another form of incorporation was a common feature of Gonja as of other West African states, namely, the incorporation of slaves. Not only did the children of slave concubines have the full status of their fathers, but the descendants of the union of two slaves eventually became freemen and the memory of their origin gradually disappeared over time. But this complex problem is peripheral to this essay on the incorporation of groups, and demands to be treated more fully at another time.

The units of an acephalous society tend to be homologous and politically equal (Fortes and Evans-Pritchard 1940: 13); in the long run there is but one slot into which migrants can fit. Centralized societies on the other hand are invariably stratified, and in most pre-industrial societies stratification is political in kind, that is, access to the kingship (and usually the major offices of state) is confined to a minority group. Only the post-monarchical party systems of modern times provide formally open means of obtaining political office, though under capitalism the economy (or at any rate its commanding heights) is still marked by a degree of ascriptive ownership of the means of production. In modern states new migrants have usually the same rights of political control (i.e. the vote) as other citizens, though it may be more difficult for them to obtain political office. But in societies where office-holding is legally restricted, the new migrants must either displace the existing rulers or accept a politically inferior status.

If they displace the governing elite (or create a new one), they do so by force or the threat of force. They create (or take over) a conquest state, of which the colonial system is one major variant. Though colonization may occasionally grow out of contractual agreement, war is its usual midwife. And the result, in every case except that of free occupation, is a politically stratified society, with the newcomers holding the reins of authority. Colonization, insists Maunier, is emigration plus government, whether this be in colonies of settlement ('habitable colonies') or colonies of rule ('colonies for exploitation', 'skeleton colonies'). But it is also government that is subordinated to that of the mother-country, which remains (initially for colonies of settlement and perpetually for colonies of rule) the homeland to which many of the migrants see themselves as eventually going back.[4]

In monarchical systems, such as prevailed in African states, the expansion that follows military conquest takes place not by means of the extension of bureaucratic rule (though the rudiments of such may perhaps be discovered in nineteenth-century Nupe and Ashanti)[5] but rather by dynastic expansion into adjacent areas.[6] A notable example is to be found in the spread and eventual fission of the Mossi (Mole-Dagbane) states from their Mamprusi homeland. Ritual ties persisted, even when government had effectively passed to the former segments of the ruling dynasty.

When home territory and dynastic offshoot are spatially separated, political ties tend to be more quickly broken off. For, under the prevailing conditions, the new state, whether formed by the losing faction in a succession dispute, by a group of mercenaries or free-booters, or by a dissatisfied outpost of empire, is independent of the mother-country for the recruitment of personnel, the provision of capital, technological services as well as for the materials of conquest, that is, the means of destruction. And the actors themselves are soon likely to want to discard rather than retain political and sentimental ties with their earlier homeland.

Gonja was just such a conquest state. A group of 'Mande' horsemen first settled to the north of the Bono kingdom in the sixteenth century and later established their own state above the Black Volta. Separated by great distances from their homeland and coming as a warrior band rather than as family migrants, they doubtless took their women from the new locality in which they found themselves and the children of these unions adopted their mothers' tongue. Mande was abandoned and Guang substituted; the assimilation of the migrants, at least linguistically, originated in the absence of women of their own kind. The conquerors had therefore to marry the conquered and linguistic change was in a downward direction.

When the Gonja state expanded northward across the Black Volta, it wrested from the Mossi-speaking states (Dagomba, Nanumba, Wa, Mamprusi and Buna[7]) a territory as wide as present-day Ghana itself. While driving out the earlier rulers, the conquerors (the NGbanya) took over their subjects, who consisted of a number of small groups, distinct both in language and in culture. In their midst, the new ruling estate established a number of divisional centres, from which chiefs were despatched to govern these alien villages.

Traditions of subject peoples such as the Vagala make it clear that political incorporation was initially effected by force of arms; indeed, such is almost invariably the case, since any state system has to establish an effective monopoly of force, not simply for military reasons but in order to back up the decision-making process. It is because they fail to achieve such a monopoly that many union governments are so ephemeral.

But in time military government gave way to a rule which was, at least partially, based upon consensus. While all important chiefships remained firmly in dynastic hands, an element of popular choice (not simply dynastic election) crept into the system of succession; or, at any rate, the approval and blessing of representative commoners constituted an intrinsic part of the installation of a new chief.[8]

The political incorporation, by conquest leading to partial consent, was followed by cultural assimilation. In general, the commoners retained their own language. Although in central Gonja some of these groups adopted the language of the ruling estate,[9] most were compact and solidary enough to retain their own speech-forms. Gonja (*Gbanyito*) was used as the language of administration, and such records as were kept were written in Arabic and Hausa; but social intercourse was very often conducted in the language of the commoners. In those Gonja divisions where a plurality of languages exist, multilingualism is frequent and even members of the ruling estate can be heard conversing among themselves in a commoner tongue.

Language, the prerequisite of all complex cultural achievement, has a certain inflexibility when compared to other forms of cultural expression. For, except within prescribed limits, you cannot mingle codes. If two groups come together they either keep the languages separate and so limit effective intercourse (unless they practise multilingualism) or else they adopt one and reject the other. You may get major changes in vocabulary over time, as in post-Norman England; but you cannot compromise with basic systems as you can (and indeed have to) mix systems of marriage, law, etc.

There is no known law which will predict the direction of linguistic change in a conquest situation; one can point to the variables, dominance, numbers, sex ratios, intermarriage, usage and self-image, but not to the relationship between them. Political dominance is certainly not enough to ensure the acceptance of one's language as the means of communication. If one looks at northern Ghana, the incoming groups (whether they have been settlers or conquerors) have generally accepted the language of the indigenes. But while they have accepted, they have also imposed; the area round Tamale seems formerly to have spoken Kpariba, a Tem language resembling Konkomba, while in eastern Gonja the language adopted by the Mande invaders is now being accepted by many of the other groups in the area.

Part of the explanation has to do with the relative numerical strength of the groups concerned. A small group, even if in a dominant position, will tend to lose out; language exists primarily as a tool of communication and only secondarily as an emblem of group existence. For similar reasons, a mass migration allows the participants the opportunity to cling to their language.

Another factor is the sex ratio. If the incoming group is more than just a handful, and at the same time heterosexual in composition, then it can operate as a breeding unit; such an endogamous group can retain its language and other aspects of culture even under adverse conditions. But if the group consists only of males, which would tend to be the case in situations of conquest, trade or hunting, then there is always the problem of the 'mother tongue', or, more significantly, the language of peers; women are generally less the explorers of new social territory than the consolidators of the old.

I argue later that marriage policy is the most important single factor in the change of language (and other cultural features) since it usually provides the social context within which this basic skill is acquired.

Meanwhile two other factors require consideration. The first is usage: if a language has special significance in religious behaviour, either for ritual or for writing, then it gains an added resistance to change. The second has to do with what I speak of (unsatisfactorily) as the self-image of the group. In some cases language assumes a heightened value as a symbol of group activity, and intense efforts are made to retain or revive the native tongue, despite the heavy pressures making for its extinction; the rescue operation carried out upon the Celtic languages is an example of what I have in mind.

Such a factor, vague as it is, seems to be needed to explain the strength of commoner tongues in western Gonja (Bole) and their disappearance in the central (Buipe) area. The main commoner group in the west of the country is the Grusi-speaking Vagala, whose traditions claim an Isala origin.[10] While contact with the NGbanya has undoubtedly modified many other features of Vagala culture, the language itself flourishes. Indeed it is spoken in many compounds of members of the ruling estate, whose mothers often belong to that group. Many Vagala men display great pride in their language, and their traditions recount how their ancestor Bangmaara strongly resisted the coming of the NGbanya, who succeeded in conquering them only by a trick.[11] Even today, the Vagala play little part in the main Gonja festivals, except as spectators, and they retain some of the spirit of opposition to authority that marks the members of many stateless communities.

This 'commoner opposition' is notably stronger here than in those parts of Gonja where there is no linguistic differentiation between rulers and ruled. This opposition is not openly 'purged' in any public ritual of rebellion but forms a recurrent theme of conversation and is often expressed in linguistic terms. Vagala elders sometimes refused to answer my Gonja greetings and often insisted on addressing me in their own tongue, knowing I could not understand.

I have described the Vagala situation at some length not because it is typical (in many respects it is not) but because I want to refer to this example in discussing other aspects of the problem of cultural accommodation in Gonja.

With regard to language, the situation is one of separateness. Whereas Gonja (Gbanyito) has but few remnants of Mande vocabulary, possibly no more than Twi,[12] Vagala is closely related to its parent tongue, Isala;[13] neither Vagala nor Gonja is much influenced by the other, even though the languages are spoken in the same town (Bole) and by the same people.

But in other areas of cultural expression, the situation is often very different. Occupationally, the NGbanya have remained rulers and the Vagala peasants; militarily, they have kept largely to their earlier weapons, and the same is true of other aspects of their technology. But in these respects their equipment and behaviour was representative of a geographical region rather than of any particular group. On the other hand, the Vagala have adopted much of the material culture associated with the centralized states and with Islam; guns have tended to displace bows, and cloths to outmode skins and fibres. Economically, both groups have adapted to local conditions and cultivate local staples, especially yams. The Gonja have ceased to depend upon rice and the Vagala upon guinea-corn, although both crops retain a certain religious significance in offerings to the gods.

Religious assimilation requires special treatment. When the NGbanya, who were probably pagan Bambara, established their conquest state, they were accompanied and helped by Muslims of Dyula origin. A mid-eighteenth-century history, the Gonja Chronicle, contains an account of the conversion of the ruling estate, and European sources of the early nineteenth century refer to the Muslim kings of divisions such as Buipe and Daboya.[14]

Whatever the situation in the eighteenth century, most Gonja rulers of recent memory were eclectic in their religious practices and beliefs.

Like their Christian and Hindu counterparts, even formally Islamic societies have their syncretistic elements.[15] But for the Gonja, New Yam festivals and the yearly celebrations of local shrines are as important, though not always as public, as the regular Muslim festivals. Muslims, whether by descent or by conversion, occupy different social roles from the princes and have different tasks in national ceremonies. While many princes pray in private, to sit with the Muslims on public occasions or to attend the Friday mosque is to forfeit any rights to chiefly office. In 1937, Jawulla, Chief of Kpembe, was removed from office when he asked leave to make the journey to Mecca. No chief can become a *karamo*, it is often said, though this is not universally true, especially nowadays. On the other hand, no chief entirely rejects Islam as do some commoner groups, like the Vagala; he has to maintain a judicious balance between various divisions of his state, religious as well as kinship, and for reasons of belief as well as of political expediency.

But the most outstanding sphere of cultural assimilation is in domestic life. The kinship system of the NGbanya bears little relationship either to the Bambara with their dominantly patrilineal kin groups (Paques 1954) or to Akan with their strong matrilineal clans (Fortes 1950); although succession to office and estate membership are transmitted agnatically, unilineal descent groups are of peripheral importance and indeed it is difficult to speak of 'corporate' kin groups at all.

The Vagala provide an even more striking instance of cultural change through assimilation.[16] In the main features of the kinship system, their parental group, the Isala, resemble the Tallensi and the Dagaba (Rattray 1932): strong patriclans, high bridewealth, widow inheritance and the prohibition of cross-cousin marriage. However, the Vagala have no important descent groups, low marriage payments, prohibited widow inheritance and preferred cross-cousin marriage. The reversal is striking and complete. And in all these features, the Vagala resemble their overlords the NGbanya as well as their fellow commoners from other ethnic groups within the state.[17]

This contrast points to one possible conclusion: that the social organization of both conquerors and conquered, of both dominant and subordinate groups, has undergone major changes in a single direction at the domestic level; differences have been ironed out and the disparate systems mutually adjusted one to another.

The result, in terms of kinship, inheritance and marriage, is broadly consistent with Islamic practice, and it should be remembered that the third 'estate', that of the Muslims, have basically the same practices. The Islamic custom of paternal parallel cousin marriage and bisexual inheritance tends to break down the boundaries of clanship (though neither custom is at all common in Gonja). Islamic practice favours the transfer of marriage gifts (*sadāq*) to the wife rather than bridewealth to her kin; and while widow inheritance is permissible, the levirate is discouraged.[18]

But there are many variations in marriage and inheritance among Islamic peoples, and many more committed Muslim societies retain features such as matriliny (e.g. the Wolof and northern Tuareg) and exogamy (e.g. the *dyamu* of the Mande) which are incompatible with Muslim law and custom. Nor has the Muslim religion as such had any direct effect upon the commoner communities of Gonja, despite the congruence of their kinship institutions.

Restricted and Unrestricted Conubium

The most significant factor in this process of change is not Islam itself but the incorporation of diverse groups in a single polity, marked by unrestricted conubium. Systems of stratification in Africa stand in marked contrast to those of Eurasia, and particularly to the caste societies of the Indian sub-continent. For endogamy is rare anywhere in Negro Africa. It is found only where northern whites are dominant over southern blacks. The example of the Union of South Africa has parallels among the Saharan Tuareg and the Bahima of Ankole, as well as in Ethiopia (Shack 1966: 8); and it is a pattern that was copied by Freetown Creoles (Banton 1965: 136).[19]

Among the Tuareg of Timbuctu, as in other caste societies, it is the 'purity of women' that is at stake (Yalman 1963); women cannot marry down (Miner 1953: 23). The Negro Bela are agricultural slaves of the Caucasian Tuareg pastoralists; a Bela can never marry a Tuareg girl. The Negro Gabibi, who are said have a slave origin, are agricultural serfs of the Caucasian Arab merchants; again a Gabibi cannot marry an Arab girl (Miner 1953: 20, 24). But unions of male Tuareg with female Bela are not uncommon and give rise to an interstitial estate known as the Daga.

A similar situation obtained among the Ankole of Uganda. As among the Tuareg and Arabs of Timbuctu, there was a sharp economic, cultural and ethnic division between pastoral rulers and subject farmers. No Bairu peasant could marry a Bahima girl; the union was repugnant and the bridewealth unobtainable, since the Bairu were not permitted to own productive cows (Oberg 1940: 130). 'Marriage' was equally impossible between a Bahima man and a Bairu girl, since it was illegal to alienate cattle to the lower orders. But such women did become concubines of a sort, again giving rise to a group of 'half-castes', known as Abambiri.

Otherwise endogamy exists only in some skilled occupational groups in Senegal, Mali and Niger (though groups of in-marrying smiths are found over a much wider area of Africa). In the eastern part of the western Sudan, that is, in northern Nigeria, the system of stratification is more flexible and does not inhibit marriage between social estates. Marriages within certain degrees of kin are prohibited and the unions of cross-cousins are often favoured, but, from the standpoint of stratification, conubium is unrestricted, not simply in law but in practice too. Men are eclectic in their choice of wives and do not confine their marriages either to their own, or to any other, social estate or ethnic group.

I do not wish to imply that Gonja marriages never have any immediate political or religious significance. Reigning chiefs do marry the daughters of neighbouring rulers, but they can more often be heard to express a distinct preference for commoner wives who are reckoned to be less transitory partners than women of the ruling estate (E. Goody 1962). In former times, slave concubinage was common for much the same reason, and a prominent chief once remarked to me, 'You know, all our mothers were slaves'. An exaggeration, it is true, but one that brings out the same kind of preference for 'low' marriage that exists in the extensive kingdom of Bariba in northern Dahomey (Cornevin 1962: 163)[20] and in many other states of West Africa (although it was probably uncommon for a free woman to marry a slave).

In Gonja, the long-established Muslim groups (i.e. the 'Gonja' Muslims) are almost as eclectic in their marriages as their chiefly counterparts. While there is a tendency for a woman's first marriage to be made with a man of the Muslim estate, their brothers are not so inhibited. As the senior Imam in Gonja recently remarked in explanation of his own maternal origin, 'Here, we Muslims (*Karamo*) marry commoners (*Njumo*), the commoners marry chiefs (*NGbanya*) and the chiefs, Muslims.' In any case, the marriage ceremony includes a rite which converts the girl to Islam.

Open conubium increases the intercourse between the various groups in the society and hence modifies the social institutions of all. For example, if frequent intermarriage occurs between two groups, one practising agnatic, one uterine inheritance, then property inevitably tends to accumulate in the hands of the former, and a whole series of further changes is likely to occur in order to meet this situation.[21] Such a process of change seems to have been at work in various parts of Gonja. But the changes are clearest in the case of marriage payments.

In the acephalous societies of northern Ghana, the marriage payments are high.[22] Whereas among the commoner groups, many of whom appear to have had a common origin with their acephalous neighbours, the prestations are greatly reduced. For reasons of reciprocity, they have been brought down to the Gonja and Muslim level; instead of the transfer of bridewealth to a woman's kin, we find marital gifts made to the woman and her parents, which are not returnable if the union is dissolved.

Free intermarriage in a stratified system also tends to emphasize a woman's attachment to her own natal group; in old age she is likely to be drawn back to an environment in which she can revert to the customs, beliefs and privileges of her youth, rather than continue to live in a conjugal setting when her days of childbearing are over. And for similar reasons, less emphasis is likely to be placed upon the unilateral allocation of children to one parent rather than another; in Gonja, kinship fostering plays a dominant part in maintaining the links between siblings separated by spatial and social distance, and indeed by the very fact of marriage.[23]

In other words, the incorporation of structurally diverse groups with frequent intermarriage leads to a mutual adjustment of domestic institutions (which is the sphere most directly influenced) and results in a kinship organization based upon the lowest common denominators. The result is the kind of 'bilateral' system found, and for much the same reasons, in other centralized states in Africa, the Hausa (Smith

1959: 243) and Nupe of Northern Nigeria, the Dagomba of Northern Ghana and the Lozi of Zambia, all of which have incorporated groups of widely different social structures.[24]

I would stress that the important factor is frequent intermarriage rather than open conubium alone. In most states no legal restrictions are placed upon intermarriage, but in contemporary societies, all of which, whatever their ideology, have some system of social stratification, the strata normally prefer to marry among themselves; as in the earlier Eurafrican slave societies of the Americas, sexual intercourse rather than marriage is the characteristic relationship with women of the lower orders.

Rural Migration

I have so far been dealing with the processes of mutual adjustment arising out of the establishment of the Gonja state, an exercise which is inevitably somewhat speculative since there are too few records to enable us to make a satisfactory reconstruction of Gonja society in the seventeenth and eighteenth centuries.

However, immigration into the area continues at the present time, and the Gonja, like any other ethnic group, have to decide upon their relationships with these newcomers—just as the strangers themselves have to decide what to do about the Gonja.

The character of contemporary migration into Gonja depends largely upon whether it is rural or urban;[25] or more precisely, according to the intended occupation of the immigrant, whether farming, trading, government service or some specialist activity such as herding, smithying, drumming, dyeing or distilling.

The rural migration is of farming groups of shifting cultivators[26] and is concentrated in the western and eastern extremes of the country.[27] In the west the migration of Lobi (i.e. LoBirifor) from the Ivory Coast began around 1917 and reached its peak in the 1940's, when they became the most numerous element in the Bole Local Council area.[28] The Konkomba migration from the Oti plains in eastern Dagomba began somewhat later and shows little sign of slackening.[29]

The reasons for these migrations were many. The Lobi were prompted by a desire to escape the poll-tax imposed in French colonies. Moreover, the area of western Gonja into which they moved had been devastated two decades earlier by the activities of Samory, the Mandingo warrior; it was fertile, as local soils go, and few inhabitants survived. The migration built up rapidly and the LoBirifor were joined by the LoDagaa (or Lobi-Dagarti) from the more heavily populated Lawra district east of the river, who had come across these empty lands on their way to work down the mines, on the railways or in the cocoa farms of southern Ghana.

In the east, the Konkomba seem to have been motivated mainly by the desire to obtain better yields, and the actual move often followed a period of wage-labour on farms in the Salaga-Krachi area. Better yields meant more cash, which could then be used to purchase manufactured goods or to circumvent the traditional system of infant betrothal which forced the junior generation into heavy dependence upon the old and meant the postponement of marriage until the age of 35 or 40.[30] So the search was not simply for new lands and for better yields, but also for a larger cash income. The move coincided with the introduction of motor transport to northern Ghana in the early 1920s. The bulky food crops of the north could now be transported at economic rates to the markets of southern Ghana, where the increasing prosperity of cocoa farmers and the larger percentage of the labour force engaged in non-agricultural pursuits led to a great demand for farm-produce, especially yams. It was not accidental that the Lobi and Konkomba, whose staple foods are cereals, were moving into areas better suited to the cultivation of yams, to become the most prosperous farmers in the north.

Both groups were ambivalently welcomed by the Gonja, whose chiefs were keen to increase the numbers under their command, for political as well as for financial reasons. But the newcomers maintained a virtually separate existence, their joint activities being largely confined to the market and the court. For both groups came from strongly 'acephalous' peoples who resent the authority vested in chiefs, and indeed in governments generally. Having been for centuries the prey of slave-raiders, they adopted a particularly hostile attitude towards the representatives of those states which had mounted attacks against them; indeed, given the technological imbalance in weapon systems, their only safeguard had lain in continual vigilance and a constant readiness to take up arms in self-defence—and in an emergency to flee across a convenient river. Their hostility to and suspicion of outsiders, their attachment to the bow and arrow which they always carried, their homes built like fortresses, all this had a firm basis in reality.

The settled Gonja are uneasy about these more mobile farmers and, like settled Europeans and the nomadic gypsies, fear them both on account of their supernatural powers and their easy recourse to violence. Even Gonja commoners, who have taken on the clothing associated with Islam and the centralized states, look down upon them as naked bushfolk, more used to skins than to cloth, to bows than to guns.[31] As a result, Gonja of all estates strongly discourage marriage with these new migrants and the number of such unions is very small.

It seems doubtful whether a migration on this scale could have taken place before the advent of British over-rule at the beginning of the century placed severe restraints upon the political activities of the Gonja. Before the Lobi and Konkomba were more valuable as potential slaves than as subjects. Colonial rule gave them some new freedoms. In this as in other respects, new states are heirs to their colonial predecessors and independence has not greatly altered the position of these peoples. But proud and industrious, oblivious to considerations of status, the Lobi and Konkomba are making a useful contribution to the economy of Ghana as well as to their own pockets; their voice will soon be heard and the Gonja hierarchy, which has neatly adapted to the new dispensation, will receive a rougher jolt from these new migrants whom it has rejected, than from the old ones whom it has assimilated long since.

Urban Migration: the Bole Zongo
If we turn from rural to urban migration, we need to take account of two further variables: firstly, the length of residence in the new environment, intended and actual, and secondly, the nature of the urban centre.

The more recent inhabitants of Bole consist of traders, migrant labourers and administrative personnel. The labourers are few in number. The administrative personnel, who are educated, regard themselves as temporarily stationed there and have elaborated their own 'civil service' life, socially separate from the local inhabitants. Most of the strangers have come by way of trade, though in many cases this has now ceased to be their major occupation.

All trade involves migration and, lying in the savannah country to the north of the Akan-dominated forest, Gonja was a natural area for the exchange of forest produce with the livestock and manufactured goods of the north. Bonnat, one of the first European visitors, was told that the great trading town of Salaga formerly had a population of some 40,000, plus a daily average of 10,000 strangers entering and leaving the town during the dry season.[32] The figure is doubtless greatly inflated, but temporary migrants were nevertheless of great importance to the social organization of Gonja, whose total population in 1960 was but 118,000. An influx of long-distance traders of this kind required a considerable degree of organization of the caravans themselves, of the main centres of trade[33] and of their provisioning. In the larger towns along the routes, men from the trading nations settled down to provide food, lodgings and assistance for their country-men, to act as landlords, middlemen and agents in the complex net-work of trade in which so many were fully engaged. These settlers were often men grown tired of the constant travelling, who had no explicit intention of making their permanent home in a new land. They had come, and they stayed on, principally for economic reasons, becoming landlords and brokers.[34]

Nevertheless, such men formed the nuclei of the 'tribal' quarters of the *zongo* or strangers' settlement. *Zongo* is Hausa for a 'ward' and it describes the strangers' sections that are found in so many towns throughout West Africa, especially those situated along the main roads. Many of these *zongos* are of recent origin; the conditions that followed the establishment of colonial rule enabled traders to expand into areas previously denied them, and increased incomes from cash crops and wage-labour made such expansion more profitable than hitherto. Babile *zongo*, next to the LoWiili settlement of Birifu, is just such a new development, separated from the autochthonous com-munity because, in such a region of dispersed compounds, strangers have to create their own nucleated townships. But some 50 and 120 miles to the south, the towns of Wa and Bole have long-established traders' quarters. And in other places, such as Salaga, Bonduku, Nalerigu and the ancient towns of Begho and Ghana,[35] there was a physical division between the King's town and the Traders' town, the former consisting of 'locals', the latter of 'strangers'; and often enough the twin towns also represented a religious dichotomy between pagan kings and Muslim merchants.

I raise the question of the social morphology of the settlement into which the migrant fits because of its effect on the process of incorporation. In a town of the size and separateness of present-day Salaga, with its population of 4,000 and situated some two miles from the King's town of Kpembe, it is possible for the inhabitants to lead a relatively self-contained existence. Marriages can be made within the town and there are few pressures to conform to local custom or participate in Gonja ceremonies. For trading purposes Hausa was more useful than Gonja and persists even as a first language among part of the community.

Even so, some adaptation to local conditions has taken place; the older residents in Salaga, the Bornu of Nfabaso, the Hausa of Sonipe and the inhabitants of Lompor, speak Gonja as their mother tongue; indeed, when he stayed there in 1888, Binger referred to all these groups as Gonja (1892: ii, 95). And it is precisely these groups that have the highest rate of intermarriage with the local population.

The same distinction between 'assimilated' and 'non-assimilated' immigrants is found in the western Gonja capital of Bole and is again linked, as one would expect, to length of residence.

The earlier migrants live in Nyimunga, a section of the old town, where their buttressed, Sudanese-type dwellings are similar in construction to the flat-roofed compounds of the chiefs and commoners.[36] The quarter is made up of peoples of various ethnic origin, the memory of which is retained in their patronymics, in their tribal names and in their oral traditions. But linguistically, and in most other ways, they are Gonja, even though, in certain contexts of social action, they are referred to as Ligby, Dyula, Wala or Hausa.

People answering to just these same tribal names are found in the *zongo* itself, the new part of Bole which includes the market area and where the houses are of the separate Ashanti type, built in cement or mud-brick, with sloping roofs of thatch or metal sheets. But the Hausa or Ligby who live there interact more with other residents of the *zongo* than they do with the old Hausa or the old Ligby of Nyimunga.

Nevertheless, incorporation is a continuous process which is beginning to take effect even among the newer migrants. In order to obtain a measure of assimilation, I examined the marriages of all residents in the Zongo ward of Bole (Ward 5) recorded in the tax registers of the Local Council and the results are listed in Tables 8 and 9.

I have no precise figures that enable me to relate length of residence with degree of intermarriage, but in any case the differences which these tables bring out cannot be explained on the grounds of time alone. The significant variable seems to be the marriage policy of the groups themselves.

At one end of the scale, we have the Yoruba (locally known as Lagosians) who are here a completely in-marrying group. Their daughters' marriages are arranged with other Yoruba living at great distances. At Christmas, 1965, two of Moses' daughters were to be married to Yoruba husbands at Bolgatanga, some 190 miles away. The same man, who has lived in Bole for 17 years, refuses even to respond to greetings in Gonja. On his walls hang Nigerian calendars displaying the photographs of prominent Yoruba politicians, while his transistor radio keeps him in constant touch with his distant homeland.

Moses has no intention of becoming a permanent inhabitant of Gonja or of contracting any persisting ties with its inhabitants. Indeed his occupation of shopkeeper would be hampered if he did so. One of the main reasons why the Gonja, like other inhabitants of northern Ghana, have difficulty in establishing stores in their own localities (and I have known some spectacular failures) is because of their wide network of kinship ties and obligations; a large number of people are linked to them in ways that are incompatible with the cool calculation of the profit and the loss, and with the preference for cash transactions or monthly settlement that are required in this highly competitive business of petty trading.

As in-marrying, as culturally distinct, and as homeward-looking as the Yoruba are two other 'expatriate' groups in Bole, one 'higher', one 'lower' in the dominant scale of values, namely the Europeans and the Fulani. Neither of these groups appears in the list of *zongo* marriages, since the former (2 marriages) live in the 'residential quarter' and the latter (4 marriages) live next to their cattle kraals on the outskirts of

Comparative Studies in Kinship

TABLE 8

IN-MARRIAGES AND OUT-MARRIAGES IN BOLE ZONGO

Ethnic group of husband	In-marriage	Out-marriage	Total
Ashanti	3	5	8
Dagarti	4	0	4
Dagomba	3	4	7
Ewe etc.	2	1	3
Frafra	1	0	1
Gonja	23	3	26
Hausa	4	2	6
Isala	0	6	6
Lobi	1	1	2
Mossi	7	6	13
Songhai	2	8	10
Wala	6	2	8
'Wangara' (Smith)	0	1	1
Yoruba	19	0	19
Total	75	39	114

TABLE 9

SUMMARY OF IN-MARRIAGES AND OUT-MARRIAGES IN BOLE ZONGO

Husband's group	In	Out
Gonja	23	3
Non-Gonja	52	36
Total	75	39

166

the town. In both groups, the marriage range is as wide as that of the Yoruba, and their kin relations are therefore equally dispersed.

In all three of these instances, the absence of out-marriage is a function not only of the homeward orientation of the groups, the theoretically temporary character of their migration and their desire to retain cultural distinctions, but also of the specialist roles demanded of their wives.

Yoruba women undertake a great deal of petty trading. In Bole, they looked after the bulk of the market stalls, while their husbands minded the stores and travelled to Kumasi to purchase supplies; in Salaga, they did the early morning rounds of the near-by King's town of Kpembe, which had neither market nor shops. These trading activities require knowledge, skill and determination; at marriage, wives are set up as traders by their husbands, who then provide them with a loan so that they can select, at cost price, those goods from his store which they think likely to sell.

Fulani women have equally specialized roles, since it is they who are responsible for milking the cattle, making the butter and selling the products in the local market. For though they have no cattle of their own, their husbands are all pastoralists who, like the Yoruba, have come to acquire some capital and then return home.

European women also have special tasks and expectations which make it difficult for women of other groups to fill their roles or for them to fill the roles of other women in the locality.[37]

At the other end of the scale of intermarriage lie the Isala, Mossi, Songhai (Zaberima) and the Ashanti. But even though most interaction is greater between the residents of the *zongo* than with other inhabitants of the town, out-marriage is overwhelmingly with the Gonja rather than with women of other ethnic groups (Table 10).

TABLE 10

OUT-MARRIAGE OF NON-GONJA MALES IN BOLE ZONGO

With Gonja	30
Songhai=Hausa	4
Isala=Degha (Mo)	1
Ashanti=Hausa	1
Total	36

Songhai men are the only ones to contract any number of out-marriages to non-Gonja women; and these are with their closest cultural neighbours, the Hausa, and can therefore be considered the best alternative to actual in-marriage. The Isala and Degha are also the closest pair from a linguistic and cultural standpoint.

Apart from the few Ashanti, the out-marrying groups are also the assimilating groups. Their migration histories show that they usually come singly, often selling their labour rather than marketing goods. Two of the groups, the Mossi and the Songhai, live outside the boundaries of Ghana, and the representatives in Bole doubtless come from the commoner elements in those stratified societies. In the past, the Isala (or 'Grunshi') were often raided for slaves and so form a significant, though mainly concealed, portion of the population of Gonja, as of Ashanti. These groups have therefore a strong incentive to assimilate and the Gonja do not reject their advances.

Any policy of intermarriage requires both demand and supply; that is to say, in the absence of force, a willingness on the part of both connubial groups. While Gonja marry Isala and Mossi, they express aversion to the idea of marrying Fulani and Lobi.[38] Since the figures give no idea whether one party or both, one sex or both, were responsible for the absence of intermarriage, I tried out a preliminary survey of marriage preferences, based on a non-random sample.[39] The responses are summarized in Table 11.

The most rejected groups are the Lobi and Fulani. None of the Fulani evidenced any desire to marry outsiders; in any case they were decisively rejected by other groups. I had at first thought that their rejection in the centralized states (for the same is reported for the Mossi) was associated with the fear that pastoral penetration might be the forerunner of military conquest; news of events in northern Nigeria certainly spread rapidly throughout the western Sudan, and other states may have wished to prevent the kind of take-over that occurred in the *jihad* of 'Uthman dan Fodio at the beginning of the nineteenth century. But the 'Dagarti' and other acephalous peoples also reject such marriages, though often admiring the beauty of Fulani girls. As I have earlier remarked, their anxiety appears to be related to the fears that settled peoples so often have of their nomadic neighbours, whose greater freedom of movement and different culture make them seem dangerous, unreliable and 'shifty' in every sense. But particularly, perhaps, they fear that the mobility of these strangers will deprive them of their wives or sisters, their children or their nephews.

The other main ethnic group of rejected partners (rejected for marriage, though not necessarily for sex) are the 'Lobi' (LoBirifor). For aesthetic reasons, Lobi women wear lip-plugs of up to an inch in diameter in both their upper and lower lips, but this practice does not endear them to the more sophisticated inhabitants of Bole and Wa. Nor does their comparative nakedness and the use of shea-butter to anoint their bodies. All of these features, combined with their farming life, lead others to dismiss them as 'dirty'.

The distinction between 'Lobi' and 'Dagarti' (Lo and Dagaa) is largely a matter of the position of the speaker relative to a whole series of cultural differences, and no hard-and-fast boundary can be drawn between them.[40] So that the lack of any marriages between Dagarti and Gonja (Table 8) may be due to the fact that, although these men refer to themselves as Dagarti, others think of them as Lobi. However, it is the case that the Gonja do not show the same antipathy for the new migrants from the Lawra district (the LoDagaa) that they do for those from the Ivory Coast (the LoBirifor), and there is no doubt that the former will be more rapidly incorporated, both into the marriage system and into the contemporary scene, especially since many of them were strongly influenced by schools and missions before they migrated southwards.

The next most frequently rejected group is the Yoruba, mainly I think in response to Yoruba separateness and the knowledge that, for a man, such a marriage would be even more fragile than most unions in Gonja, with the additional possibility of losing all one's children, or alternatively one sister's children.

I have as yet few responses from women, and the only additional comment I can offer here is that a woman's marriage policy becomes more liberal the older she gets. However, there is no evidence to show that Gonja women who make *zongo* marriages are any lower in status than those who marry their own kind. In the first place, there are many important men in the *zongo* who hold positions of economic, religious and, nowadays, political power. In any case, as in Ashanti and Techiman, Gonja women of the ruling estate were eclectic in their choice of mates, also having perhaps some sexual preference for the men from the north.

The situation of open conubium and free intermarriage that obtains in Gonja, Hausaland and most of Africa contrasts strongly with the city of Timbuctu and the Ankole of Uganda, where closed conubium is practised by the ruling groups. Although high-status men have liaisons with lower-status girls, the sexual and marital relationships of their women are severely restricted; as Yalman has remarked of India, there is a 'structural necessity to safeguard the women in a caste system' (1963: 48).[41]

The apparent correlations of such a system are significant, for in both Timbuctu and Ankole you find considerable ethnic heterogeneity. In Timbuctu, intergroup marriages are few and 'sexual relations are primarily organized through prostitution' (Miner 1953: 277,280). So that distinct groups, each with their own languages and traditions, operate in virtual separation one from another except in the field of market activities. The situation is basically the same as Furnival's well-known description of a plural society:

> In Burma, as in Java, probably the first thing that strikes the visitor is the medley of peoples—European, Chinese, Indian and native. It is in the strictest sense a medley, for they mix but do not combine. Each group holds by its own religion, its own culture and language, its own ideas and ways. As individuals they meet, but only in the market-place, in buying and selling. There is a plural society with different sections of the community living side by side, but separately, within the same political unit. Even in the economic sphere there is a division of labour along racial lines . . . There is, as it were, a caste system, but without the religious basis that incorporates caste in social life in India . . . The obvious and outstanding result of contact between East and West has been the evolution of a plural society (1948: 304–5).

That the continuing ethnic diversity of Timbuctu depends largely upon marriage policy can be seen from the history of one of its main elements, the Arma. These are the descendants of the Moroccan army, consisting partly of renegade Christian gunmen, that crossed the Sahara and conquered the upper Niger in 1591. As an entirely male garrison of professional soldiers, some thousand miles distant from their base, they were forced to take their women from the vanquished Songhai, whose language they had also to adopt.

A similar contrast with contemporary Timbuctu is seen in Hausaland, where the Fulani conquerors, freely intermarrying, acquired the Hausa language, and ethnic distinctions all but disappeared. Among the Interlacustrine Bantu of Uganda, the same contrast exists between the Ankole and the Buganda, even though the ruling dynasties claim a common origin. In Ankole closed conubium is associated with the retention of ethnic differences, and in Baganda, open conubium with their disappearance.

This process of cultural incorporation through marriage usually works both in a downward and in an upward direction, leading to a reconciliation of diverse cultural practices. Where the groups involved are solidary, and by this I mean to exclude the case of slaves whose incorporation makes but little contribution to cultural change, each gives something to the resulting culture. As a result the process of Islamization that in the West African savannahs often accompanies inclusion in a centralized polity, is perhaps less unidirectional than the corresponding process of Sanscritization that occurs in India, where social and sexual intercourse with the religiously impure is severely restricted.

Conclusions

In the acephalous societies of northern Ghana, political incorporation means cultural assimilation. In the state systems it may entail no more than co-residence, though the degree of cultural assimilation clearly affects a man's political role.

In such differentiated societies, there is a sense in which incorporation is never complete, except for the dominant minority; the significance of membership of the body politic varies with status, and alienation is in part a function of the division of labour, including differential access to armed force. Nevertheless, if we stick to immigrant groups, it is clearly possible to make a rough assessment of the degree and rate of incorporation among them.

While there are a number of factors involved in these differences in incorporation, marriage policy is overwhelmingly the most important; for most purposes the situation in northern Ghana can be summarized in the proposition that the rate of incorporation (I) varies directly with the rate of out-marriage (OM); that is, $I = OM$. For out-marriage is more than an index of assimilation; it is the main mechanism whereby integration is achieved. This it does in two interrelated ways, by affinity and by kinship.

In terms of affinity, marriage and the domestic environment create the kind of cathexis (though the hostilities are numerous) that generally leads to the mutual adjustment of attitudes,[42] and such accommodation may flow over to more distant affines. In terms of kinship, marriage usually establishes the domestic group that forms the template of culture, the unit of socialization, that is, of cultural incorporation.

In nation-states socialization is partially shifted on to the school, which becomes an indispensable medium of cultural indoctrination; quite apart from the teaching of national history and literature, there is the saluting of the flag, the saying of prayers, the lining of streets and the celebrating of state occasions. It is the school on which new nations, like the old, rely for the inculcation of national unity as against tribal or religious solidarity. Here they are dealing not with the assimilation of immigrants (whose presence is often discouraged) but with the incorporation of the diverse elements brought together by European conquest. For 'Balkanization' is a function not so much of colonial rule as of pre-colonial divisions.[43] The new nation-states are the heirs to colonial governments in their boundaries as in other respects, but the problem of incorporation becomes more acute when power no longer rests in the hands of outsiders, who, as far as the internal balance of peoples is concerned, are mainly, though not entirely, ethnically neutral.

In pursuit of national unity, which is often fragile enough, the new states of Africa try to eliminate sectional politics, whether based on religion, tribe or region, and have usually opted for a one-party state. Meanwhile, a corollary of the stress of national unity is the emphasis placed upon the sanctity of existing boundaries, anomalous as these may be.

But the problems of incorporation are a challenge to old nations as well as to new. Some are frankly incorporative (though always selectively so), seeking new members from outside rather than waiting for natural increase alone. Others are exclusive, attempting to maintain the 'purity of the nation', unwilling to mix with peoples of other physical features or cultural habits, for social and doctrinal as well as for racial reasons.

The social problems, at least, are not altogether imaginary. If we look at the process of decolonization, the greatest difficulties in the final stages of the progress towards independence have often been in those countries with major internal problems of assimilation, for example, in Guyana, Fiji, Mauritius and Zimbabwe. Though countries like Brazil have gone some way towards solving problems of this kind, largely by marriage policy, it is not surprising that many others attempt to avoid difficulties by expelling, excluding or limiting other breeds, or by promoting slogans such as 'one country, one faith, one people'. Indeed the insistence on national, or even continental unity (the European idea or the O.A.U.) may have the side-effect of racializing politics and thus militating against the fuller incorporation of nation-states or regional groupings into even wider political units.

If incorporation increases with the rate of intermarriage, then the socio-political implications are clear. The unity of a state can be nurtured by encouraging marriage between the most socially distant members of the nation, tribal groups in West Africa, immigrants in Europe. Alternatively it can be fostered by discouraging the immigration of physically, culturally or doctrinally distinct peoples. But on a wider canvas, in terms of a world strategy, the distinctions continue to exist, whether or not immigration occurs, and a major mechanism for dissolving them, if this goal is a desirable one, is by increasing marital and sexual relationships. International co-operation can be promoted through international copulation. To achieve such ends, nationally or internationally, barriers to intermarriage should be broken down, and the union of cousins, cross and parallel, should be proscribed, like other in-marriages. The legal enforcement of exogamy presents obvious objections and difficulties; but positive sanctions, such as tax relief, could be equally effective in the long run as a way of increasing the import and export of women.

As Tylor long ago pointed out, endogamy is a policy of isolation and the progress of mankind has depended to a significant measure upon the substitution of marrying-out for killing-out. Tylor realized that every marriage was by implication a political act.[44] Nor was this true only in the childhood of mankind. 'Even far on in culture', he wrote, 'the political value of intermarriage remains. "Matrimonial alliances increase friendship more than aught else", is a maxim of Muhammed.

"Then we will give our daughters unto you, and we will take your daughters to us, and we will dwell with you, and we will become one people", is a well-known passage of Israelite history' (1889: 267). This statement expresses in concrete terms what is meant by marriage policy, the consequences of which I have tried to examine for the Gonja and some other African peoples.

Acknowledgements
I wish to thank the Trustees of the Leverhulme Foundation for a grant which enabled me to continue my fieldwork in Ghana in 1965 and 1966. For a general account of the LoDagaa, see J. Goody, 1956, and of the Gonja, J. Goody, 1967.

APPENDIX

In March, 1966, I had an opportunity to follow up the preliminary survey of marriage preferences in a rather more systematic way, helped by some University students from Gonja; the earlier questionnaire was administered by two Europeans, with Dagarti and Vagala assistants. I mention the identity of the interviewers (who were all well known in the community), since this is bound to affect the responses on so sensitive an issue.

The survey was carried out both in Western Gonja (Bole) and in Eastern Gonja (Kpembe-Sala). The results are summarized in Tables 12 A, B and C.

The data are largely consistent with the preliminary study. In Bole the most rejected groups were:

1. Fulani, 2. Lobi, 3. Dagarti, 4. Hausa, 5. Yoruba.

The Dagarti are less desirable as marriage partners than in the earlier survey, partly because of changes in the interviewing staff (who were now non-Dagarti); in any case, this figure is likely to fluctuate because of the difficulties in discriminating them from the Lobi (the problem of the 'LoDagaa continuum'). The Hausa also appear as more rejected, the Yoruba as less.

In eastern Gonja, the results conform more closely to the original survey. It is the Yoruba who are most rejected, followed closely by the Fulani. Then come the Konkomba, who occupy the same structural position as the Lobi-Dagarti; they are the new, immigrant farmers from acephalous communities. After them come the 'Grunshi' (ex-slaves) and the Ashanti (ex-conquerors).

In the Kpembe-Salaga material, the preferences were the mirror opposite of the rejections. Throughout the district, the politically dominant minority were held to be the most sought-after marriage partners, other than one's own group, except by the in-marrying Fulani and Yoruba; the Gonja are rejected only by the Yoruba, the Fulani and by one Hausa and one Ashanti.

There is one figure out of keeping with the general picture, namely the Yoruba in Tables 12A and B who stress 'marriage for love', an attitude that stands in contrast to the actuality of most Yoruba unions. The discrepancy can perhaps be explained by the fact that the respondents were relatively young and were not anxious to appear different (even though they behaved so), especially as foreigners at a time of political crisis: the Nkrumah government had just been overthrown.

The Yoruba are probably the most deliberately organized of the alien Africans living in Ghana; most parts of the country, including Bole and Salaga, have been visited by Nigerian High Commission staff who have encouraged their nationals to take out passports.

TABLE 11

MARRIAGE REJECTIONS OF BOLE MEN (BOLE, AUGUST 1965)

Respondents		Tribe rejected								
Tribe	Number	*'Dagarti'*	*Fulani*	*Gonja*	*Hausa*	*'Lobi'*	*Mossi*	*Yoruba*	*No rejects*	Total responses
'Dagarti'	10	—	6	4	—	7	2	4	3	26
Degha (Mo)	1	—	1	—	1	1	—	—	—	3
Fulani	1	—	—	—	—	—	—	1	—	1
Gonja	9	4	8	—	5	8	4	7	—	36
Hausa	1	1	1	1	—	1	1	1	—	6
Isala	1	1	1	1	—	1	1	1	—	6
'Lobi'	1	—	1	1	1	—	1	1	—	5
Mossi	1	—	—	—	—	—	—	—	1	1
Songhai	1	—	—	—	—	—	—	—	1	1
Vagala	2	—	1	—	2	2	2	2	—	9
'Wangara'	1	1	1	—	—	1	1	1	—	5
Yoruba	1	1	1	1	1	1	1	—	—	6
Total	30	8	21	8	10	22	13	18	5	105

PATERNAL PREFERENCES FOR DAUGHTERS' MARRIAGES
(BOLE, MARCH 1966)

Respondents		Tribe preferred										
Tribe	Number	Ashanti	Dagarti	Dagomba	Fulani	Gonja	'Grunshi'	Hausa	Lobi	Yoruba	For love	Total responses
Ashanti	2	2	—	—	—	1	—	—	—	—	—	3
Gonja	7	5	1	5	—	7	3	5	—	3	—	29
Isala	3	1	—	—	—	3	—	—	—	—	—	4
Vagala	10	8	3	9	—	10	4	3	2	—	—	39
Yoruba	3	—	—	—	—	—	—	—	—	1	2	3
Total	25	16	4	14	—	21	7	8	2	4	2	78

TABLE 12B

PATERNAL REJECTIONS FOR DAUGHTERS' MARRIAGES
(BOLE, MARCH 1966)

Respondents		Tribe rejected										
Tribe	Number	Ashanti	Dagarti	Dagomba	Fulani	Gonja	'Grunshi'	Hausa	Lobi	Yoruba	For love	Total responses
Ashanti	2	—	1	1	1	—	1	1	1	1	1	8
Gonja	5	2	5	1	5	—	4	1	5	1	—	24
Isala	3	—	2	1	3	—	2	3	2	3	—	16
Vagala	8	1	4	1	7	—	3	2	5	1	1	25
Yoruba	3	—	—	—	—	—	—	—	—	—	3	3
Total	21	3	12	4	16	0	10	7	13	6	5	76

N.B. The preliminary survey asked about the respondent's own marriage, the later survey for his daughter's; there seemed to be some advantages in a less direct approach.

TABLE 12C

PATERNAL REJECTIONS FOR DAUGHTER'S MARRIAGES
(KPEMBE-SALAGA, MARCH 1966)

Respondents		Tribe rejected											
Tribe	Number	Ashanti	Dagomba	Fulani	Gonja	'Grunshi'	Hausa	Nchumuru	Yoruba	Konkomba	No rejects	Reject all	Total responses
Ashanti	4	–	1	3	1	2	2	–	3	3	1	–	16
Busanga	2	–	–	–	–	–	–	–	–	–	2	–	2
Dagomba	2	2	–	2	–	2	–	2	2	1	–	–	11
Ewe	1	–	–	–	–	–	–	–	–	–	1	–	1
Fulani	3	3	3	–	3	3	1	3	–	3	–	–	19
Gonja	27	7	1	13	–	10	6	9	14	13	3	–	76
'Grunshi'	4	1	–	3	–	–	1	2	3	2	1	–	13
Hausa	1	–	–	–	–	–	–	–	–	–	–	1	8*
Konkomba	5	4	4	5	–	4	4	4	5	–	–	–	30
Mossi	1	–	–	1	–	–	1	1	1	1	–	–	5
Nawuri	1	–	–	–	–	–	–	–	–	–	1	–	1
Nchumuru	1	1	1	1	–	1	–	–	1	1	–	–	6
Yoruba	4	1	1	–	1	1	1	1	–	1	–	3	31*
Total	56	19	11	28	5	23	16	22	29	25	9	4 (32*)	219

* Total possible rejections = 8 for each respondent. Thus each unit in the column 'rejects all' stands for 8 'responses' and is included as such in the totals.

NOTES

1. The LoDagaa migration, formerly into the northern Ivory Coast and Upper Volta, now into western Gonja, is mainly caused by pressure on the land.

2. The migration stories of the Degha and other Grusi-speaking peoples often relate how the migrants left their homeland following a quarrel over the ownership of the head of a dog they had jointly sacrificed.

3. The southward movement of peoples (the Degha, Vagala, Tampolense) to form the Grusi wedge was probably the result of pressure from the Mossi (Mole-Dagbane-speaking) group of states, especially Mamprusi, Dagomba and the Mossi themselves. An indication of the devastation caused by the activities of these states can be found in a contemporary Hausa account of the wars which were conducted by the Songhai free-booter, Gazari, his successor Babatu and their 'overlords', the Dagomba, in Isala country during the latter part of the nineteenth century (G. A. Krause 1928: 53–60).

4. In every colony we therefore find the colonizers as the conquerors, the governors, the exploiters, the progeny of old countries, coming from afar, and claiming to bestow on the new countries the benefits of the development of their riches. And we find the earlier occupiers, the dominated, the governed or the colonized, who, by the very fact of their country's being occupied, are reduced to a position of legal or actual tutelage.

From this point of view, colonization seems to us both a primitive and a general phenomenon (Maunier 1949: 6).

5. Nadel 1942; Wilks 1967.

6. The recognition of common interest also led to a system of international alliances, and military force to a network of tributary relationships, but neither relationship meant emigration, and 'government' was only peripherally involved in the collection of tribute.

7. Being an offshoot of Wa, the dynasty of Buna originally spoke Dagari, but like the NGbanya, they adopted the language of the indigenes, in this case Kulango (Goody 1954: 13).

8. The public expression of such approval is an important part of the installation ceremonies of the Mossi states. For example, in the Wa division of Wechiau, the chief is actually enrobed by the representatives of the Muslim and commoner estates, the Imam and the Earth Priest.

9. The Mpre and Mpur adopted the language of the ruling estate; in Eastern Gonja, the Nanumba Earth Priest of Salaga, and possibly some early Konkomba inhabitants, made the same change.

10. The other main commoner language in the Bole area is Safalba, a language of the Mossi group. Many of the inhabitants can understand all three; in addition, others speak Ligby, Hausa and English. In some types of song such as *Aguro*, a singer's prestige in enhanced by the number of languages he can use. For a stranger, the linguistic situation is bewilderingly complex.

11. The only published account of the traditions of the Vagala of Bole is given in Rattray (1932: **ii**, 516).

12. For Gonja, see Duncan-Johnstone 1930: 30, quoted in Goody 1954: 12; for Twi, see Wilks 1962.

13. See word lists in Rattray, 1932, where it is stated 'there is no doubt that the Isala, Vagala and Tampolense were originally one stock' (**i**, 122).

14. Goody 1954: 36 ff.; Dupuis 1824: 248.

15. For West Africa, see Trimingham 1959: 40 ff.

16. Throughout this essay I have distinguished between a change in culture and a change of culture. A group of people moving from one locality to another may adopt the practices of their hosts *in toto*, and so effect a change of culture; but in the process they are also likely to modify the receiving society in some way (and so produce a change in culture). It is the second that is usually referred to as social (or cultural) change; the former is a type of social (or cultural) mobility. Mobility is often connected with change but has no necessary relationship to it.

17. The implications of this contrast are discussed in chapters 7 and 8.

18. Greenberg 1946; Trimingham 1959: 127ff., 165ff.

19. In 1894 Bishop Ingham wrote of the Creoles and immigrants: 'The latter form a class for the most part below them. They are their servants. Illicit connection there may be, but not intermarriage.'

20. Lombard, quoted by Cornevin (1962: 163–4), states that 'the king took his wives from families of low status.'

21. According to my inquiries, the patrilineal Guang speakers of Larteh in southern Ghana attempt to forbid the marriage of their daughters with the matrilineal Akan since their offspring would be without inheritance. Huber also records that among the neighbouring Krobo, no father would formerly give his daughter in marriage to an uncircumcized man 'which, *in concreto*, means to a member of the *Akan* tribe' (1963: 96); Huber attributes this to long-standing enmity, but property considerations would certainly explain the same phenomenon (see chapter 5).

22. e.g. Tallensi (Fortes 1949), LoDagaa (Goody 1956, 1962) and Isala (Rattray 1932).

23. Goody, E. 1960, chapter 6; 1966.

24. Neither the definition of bilateral nor the comparative analysis can be expanded here.

25. The 1960 Census Report on *Statistics of Towns* (1964) includes as urban those communities with a population of 5,000 or over; only one town, Damongo, met this figure. But before 1874, the population of Salaga was perhaps 8 times this size and in 1888, the first European visitor to Bole described it as bigger than the well-known market town of Bonduku.

Numbers, however, are not all. The Gonja themselves make no terminological distinction between towns and villages; both are *nde* (sing. *kade*). But in most divisional capitals of Gonja, however small, an ethnically mixed population gives a certain cosmopolitan air; and the structure and ambience of a town like Bole are certainly different from those of the farming villages that surround it.

26. The term 'shifting cultivator' requires some comment. Many LoBirifor and Konkomba live in relatively permanent villages, farming the surrounding land by rotation and by fallow. But if yields drop and circumstances allow, most of them are quite prepared to abandon their elaborate compounds and move to foreign parts.

27. See Tait 1961. The Konkomba inhabited what was formerly Togoland under U.K. Mandate, which was later included in Ghana after a U.N. plebiscite.

28. The figures in the 1960 census for the whole of Western Gonja are: 'Gonja', 30,670 (49.1 per cent), Lobi, 10,390 (16.6 per cent). In 1948, there were 7,333 Lobi in Gonja. The 1931 census does not record ethnic distribution.

29. The figures in the 1960 census for Eastern Gonja Local Council are: 'Gonja', 18,800 (33.7 per cent); Konkomba, 16,050 (28.8 per cent). In 1948, there were 7,832 Konkomba in Gonja, including the part under U.N. Trusteeship.

30. Tait, 1961; see below, chapter 7.

31. Weaving, which is common in the Vagala villages of western Gonja, is completely unknown to the LoDagaa, to the LoBirifor and to the Konkomba, among whom all cloth is foreign.

32. M. J. Bonnat, *Liverpool Mercury*, 12th June 1876. In 1940, the population of Timbuctu was only 6,000 and Miner claims that it was never more than double this figure (1953: 14).

33. On the organization of the caravans, see the Hausa documents collected by G. A. Krause, 1928, especially No. 41 (Mustapha and Goody, 1967).

34. On the roles in trading communities, see Cohen (1965) and Hill (1966). The large number of persons engaged was partly due to the bulky nature of the commodities and partly to the absence of wheeled transport. South of Salaga, donkeys were of little use, owing to the presence of tsetse, and goods had to be manhandled, usually by slaves or pawns.

35. Bono-Mansu, capital of the forerunner of Techiman, was also perhaps a twin town.

36. The eastern Gonja have round thatched huts, set in an open circle, rather like the neighbouring Dagomba. A striking example of the mutual adjustment of which I have spoken is the fact that in eastern Gonja, chiefs, Muslims and commoners all have round huts, while in western Gonja they all have flat-roofed compounds.

37. Except for a priest, whose role prescribed celibacy, the Europeans were transients rather than migrants and their roles too diverse to consider here.

38. The Lobi-Gonja marriage recorded in Table 8 was exceptional in character and lasted only a short while. I am indebted to Yakubu Saaka for his help with this survey.

39. I am grateful to Keith Hart and Birgitte Rode-Møller for their assistance in administering the questionnaire, and also to Esther Goody for her help and advice. The smallness of my numbers is due to the lack of time at my disposal; but the investigation needs to be pursued in greater depth, with more subtlety and with better statistical techniques. See Appendix for later information.

40. For a discussion of the complexities involved see Goody, J. 1956; chapter 1. Like the LoDagaba, the LoBirifor inherit movable property matrilineally, so that intermarriage raises some of the same problems it does for the Krobo, the Guang and the Akan (chapter 5).

41. I use the word caste without religious implications (such a system has no warrant in Islam) to indicate one of a hierarchical series of endogamous status groups.

42. There appears to be no adequate study of the attitudes of spouses before and after marriage, but there is plenty of evidence of the high correlation of social and political attitudes between husband and wife (91 per cent agreement in

Newcomb's re-study of Bennington students) and of the adjustment of attitudes of strangers one to another (Newcomb 1962; see also Homans 1950).

In its most general form, that of balance theory, the process has been summed up as:

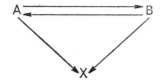

A and B are social persons, X a social object. Where A's attitude to X and B's attitude to A are positive, then B's attitude to A will, given continuing inter-action, tend to change in the same direction (Newcomb 1953).

43. In the establishment of their rule, colonial governments united rather than divided, although in the exercise of power, they often exploited cleavages in order to gain their ends.

44. The political implications of contemporary marriage are explicit in the policy of the major world powers. The Soviet Union clearly disfavours the out-marriage of its women, while at the height of the Cold War, affinal connections with former citizens of Russia were enough to place an Englishman's visa in jeopardy, should he wish to visit the United States.

REFERENCES

Banton, M., 1965, 'Social Alignment and Identity in a West African City', in *Urbanization and Migration in West Africa* (ed. H. Kuper), Univ. of Calif. Press.

Binger, L. G., 1892, *Du Niger au Golfe de Guinée*, Paris.

Cohen, A., 1965, 'The Social Organization of Credit in a West African Cattle Market', *Africa*, **35**, 8–20.

Cornevin, R., 1962, *Histoire du Dahomey*, Paris.

Dupuis, J., 1824, *Journal of a Residence in Ashantee*, London.

Eisenstadt, S. N., 1954, *The Absorption of Immigrants*, London.

Fortes, M., 1949, *The Web of Kinship among the Tallensi*, London. 1950, 'Kinship and Marriage among the Ashanti', in *African Systems of Kinship and Marriage* (eds. D. Forde and A. R. Radcliffe-Brown), London.

Fortes, M., and Evans-Pritchard, E. E., 1940, *African Political Systems*, London.

Furnivall, J. S., 1948, *Colonial Policy and Practice*, Cambridge.

Goody, E., 1960, *Kinship, Marriage and the Developmental Cycle among the Gonja of Northern Ghana*, Ph.D. thesis, University of Cambridge. 1962, 'Conjugal Separation and Divorce among the Gonja of Northern Ghana', in *Marriage in Tribal Societies* (ed. M. Fortes), Cambridge. 1966, 'Fostering in Ghana: a Preliminary Survey', *Ghana J. of Sociology*, **3**.

Goody, J., 1954, *The Ethnography of the Northern Territories of the Gold Coast, West of the White Volta*, London. 1956, *The Social Organization of the LoWiili*, London. 1962, *Death, Property and the Ancestors*, Stanford. 1967, 'The Over-kingdom of Gonja', in *West African Kingdoms* (ed. D. Forde and P. Kaberry), London.

Goody, J. and E., 1966, 'Cross-Cousin Marriage in Northern Ghana', *Man*, **1**, 343–55. Reprinted as chapter 8.

Greenberg, J. H., 1946, *The Influence of Islam upon a Sudanese Religion*, New York.

Hill, P., 1966, 'Landlords and Brokers: a West African Trading System', *Cahiers d'Ét. Afr.*, **6**, 349–66.

Homans, G. C., 1950, *The Human Group*, New York.

Huber, H., 1963, *The Krobo* (Studia Instituti Anthropos, **16**), St. Augustin, near Bonn.

Krause, G. A., 1928, 'Haussa-Handschriften in den Preussischen Staatsbibliotek', *Mitt. Seminars für Orientalische Sprachen*, **31**.

Maunier, R., 1949, *The Sociology of Colonies: an Introduction to the Study of Race Contact*, (1st French ed. 1932–42), London.

Miner, H., 1953, *The Primitive City of Timbuctu*, Princetown.

Mustapha, T. M. and J. Goody, 1967, 'The Trade Route from Kano to Salaga', *J. Hist. Soc. Nig.* **4**, 611–16.

Nadel, S. F., 1942, *A Black Byzantium*, London.

Newcomb, T. M., 1953, 'An Approach to the Study of Communicative Acts', *Psych. Rev.*, **60**. 1962, *The Acquaintance Process*, New York.

Oberg, K., 1940, 'The Kingdom of Ankole in Uganda', in *African Political System* (ed. M. Fortes and E. E. Evans-Pritchard), London.

Paques, V., 1954, *Les Bambara*, Paris.

Rattray, R. S., 1932, *The Tribes of the Ashanti Hinterland*, Oxford.

Shack, W. A., 1966, *The Gurage*, London.

Smith, M. G., 1959, 'The Hausa System of Social Status', *Africa*, **29**, 239–52.

Tait, D., 1961, *The Konkomba of Northern Ghana*, London.

Trimingham, J. S., 1959, *Islam in West Africa*, Oxford.

Tylor, E. B., 1889, 'On a Method of Investigating the Development of Institutions; applied to Laws of Marriage and Descent', *J. Anthrop. Inst.*, **18**, 245–69.

Wilks, I., 1962, 'The Mande Loan Element in Twi', *Ghana Notes and Queries*, **4**, 26–8. 1967, 'Ashanti Government in the 19th Century', in *West African Kingdoms* (eds. D. Forde and P. Kaberry), London.

Yalman, N., 1963, 'On the Purity of Women in the Castes of Ceylon and Malabar', *J.R. Anthrop. Inst.*, **93**, 25–58.

CHAPTER SEVEN

The Circulation of Women and Children in Northern Ghana

(WITH ESTHER GOODY)

IN this chapter we consider some interconnected aspects of domestic organization among the societies of northern Ghana which relate to the circulation (or spatial movement) of women and children. As the result of recent fieldwork among the LoWiili and the Gonja we were led to compare a set of kinship factors. These are: the nature of marriage prestations (bridewealth etc.); the pattern of divorce; the presence of widow inheritance (or levirate); the extent of kinship fostering; the concepts of paternity; the kind of kin groups.

We observe that the LoWiili and Gonja display two distinct clusters of these variables, and that the same two clusters are found in all of the societies we discuss with some relatively minor exceptions. We seek to understand why these variables should be grouped in these two ways, what is their influence on residence and what is the explanation for their distribution.

The discussion of these interrelationships continues our earlier lines of research on fostering (E. Goody 1960; 1966), divorce (E. Goody 1962), descent (J. Goody 1962; in 1968) and cross-cousin marriage (Chapter 8). Though it is specific in its ethnographic reference, the analysis relates to the general theme pursued by Radcliffe-Brown, Fortes (1949a; 1950), Gluckman (1950), Leach (1957), Fallers (1957), Stephens (1962), Lévi-Strauss (1963), Lewis (1962) and many others concerning the relative strength of conjugal and sibling bonds. We are concerned with this problem not in the abstract but in so far as these ties are explicit in patterns of residence. We wish to make the general point that the residence pattern must be viewed not simply in relation

184

to the post-marital residence of women (virilocal, uxorilocal etc.) but as a whole, that is, over the entire life-cycle, so as to include the return to natal kin (by divorce) as well as the earlier separation from them (by marriage). It must also include an analysis of the factors determining the residence of the children of the union; for the bonds between siblings that have been loosened by marriage may be strengthened by bringing up (fostering) one another's children or by arranging marriages between them; indeed, we regard some forms of preferential cross-cousin marriage as just such an attempt to perpetuate the brother-sister tie in the following generation—the compensation for the incest taboo at one remove.[1]

Methodologically we set out to continue the tradition of limited comparisons (using a few societies) that has already proved itself of some value in furthering our understanding of divorce (Gluckman 1950; Leach 1957), witchcraft (Nadel 1952; Wilson 1951), cross-cousin marriage (Radcliffe-Brown 1930; Leach 1951), matrilineal systems (Richards 1950), incest (Chapter 2) and a number of other topics. We then extend the scope of the essay to consider the other groups in the area that have been the subject of detailed study, namely the Tallensi and the Konkomba. These intensive comparisons are aimed at illuminating the interrelations among the variables in each of the two clusters A and B, and their bearing on the questions of kin group structure, sibling and conjugal roles, and shifts in residence (see Table 13).

Finally we test our conclusions by means of a systematic, inclusive, regional comparison, that is, against all the societies in northern Ghana on which reports, however fragmentary, exist. The purpose of this final exercise is to establish the distribution of the clusters observed in the intensive comparisons and hence to provide a local test of the firmness of the association. The results of the extensive comparisons are presented in Table 14, which is deliberately similar in construction to our table showing the distribution of cross-cousin marriage in the same area, in order to permit cross-reference (Chapter 8).

We begin the analysis with a statement of the general differences between the LoWiili and the Gonja, and then examine certain features of their kinship systems which we see as interrelated.

TABLE 13

KINSHIP VARIABLES AMONG THE LoWIILI AND GONJA

Set	Variable	Cluster A: LoWiili	Cluster B: Gonja
1. Unilineal descent groups		Present	None, except dynastic descent groups
	Ratio of sibling residence	Lower	Higher
	Widows	Levirate	Inheritance banned: widows ousted
2. Residence of women	Divorce prestations	Return of bridewealth	No legalizing act
	Divorce patterns	High→medium→low	High→high→high
3. Residence of children	Marriage prestations	High	Low, virtually non-existent
	Paternity	'Social'	'Biological'
	Fostering	None: occasional nurse-girls and care by substitute mother in crisis	Frequent
4. Residence of men		Largely agnatic	Partly agnatic

The General Contrast Between LoWiili and Gonja
a. Political Organization. Before 1900, the LoWiili had no chiefs, their social organization was segmentary in that the constituent units were relatively homologous and politically equal (Fortes and Evans-Pritchard 1940).

The Gonja were stratified into ruling, Muslim, commoner and slave estates, forming parts of a loose but complex state.

b. Economic Organization. Before 1900, the LoWiili were almost entirely agriculturists, living in dispersed settlements and deriving their living from hoe farming.

While most Gonja were farming, on land which is in general less fertile but less populated than that of the LoWiili, others existed by trade, crafts, the exaction of tribute and by the possession and exploitation of slaves. They lived in nucleated villages, which, in areas of concentrated political and commercial activity, developed into the kind of 'poly-ethnic town' found elsewhere in the western Sudan; indeed, Salaga, the main commercial town of Gonja, was called the Timbuktu of the south and was the entrepôt through which Ashanti kola was sold to traders from the Mossi and Hausa states to the north and north-east.

c. *Religious System.* The LoWiili are 'pagan', that is to say, they lack any commitment to one of the major world religions.

The Gonja are religiously stratified, the commoners being pagan, the traders Muslim, and the chiefs accepting aspects of all faiths held by their subjects, though there is a mounting tendency for them to increase their commitment to Islam, a trend that earlier appeared among freed slaves.

d. *Kin Groups.* The LoWiili place considerable emphasis on unilineal descent groups (UDGs), and both patrilineal and matrilineal descent groups are found side by side; only the patrilineal groups are property holding, i.e. inheritance takes place within the group and is thought of in these terms.

Among the Gonja, on the other hand, the ruling estate is organized into dynastic descent groupings of an agnatic kind that operate on the political but only marginally on the domestic level. Unilineal descent groups in the usual sense are absent and from the present point of view (although this problem requires a more detailed analysis) Gonja can best be 'placed' as a 'bilateral' system.

But both societies display a good deal of patrifilial emphasis (not necessarily patrilineal, by which we refer to social action associated with unilineal descent groups recruited agnatically). For example, marital residence in both is overwhelmingly virilocal, that is to say, when the conjugal unit constitutes a residential group, its location is determined by the husband rather than the wife.

We are concerned, then, with the contrast observed between the pagan, non-stratified, acephalous LoWiili where male agnates occupy neighbouring compounds in a dispersed farming settlement, and the Gonja, whose centralized, stratified, ethnically and religiously complex organization is associated with a bilateral kinship system which links together individuals living in nucleated villages and towns, the latter supporting an economically diversified population.

The Specific Contrast Between LoWiili and Gonja

a. The Residence of Married Women. On the domestic level the first difference that struck us again, moving between these two societies that we had known over a number of years, had to do with residence. We first want to consider (in schematic form) some of the factors that 'complicate' patterns of post-marital residence.

1. Complicating factors in residence. 'Complex' residence patterns arise in two main ways, by the circulation (physical movement) of adults and by the circulation of children. The prohibitions on sex and marriage between brother and sister mean that, in all but a few marginal cases, one or the other has to make a residential shift. In most systems this occurs at or during marriage and establishes the conjugal unit as a dwelling group.

Societies with patrilineal descent groups normally have a 'simple' pattern of residence and this is the case among the LoWiili.[2] Men usually live with their fathers (i.e. patrilocally) and women with their husbands (i.e. virilocally). The domestic unit thus contains a male core which persists over the generations, unless men go off to find new farmlands in other parts.

But in all matrilineal, and in many bilateral, societies the pattern is a complex one. If 'matrilineal' men circulate, then the differing pulls of their lineage and conjugal ties are likely to make for flexibility. In the course of his marital career a man has to split his available space-time between kin and conjugal roles. To do this he may reside alternately in the two places (e.g. Dobu), or he may make frequent visits between them (e.g. Hopi); in these cases the pulls work diffusely over the whole of his married life. On the other hand the effects may be concentrated at quite different phases of the life-cycle, leading to a general shift from uxorilocal to virilocal residence (Bemba) after the marriage has matured. When the 'matrilineal' women circulate (i.e. by virilocal marriage), then it is the male children, not the male adults, whose residential loyalties are split. A lineage home can be maintained only by the institution of 'child return'; children circulate in the opposite direction to women.

The residential patterns of matrilineal societies are invariably complex not only because of these different forms and their associated problems of bride, groom, and child removal, but also because in any one instance they are unlikely to follow a single 'rule'. In many cases the resultant distribution is a function of the strength of opposing forces at different stages in the domestic cycle (Fortes 1949a).

In those bilateral societies where claims to fixed resources are inherited through both sexes (i.e. that practise 'diverging devolution', see J. Goody 1962: 317), a married couple is likely to be offered the alternative of residing with the kin of either the husband or the wife, and perhaps with the kin of their parents as well. Other factors, too, may determine the location of a marriage. A small bridewealth or a large dowry may give a woman and her kin the right to remove the groom or acquire his offspring. For the Bemba 'wealth consists of the power to command service' (Richards 1956: 46); through his daughters a man obtained the services of a son-in-law. But property in land is perhaps the most important of the factors behind the determination of residence in what have been called (misleadingly in some respects) 'loosely-structured' societies.

2. The residence of LoWiili and Gonja women. Among the LoWiili, women play primarily a wifely role; of course, they pay short visits to their natal kin, after seeking permission from their husbands, but such permission is reluctantly given and the visits are short. Occasionally a woman may be recalled by her kin to enforce a bridewealth payment or other debt. The LoWiili husbands see themselves as having obtained the right to have their wives living with them (the right of bride removal) through the heavy bridewealth payments and farming services which they have rendered. They also see themselves as having acquired the same control over their children, although the daughters, who in any case quit after marriage, may return to their mother's family as brides, if they marry the mother's brother's son.

In Gonja (and in the other states of northern Ghana) fixed resources are negligible, most land being free and unimproved. The residence of a couple at marriage is not at issue: a woman joins her husband. What complicates the pattern is 'woman return' and the circulation of children. A woman may return to her kin during or after a marriage, and then live as a sister rather than as a wife. This happens, to some degree, in all societies, but the proportion of time spent one way rather than another is a significant variable in the comparison of societies. At this stage we have not completed the analysis of our survey data, but it is clear that a Gonja woman spends a very substantial part of her life not living with husbands.

3. The ratio of sibling to conjugal residence. The relative frequency with which a woman is found residing as sister and as wife we refer to as the ratio of sibling to conjugal residence and is to be distinguished from the divorce rate with which it is often confused.[3] It is a high ratio of sibling residence rather than high divorce as such that could be taken to indicate the strength of the relationship between brothers and sisters. In Euro-American societies, a divorcée does not normally return to live with her parents or her brother; she either gets another husband or lives as a *feme sole*, so that high divorce is not related to the strength of kinship ties. Among the LoWiili, the role of an adult woman (in residential terms) is as a wife; she leaves her husband when she wishes to marry another one and only the rejects (mainly witches) return to their kin for more than a short time. Among the Gonja a woman will have as many, if not more, husbands as a LoWiili woman, but the former spends less of her adult life living as a wife and more as a sister.

The difference between these three basic situations (Gonja, LoWiili, and Euro-American) is brought out in a number of ways: in the length of a woman's visits to her home, in the treatment of widows and in the patterns of divorce.

b. Patterns of Divorce. We are unable at present to give any refined figures, although analysis of a recent survey is in progress. But the pattern if not the rate is clear.[4] In the early stages of marriage, LoWiili wives quite often leave their husbands; girls who have been persuaded into a certain marriage may find a more congenial spouse. Since divorce is usually initiated by women throughout this area (polygyny means they are always in short supply), its frequency partly reflects the extent of the control exercised by male kin. For if a woman who wishes to end a marriage is not allowed to remain with her natal kin but is returned by them to her husband's house, incipient divorce is often smothered in the early stages. While her male kin may be willing for her to go to a new husband who will refund the bridewealth and so relieve them of embarrassment in this respect, such alternative spouses are less easy to find as a woman grows older, even though bridewealth would be reduced. For this reason, and because of the birth of children and the growing affection between the spouses as time goes on, the marriage becomes increasingly secure, until in old age it is virtually unbreakable. This we describe as a high (H), medium (M), low (L) pattern of divorce. It is associated with a low ratio of sibling residence. But it is not necessarily associated with the loss of control of a daughter by her natal kin-group. What often keeps a daughter not only in the married state but also in a particular marriage is pressure from her kin. Thus, in contradistinction to other writers on this subject we do not necessarily see low (middle and terminal phase) divorce rates as linked with a detachment of a woman from the control of her siblings or other kin, much less her absorption or incorporation in her husband's clan. Low divorce may indicate a high degree of kin control; here we have 'strong' patrilineal descent groups in a sense other than is meant by Fallers, Lewis, and others. For this reason it seems advisable to use the idea of strong descent groups, as Lewis has recently concluded (1965), only in respect of specific criteria.

In Gonja, by contrast, divorce is common throughout a woman's life, before the birth of children, during the years of active childbearing, and later in what we have called terminal separation. This latter is the *de facto* dissolution of marriage on the initiative of the woman when childbearing is done and is very common among the Gonja. Between the ages of forty-five and sixty, women of the ruling and Muslim estates and, to a lesser extent, the commoners, make prolonged visits to their kin, usually a real or classificatory brother, from which they never return to the houses of their husbands. This is so common a practice that it is rare to find a woman of fifty-five or over living with a husband.[5] English speakers refer to this as 'retiring from marriage', but in Gonja it is simply said that 'because the woman was old she went to "sit" with her kinsmen' (E. Goody 1962). Terminal separation is a major contributory factor in the high ratio of sibling to conjugal residence among the Gonja, as is the high (H), high (H), high (H) pattern of divorce.

c. The Residence of Children. Among the LoWiili children are brought up by their own parents,[6] and immediate kinship ties tend to be localized. If a LoWiili woman leaves her husband she loses touch with her older children; although she may take very young children with her, they will be sent back to the father when old enough to look after themselves. When a man dies his lineage makes a token bridewealth payment to the wife's kin to stress its continuing rights over the widow and her children. That such a payment is necessary makes it clear that the LoWiili woman retains a role—as daughter, sister, and aunt—in her natal lineage as well as of wife and mother among her husband's people. The difference is brought out by the fact that among the LoWiili the roles of daughter, sister, and aunt have little effect on the residential pattern. Nuclear families are not broken up by the obligation to send children to other kin, nor by prolonged visits of a woman to her relatives.

In Gonja it is children as well as women who circulate. Great emphasis is placed on the institution of kinship fostering whereby, from the age of about five, children are sent to be brought up by non-parental kin. Claims to a foster child are formally expressed as the rights held by a man in his sister's children (more particularly, in their sons) and by a woman in her brother's daughters. But in practice children are reared by a wide range of kin and girls in particular are often asked to go and stay with a grandparent.

Fostering tends to split up the sibling group at an early stage and often over long distances. Social relationships in Gonja extend over a very wide spatial field. There, members of the ruling and Muslim estates in particular marry widely and therefore foster widely.[7] The institution of fostering seems to us most likely to be found in the absence of such 'strong' unilineal descent groups, anyhow patrilineal ones. For while kinship fostering could take place entirely within the unilineal descent group (we might then speak of 'descent fostering'), we know of no such limitation in practice.

Easy and relatively frequent divorce also means that the nuclear family is always on the point of dispersal; most homes (from the western standpoint) are broken homes. In fact, children are often living with non-parental kin. While political status is given by the Gonja father, there is no real problem of the unilineal affiliation of the children and no great anxiety over their whereabouts. One consequence is that if a woman returns to her natal kin (and this is in many ways a praise-worthy act), she may well find a child of hers living there.

Adult brothers in Gonja are often widely separated, though they may come together at annual festivals and on 'family' occasions. There is not the constant interaction that exists in the joint agnatic household of the LoWiili (or any similar society); brothers are less often in each other's company, though they continue to have close ties, which among the ruling group are manifest in political support (J. Goody 1967). The difference is also manifest in cross-sibling (brother-sister) relationships and in sororal ties. For LoWiili women, once married is always married, though not necessarily to the same man. But among the Gonja, a woman often returns to her kin (sometimes for many months) after the birth of her children, between marriages, and when she has given up marriage as a career. She can live as a sister, not only as a wife. And her brothers must find a room and food for her as long as she wishes to live with them.

d. Widows. In all farming societies the aged have to be supported out of the current production of a kin group, which forms the basic productive unit. Indeed, this is equally true of all dependants, the young as well as the old, and women, too, unless they take part in productive or money-making activities.

For women the alternatives are support by the husband, by the brother or, at a later stage, by the children. Before the menopause there is no great problem, since the coital and usually the reproductive services of women are in effect exchanged for support (among other things) in the economic sphere, although there are clearly important variations in the dependence on 'kin' or 'affines', husband or brother, which are correlated with (among other factors) the inheritance of property. In northern Ghana virilocal residence at marriage is virtually universal; when the conjugal pair forms a residential unit, the wife joins the husband. Because of this the problems of residence in old age centre upon women rather than men, on widows rather than widowers.

Among the LoWiili the rights which a husband (and his group) acquire by bridewealth payments persist after his death. All children born to the widow belong to the dead man, unless the bridewealth payment is returned. She is expected to make a leviratic 'marriage' and women in general accept this position. In 1965 we found the widows of Bonyiri still living in his compound seven years after his death (J. Goody 1956a: 45). And fifteen years after the funeral of the late chief,

Gandaa, a number of his widows remained in his house. There are certain advantages for these women. Nominally they are all leviratic wives,[8] but some in fact are certainly there because of their sons and grandchildren. 'He's not my husband', said one widow, referring to the dead man's brother who had become her leviratic spouse, 'my son is'. And a woman will possibly see more of her daughters, too, when she is living at their lineage home.

The contrast in the treatment of widows is most striking. For whereas the LoWiili encourage a widow to stay where she is, the Gonja in effect forbid it. Widow inheritance is banned; death dissolves the marriage and a woman is forbidden to marry any of her dead husband's close kin. Death divorces a woman from all her classificatory husbands. She has to return home to marry elsewhere, although in some cases her children may support her in her own compound. In any case, the ban on remarriage to her children's paternal kin means in effect that she has to quit her late husband's compound, where there is no role that she can easily fill. If she is of marriageable age she offers a forbidden temptation to her late husband's brothers. If she is past the menopause her place is with her own brothers. So the widow is ousted.[9]

Unless she goes straight to a new husband the Gonja widow returns to her natal kin where she settles down with a child (usually a son) or with another kinsman. Sometimes a widow establishes a compound of her own. When she does so it is usually sited near the house of a kinsman of which it is regarded as an offshoot. If a woman chooses to join her brother, even a classificatory one, he will find her a room and provide her with food. Indeed, in some parts of Gonja it is said that one reason why an adult son may be living with his maternal kin is so that he can farm for his mother in her old age.

e. Marriage Transactions. Among the LoWiili bridewealth is very high relative to a man's total holding of capital; the average number of cattle in a compound was four (one to every 2·5 persons in the community), while the bridewealth payments consisted of 20,000 cowries and 2 to 3 cattle. An investment of this kind cannot come out of what a young man makes by selling his surplus grain and cash crops. It has to come from 'corporate' funds, most usually from members of the senior generation, father and mother's brother, possibly from more distant kin; in this case a debt is contracted which is extinguished at death.

Again, corporate funds are not sufficient to sustain many payments of this kind unless there is a counterbalancing intake from the marriages of sisters who are thus cattle-linked, although never in the specific sense of the Lovedu; an individual is dependent either upon his sisters or upon the senior generation.

The outgoing funds are not only—nor even perhaps primarily—for sexual (i.e. coital), domestic, or economic services, but relate to the proven procreative powers of the woman. For the payments are not made in a lump sum but by instalments, as the children are produced. A barren woman earns no bridewealth, apart from the initial transfer, a fact which makes her barrenness a matter of concern to her brothers as well as her husbands. Bridewealth is largely childwealth.

It is not surprising then that fostering should be uncommon in such a system. The co-resident corporation is always agnatically based in these societies, so that its core is formed by the males of a patrilineage. Its resident male members supply bridewealth for each other, bridewealth which is produced by the out-marrying females. Members have joint interests, financial and otherwise, in each other's marriages and in the offspring that result; they are unlikely to want the care and control to pass into the hands of other, non-lineage, kin. There is of course always a certain number of sister's sons living with maternal kin, but this is refuge (or crisis) fostering. Children are rarely, if ever, sent to maternal kin by their parents, but occasionally run there to get away from them; or young children accompany their mother when her marriage is dissolved.

Among the Gonja a man's outlay at marriage is basically the wedding expenses, a matter of entertainment and display, plus bridal gifts and presents to in-laws, which are rarely recoverable in the event of divorce.[10] There is little incentive to accumulate property for marriage; young men are less dependent upon their parents' wishes and do not need to farm for kinsfolk in order to get help with marriage payments. Not that Gonja youths are unsolicitous of their senior kin, but filial piety is more relaxed, less complicated by pecuniary considerations, and dead ancestors do not play the central role in an individual's life that they do among the Tallensi or the LoWiili.

There may be family pressures on women, formerly supported by force, to marry the children of close kin, either cross-cousins or occasionally (among Muslims) paternal parallel cousins. Such marriages were often sanctioned by supernatural forces too, since the close ancestors, particularly the maternal ones, are concerned to ensure that their descendants do not fall out. But a woman is held neither to a particular marriage, nor to marriage in general, by a background of heavy transactions which have to be repaid in the event of divorce.

It will be seen that the presence of high, fixed bridewealth, like infant betrothal (e.g. among the Konkomba), places considerable restraints upon the junior generation in making marital arrangements. Unlike the Gonja, the LoWiili find it very difficult to raise the marriage prestations themselves. Unless they depend upon kin they have to work in the south in order to acquire the necessary funds or else migrate to an area where land is more plentiful.

f. Divorce Transactions. Important here is the nature of divorce transactions, by which we mean the counterpart of marriage transactions. Bridewealth, dowry, wedding gifts, are these returned or retained on divorce?

Among the LoWiili bridewealth relates to the whole period of the marriage; if this is dissolved the prestations are returned, perhaps with some deductions for the expended portion of a woman's marital career. It is not surprising that, given the nature of these transactions, LoWiili divorce rates should display the kind of pattern that Fortes notes for the Tallensi: initially high, then medium, then low, a pattern that is almost the inverse of the scheme of bridewealth payments (Fortes 1949*b*: 85–7). For the return of bridewealth is an enormous charge on a brother's funds. The LoWiili cannot afford to have their sisters around their compounds, not if they want partners themselves. The only occasions on which this happens is when a man with few children discourages his daughter from marrying until she has produced a child on his behalf; this is the 'house-child', who has at once a privileged and an underprivileged status (J. Goody 1956*a*: 62; 1962: 223). A woman sometimes lives with kin when she is divorced by her husband; but if the husband initiates divorce, he loses the right to claim the return of bridewealth, so that examples of this are rare.

In Gonja gifts are not usually returned in actual practice. They are made once and for all, to please in-laws, to initiate intercourse and to secure the removal of the bride. Thus a father is under no economic pressure to persuade his daughter to 'try again', nor, on the other hand, to recall a daughter from a man who has been slow with his bridewealth payments. Consequently affinal relations, particularly with the senior generation, take on a different quality and do not display the same pattern of respect that is reported for the LoDagaa and the Tallensi. One can hear a woman refer to a son's wife as her 'grandchild' and treat her in the joking manner appropriate to this category of kin. However, the easy relationship with mothers-in-law may also be affected by the fact that they are seldom found in the same compound as their sons' wives: even if a woman is still living with her husband her sons are likely to have moved out of their father's compound by the time they marry. But it is all affinal relations, not only those between mother and daughter-in-law, that are more diffuse, more relaxed. So the presence or absence of high bridewealth appears to have considerable ramifications for the whole set of kin relations.

g. Paternity. One further aspect of the contrast between the LoWiili and the Gonja associated with this set of variables concerns the concept of paternity. The critical case here is the fate of the adulterine child. Among the LoWiili, as in other societies with 'strong' unilineal descent groups, a man's jural father (*pater*) is his mother's jural husband, no matter who is the actual genitor. Among the Gonja a man's jural father is his genitor; if a chief's wife sleeps with a commoner, then the child is a commoner; as in earlier England it becomes possible to bastardize the offspring of a married woman and thus exclude him from the enjoyment of the property and status of his mother's husband. Although the Gonja affirm that 'a thief doesn't own the thing he steals', it is seldom that an adulterine child is accepted by his mother's husband; a boy is usually forced to seek out his genitor. A husband's rights are in no sense exclusive even over his legitimate offspring, for they are shared with maternal kin. Traditionally it was the mother's brother who had the right to pawn or sell the children into slavery, not the father. This provides the charter not only for claims on particular children for fostering, but for the strongly held sense of 'ownership' of, or rights in, one another's children which characterizes the groups of both full and half-siblings. Clearly, overlapping claims are present, for siblings of both parents feel that they share rights in the same children.

This idea is sometimes expressed by saying that half the children (the 1st, 3rd, 5th etc.) belong to the father's side and half (the 2nd, 4th, 6th etc.) to the mother's, but no such strict allocation is in fact adhered to. One reason for this lack of exclusiveness, as some of the actors themselves explain, is the nature of the marriage prestations.

Among the LoWiili the corollary of the fact that bridewealth transfers rights in a woman's procreative powers to the husband's lineage is the idea that a woman's natal kin have the exclusive ownership of children before these payments are made. 'Housechildren' are not in fact illegitimate; rather their legitimacy (albeit restricted) resides in their natal lineage. A man may deliberately use his daughter to produce children on his behalf; these are what the LoWiili refer to as *yirbie* and the Nankanse as *yi-yeen bia*, 'the children of the house'. 'This is not a marriage', writes Victor Aboya, 'It is only a sowing of seed' (Rattray 1932: 1, 161–2). Among the Gonja, on the other hand, a man has a claim upon his children by an unmarried girl, for paternity and ownership are not determined by bridewealth, nor, indeed, by 'marriage'.

h. Unlineal Descent Groups. Table 13 summarizes the main differences between the LoWiili and the Gonja in terms of the two clusters of kinship variables. Logically consistent with these is the fact that the LoWiili have 'strong' (i.e. multifunctional) unilineal descent groups, the Gonja none; indeed, apart from the dynastic descent groups of the ruling estate and the residual patronymic groups of the Muslims, they can hardly be said to have boundary-maintaining kin groups (as distinct from kin ranges) at all.

Low marriage payments, the prohibition on widow inheritance, a high ratio of sibling residence, and 'biological' paternity (cluster B) all fit with the absence of unilineal descent groups. Whereas high marriage payments, the levirate, a low ratio of sibling residence (rather than a low rate of divorce in itself), and 'social' paternity (cluster A), all these are consistent with the 'strong' unilineal descent groups.

Other Intensive Studies

The other intensive sociological studies of communities in northern Ghana are of the Konkomba and the Tallensi. In terms of the institutions we have been isolating the Komkomba represent a more extreme case than the LoWilli. The stability of marriage, writes Tait, is regarded as absolute and is in fact 'remarkably high' (1961: 180). Inheritance of widows (and even betrothed) is very frequent as a result of the disparity in age between husband and wife. Because of this children often have to be redistributed at the death of the father, a situation that is dealt with by a special form of 'crisis fostering' where the orphans are looked after by close agnatic kin of the deceased.[11] In his discussion of the development of the household Tait writes of the assignment of adolescents and young adults of both sexes to reinforce the existing members of a newly established household on the farm and in house-work. This is essentially an allocation of the labour available to a minor lineage after the death of a male member. There is no question of control of either widows or children passing outside the lineage that has acquired rights in them; both are physically retained within the unilineal descent group, or rather, the lineage home.

Bridewealth payments and services are relatively high among the Konkomba. In 1952 Tait estimated their total value at £32, while marriage to a woman of the neighbouring Kabre tribe involved an outlay of four cows, at a value of £40 to £50. A major difference exists in the kind of transaction that was made; internal marriages between Konkomba involve the transfer of perishable foodstuffs (guinea-corn) rather than cattle or cowries. The payments of grain, however, could be commuted (on some traditional system of reckoning which was clearly not keeping up with contemporary inflation) to cash payments amounting to £6.[12] While the average cash income of a compound head was less than £10 a year, this sum could be earned by two weeks' work on a farm in the south (Tait 1961: 95). It would appear that the outlay on brides was formerly considerable, but that labour migration has led to an easing of the situation.

There does not seem to be any return of marriage payments in the event of divorce, perhaps because the latter was so rare and the former so perishable. In any case a runaway wife had to seek some distant haven where such claims were unlikely to be effective. If she goes back to her natal home, her brothers 'accept her for a short period only and will then return her to her husband' (1961: 183); for nearly every Konkomba marriage is an arranged marriage, since girls are betrothed in their infancy to men already of marriageable age; and when the time comes for them to join their husbands, 'all are reluctant to go, most of them seek to delay their going, and in the end they go weeping bitterly' (1961: 182). The pre-emption of sexuality involved in infant betrothal leads to a maximization of parental control and Tait concludes that 'the low rate of broken marriages is due to the controls exerted over both spouses and is in no way due, in the early years of marriage, to happy and close personal relationships' (1961: 182). This control is exercised in a wife-providing (and wife-getting) direction, rather than in the retention of rights over women as sisters.

The Tallensi case is most illuminating on this subject and its value is particularly high because of the depth of Fortes's fieldwork and analysis. These people display the same set of characteristics as the LoWiili and Konkomba; widow inheritance, absence of fostering, high bride price. Marriage tends to be 'unstable in the initial stages' (Fortes 1949b: 84), but 'despite these initial pitfalls of marriage, families do get established and remain stable' (85). In the absence of precise rates it would be difficult to say that the Gonja situation was much different up to this point, though we have rated Tallensi divorce in the middle stage as medium and Gonja as high. But in the final stage the contrast with the Gonja is clear, for when a woman has borne two or three children this link through the offspring becomes 'a really effective force in maintaining the marriage' (87).[13] Moreover, a father is under a similar sort of pressure as his LoWiili counterpart, i.e. partly 'economic', to encourage his daughter to remain in the married state.

Extensive Comparison
In Table 14 we present the information we have been able to gather from published material, unpublished papers and fieldnotes on the peoples of northern Ghana. The initial classification, on the basis of the presence and type of unilineal descent groups, we do not discuss at length here since we do so in the chapter on cross-cousin marriage (p. 216).[14] We simply point out that the horizontal subdivisions 1, 2 etc. have the following significance:

1. Patrilineal descent groups.
2. Patrilineal descent groups plus unnamed matrilineal descent groups (e.g. Tallensi *soog*).

3. Patrilineal descent groups plus matrilineal descent groups, but property is only inherited within the first.
4. Patrilineal descent groups, plus matrilineal descent groups, both corporate with regard to property, i.e. double inheritance (transmission down both lines).
5. Patrilineal descent groups, of limited significance (ethnic groups of commoners within centralized societies).
6. Unilineal descent groups absent, or very limited, except in a dynastic context (centralized societies).

In the two latter cases, the unilineal descent groups (in so far as they exist at all) have few functions, although in group 6 dynastic descent groups control eligibility to high office. So we speak of them as 'limited' or 'weak'. Moreover, group 6 consists of centralized states and group 5 of linguistically distinct peoples subordinate to those states; the same is true of at least one part of the Chakalle, a people about whom our information is minimal. With the possible exception of the Chakalle, groups 1, 2, 3 and 4 all consist of stateless societies.

The two clusters of variables that emerge from the intensive studies are also found in the societies which have received less attention from sociologists. For example, writing of the Vagala, Rattray mentions a system of 'adoption' which is in fact precisely the same as what we have called fostering. It is the only society of the 'Gonja type' with whose domestic organization he deals and he specifically remarks upon adoption and widow remarriage, linking this with the bridewealth transactions, viz., 'The position of widows regarding remarriage is unusual, but in keeping with the fact that bride-price was not paid for them on marriage. The heir may not take them ...' (1932: 2, 521).

There are three cases in the table which do not altogether fit the Gonja and LoWiili models. In Mamprusi, according to both Rattray and MacKay, widow inheritance is allowed; however it seems to be rare, treated with ambivalence and absent from some Muslim groups (Brown, private communication). The greater stress placed here on persisting rights over women may be related to the somewhat greater emphasis placed on unilineal descent groups; segments of the royal dynasty are exogamous up to a depth of three generations. A similar

TABLE 14. KINSHIP VARIABLES IN NORTHERN GHANA

	Pattern of divorce			Marriage prestations (total)	Fostering (other than crisis fostering)	Widow inheritance	Paternity (status of adulterine child)	Exogamous kin groups	Sources
	Initial	Middle	Terminal						
Type 1									
1. Konkomba	O	O	O	H (£22+Farming)	O	+	S	+(P)	Tait
Isala				H (30 c or 2 C)		+		+(P)	R.501, 505, 466
Awuna (Fra)				H (2 C+5 c)		+		+(P)	R.528, 529
Awuna (Nagwa)				H (3 C+25 c+S)		+			R.533, 536
2. Tallensi	H	M	L	H (4 C)	O	+	S	+(P+m)	Fortes
Namnam				H (4 C)	O	+		+(P+m)	G.f.
Nankanse	H	M		H (4 C)	+(?)	+		+(P+m)	R.283, 267; G.f.; Cardinall 74
Kusase	H	M		H (2–5 C)	O	+		+(P+m)	R.388, 385, 375; G.f.
Builsa	H	M		H (2 C+2S)	O	+		+(P+m)	R.399; G.f.
Dagaba	H	M		H (30–50 c)	O	+		+(P+m)	R.414, 422; G.f.
Kasena	H	M		H (2 C)	O	+		+(P+m)	R.545, 539; G.f.
3. LoWiili	H	M	L	H (20 c+2–3 C+F)	O	+	S	+(P+m)	G 1956a

				Stock					Sources
4. LoBirifor	M			H (3 C+F)	O (?)	+	S	+(P+M)	Labouret 279, 287; G.f.
LoDagaba	M	M	L	H (13–20 c+) 2–3 'L	O	+	S	+(P+M)	G.f.
Chakalle (?)	H	H	H		+	O		+(P+M)	G.f.
Type 2									
5. Tampolensi				No information					
Vagala	H	H	L		+	O		O	R.521, 520; G.f.
Safalba	H	H	L		+	O		O	G.f.
Degha	H	H	L		+	O		O	Tauxier 407; G.f.
Choruba	H	H	L		+	O		O	G.f.
6. Gonja	H	H	H	L	+	O		O	G.f.
Dagomba	?	H	H	L (4 c)	+	O	B	O	R.460; Oppong f; Blair
Mamprusi	H	H	H?	L	+	+/O		(O)	Brown f.; R 460, 463; MacKay
Wala	H	H	L	L	+	+		(O)	G.f.
Nanumba	H	H	L	L	+	O		O	G.f.; Amherst 38

Legend:

H = high
M = medium
L = low
+ = present
O = absent
P = patrilineal descent group
p = patrilineal complementary (i.e. unnamed) descent group
M = matrilineal descent group
m = matrilineal complementary descent group
C = cows
S = sheep
c = cowries (in thousands)
F = farming
S = 'social' legitimacy
B = 'biological' legitimacy
f = fieldnotes.

Sources: R = Rattray 1932.   G = Goody (J. or E.).

situation obtains in Wa, which was probably an offshoot of the Mamprusi kingdom.

The case of the Chakalle of the eastern Wa district (group 4) is possibly anomalous because of the nature of the available material. This ethnic unit consists of a western group, speaking Dagaari (Wala), who have undergone much Muslim influence and were under the hegemony of Wa; and an eastern group, speaking Chakalle (a Grusi language), who are predominantly pagan and were under Gonja domination. The information on these people was collected (by J. Goody) during the course of several brief visits and the apparent inconsistencies may be due to differences between the two groups which certainly require further investigation.

Finally, there is the case of the Nankanse. Of these Victor Aboya writes that some children are brought up by their paternal grandparents and some by their mother's brother.[15] This situation is very different from that obtaining among their immediate neighbours, the Tallensi where, out of 170 children under sixteen, only 2 per cent were not living with at least one parent and these were all orphans. Fortes is very clear on this point: the vast majority of Tallensi children grow up with their natural parents (1949*b*: 136). However, the Nankanse appear to send children to be socialized not only to parental grandparents but also outside the lineage, to maternal uncles. We offer no explanation for this apparent anomaly, although we would add that our own enquiries reveal a situation much closer to the Tallensi pattern.

With the possible exception of the Nankanse, the situation found in northern Ghana can be seen in terms of the presence and functions of the unilineal descent group. The 'descent' societies retain residential control over their wives at the expense of not seeing their sisters; if they prevent their wives from spending much time with kin, then they in turn will see little of their sisters. Control over the wife carries with it control over the children, who are rarely sent out in 'voluntary' fosterage. But although control of women as wives is linked to the control of women as sisters, the roles are not substituted for one another at marriage; in some measure, the role of wife, and later mother, is an incremental addition to a woman's status.

Discussion

There are two aspects of general theoretical relevance which need to be considered here. The first has to do with the relationship between bridewealth (or brideprice) and divorce; the second the relationship between divorce rates and the system of kinship or descent.

In pointing out that a high bridewealth enables men to control the movement of women (or anyhow of their genetricial rights), we see such payments as helping to sustain not so much a low divorce rate as a low rate of sibling residence. However frequently women circulate in the high bridewealth groups, they do not stay long with kin. In these same societies in northern Ghana there is also a relatively low divorce rate, anyhow in the middle and later stages of a woman's marital career. We recognize that this is not a universal correlation; Gluckman (1950) and Lewis (1962) cite a number of examples to the contrary, though we think these need examining to differentiate those cases where the bridewealth is *a*. returnable; *b*. jurally high (i.e. fixed at a high amount relative to total resources); *c*. not simply part of the wedding celebrations or an indirect endowment of the bride.[16] A jurally high bridewealth, such as we find among the LoWiili and similar groups in northern Ghana, is linked (by the actors and as the result of regional comparison) with the transfer of genetricial rights in the bride to the husband's lineage; it defines the status of children in relation to a series of unilineal descent groups; it is a form of childwealth.

While it is true, as Lewis maintains in his discussion of Mitchell's thesis, that the transfer of genetricial rights need not necessarily be permanent (1962: 42), the presence of a high bridewealth that is both fixed and returnable must militate in favour of jurally stable conjugal unions (Schneider 1953). Other factors may well pull in a contrary direction; the degree to which a wife retains her pre-marital legal status (Lewis 1962), the absence of exogamous descent groups, the presence of diverging devolution,[17] and 'the vagaries of the pastoral life' (Stenning 1959: 188).

The role we allocate to bridewealth in the societies of northern Ghana cannot, we think, be dismissed as 'economic blackmail' (Evans-Pritchard 1965: 184); it depends upon the exigencies of the system of 'indirect exchange' (to which Evans-Pritchard himself draws attention), on the effect of a bridewealth which requires the assistance of persons other than the husband himself (which again Evans-Pritchard remarks upon). This admission, which Gluckman (1950: 191) and Leach (1957) support, would seem to suggest that high marriage payments may indeed inhibit divorce, though other factors are certainly involved. The factors that militate against divorce on an individual level are those that work in favour of a low divorce rate.

If we stress some of the economic aspects of high bridewealth payments we do not wish to imply that we regard 'wife-purchase' as a satisfactory term for analytic purposes (Gray 1960). In the first place, a wife in these 'descent' societies of northern Ghana is never completely 'incorporated' into her husband's lineage; in the second place, unlike chattels, she is always herself a right and duty bearing *persona* and hence acquires rights in her 'purchaser' as well as he in her.[18]

The second general point has to do with the relationship of divorce rates and other kinship variables. Using a similar set of variables to that which we have isolated, Gluckman surveys a number of societies and notes an association between (strong) patrilineal descent groups,[19] rare divorce and high marriage payments. In making a detailed comparison of the Lozi and the Zulu he concludes that the 'types of marriage and the forms of the family, with inheritance of property, rights of children in father's and mother's lines and the rights of these lines to claim them, laws of betrothal, destination of widows, rates of divorce, status of wives in their husband's homes are all consistent with certain types of kinship system' (1950: 202).

Certain modifications in the hypothesis have been suggested by Fallers, Leach, Lewis, and others[20] on the basis of societies in which they have worked. Basically these modifications turn on the fact that some 'patrilineal' societies are characterized by unstable marriage, a fact that has been related to the 'solidarity' of male and female members of the same lineage (Fallers 1957: 119) and the strength of the cross-sibling bond particularly as it affects the locus of jural control of a woman, whether this is ultimately vested in brother or husband (Leach 1961: 119). Lewis explains the high divorce of the Somali in similar terms, where responsibility for avenging a woman's death remains in the hands of her natal lineage.

Our material presents a contrast very similar to that between the Lozi and Zulu. We have tried to keep our analysis on the level of the interrelationship between specific variables, since there seems a great danger, in sociological analysis, of jumping from empirical to synthetic generalization. When Gluckman states that both a high divorce rate and high marriage payments are 'rooted in the kinship system', when Fallers explains differences in divorce rates in 'patrilineal' societies in terms of differences in the degree of 'incorporation', when Leach explains the weakness of the affinal bond by the strength of the sibling bond, when Gibbs maintains that the 'epainogamous' society (low divorce) is tightly structured, the non-epainogamous society loosely structured (1963: 553)[21]—then the issue is hardly clarified if the second term is defined by reference to the first, since the resulting 'explanation' is tautologous.[22]

Appreciating this point in connection with the transfer of genetricial rights (1962: 42) and the concept of incorporation (1962: 43), Lewis relates divorce rates to the distribution of legal responsibility between a woman's natal lineage and that of her husband, showing that among the Somali responsibility can be assessed 'directly and even qualitatively' by reference to blood-wealth payments.

He speaks of the Somali as having 'strong' descent groups because the woman is strongly attached to her natal clan, whereas others see 'strong' descent groups as 'incorporating' their wives and loosing their sisters. As Lewis notes elsewhere, 'a system which is "strongly" patrilineal or matrilineal in one respect is not necessarily so in another. Thus ... any comparative analysis ... must compare the specific functional respects in which unilineal descent is significant in each case' (1965: 108–9).

We do not use the concepts of 'strong' and 'weak' descent groups in the same way as these writers but only to indicate the multifunctional character of the groups as distinct from the limited character of, say, the dynastic units of the Gonja. We feel that the explanation of the differences between the Somali and the Nuer (or Zulu) is only obscured by recourse to a vaguer set of concepts such as 'strong' and 'weak', as indeed Fallers and Lewis are fully aware.

The same appears true of attempts to assess the strength or weakness of the sibling as against the affinal bond. There is no iron law that demands that a woman's role as sister diminishes in proportion to the acquisition of new responsibilities as wife and mother; individuals adopt additional, not simply substitute, roles as they progress through the life-cycle. And in any case the strength of kinship ties does not depend only upon residential proximity; in the LoWiili situation a man's jural control over his sister or daughter is partly directed towards keeping her residentially a wife rather than a sister.

We are dealing here with a complex set of variables, so that we do not suppose that a single measure or a single factor will be equally relevant in all cases. Our own material supports Gluckman's analysis of the factors in marriage stability among the Zulu and Lozi. There are two main differences. Firstly, though the LoWiili and Tallensi unambiguously transfer genetricial rights, they do not do so permanently, as he claims happens among the Zulu. Secondly, while inheritance is agnatic among the LoWiili and 'bilateral' among the Gonja, it is not of crucial importance in this comparison as the major resource, land (particularly in Gonja), is not in short overall supply, as among the Lozi.

Our data have nothing directly to add on the differences among 'patrilineal' societies pointed out by Fallers, Leach, and Lewis. We feel that before the discussion of divorce can be carried much further, it will be necessary to move away from vague attributions of 'high' and 'low'. Even when writers have the kind of overall figure that Barnes (1949) proposes, they still differ in their assessments of what is 'high' and 'low'. This is partly because they fail to elicit the pattern of divorce in age-specific terms. It will be clear that a high divorce rate in the early 'experimental' stage of a woman's marital career has quite different implications for the relationship between husband and wife, between members of the sibling group, and between parents and children (particularly father and son) than in the case of a divorce rate that remains high after childbearing has begun.

Only when variables such as the rate of divorce have been made less impressionistic will it be possible to make any substantial advance. Meanwhile it seems worth while to attempt more precise studies, through inclusive regional surveys, of the factors involved in the circulation of women and children, of which divorce is one of the elements.

Conclusions

From the standpoint of marriage transactions, fostering, paternity, divorce, widow inheritance, and kind of kin group, the societies of northern Ghana display two main clusters of variables which are summarized in Table 15.

TABLE 15

SUMMARY TABLE, KINSHIP VARIABLES IN NORTHERN GHANA

Unilineal descent groups	Marriage pre-stations	Pattern of divorce	Widow inheri-tance	Paternity	Fostering	Exo-gamous kin groups	Excep-tions
Type 1 1 unilineal descent groups present	A	A	A	A	A	A	
2	A	A	A	A	A	A	? Nank-anse foster-ing
3	A	A	A	A	A	A	
4	A	A	A	A	A	A	? Cha-kalle
Type 2 5 unilineal descent groups 'weak' or absent	B	B	B	B	B	B	
6	B	B	B/A	B	B	B/A	? Mamp-rusi ? Wala

N.B. The anomalous cases are discussed in the text.

Type 1, e.g. *Tallensi (or Lo Wiili)*. These societies have patrilineal descent groups, high (returnable) bridewealth, low fostering, 'social' paternity, increasingly stable marriage, high ratio of conjugal residence, and widow inheritance.

Type 2, e.g. *Gonja*. These societies have no unilineal descent groups (or only weak, non-exogamous ones), low (non-returnable) marriage payments, 'biological' paternity, high fostering, consistently high divorce, high ratio of sibling residence, and no widow inheritance.

As they affect residence, these variables form two overlapping groups, those primarily influencing the circulation of women, and those bearing on the circulation of children.

Residence of Children: In societies of type 1 bridewealth serves to transfer rights in children and legitimacy is automatically conferred upon all offspring a wife bears; children live with their parents, or with lineage proxy-parents. In societies of type 2 low marriage prestations are not associated with any transfer of rights *in genetricem*, and there is no distinction between 'social' and 'biological' paternity. Rights over children are diffused among the kin of both parents and kinship fostering is widespread. Just as in societies of type 1 the relatively low divorce rate of fertile marriages makes for continuity in the nuclear family, so the high divorce rate in societies of type 2 often gives a wide dispersal to the children of one man or one woman.

Residence of Women: In societies of type 2 a high divorce rate throughout life and the ban on widow inheritance are associated with a high ratio of sibling to conjugal residence. Women live with their kin at intervals throughout their lives and nearly always return in old age. The opposite pattern is found in societies of type 1, where the increasing stability of marriage, the refundability of bridewealth, and the inheritance of widows are all linked with the virtually fixed residence of women with their husbands and sons in the agnatic extended family. The ratio of sibling to conjugal residence is markedly low.

These two groupings are obviously not themselves discrete. Apart from the duplications of particular variables in both sets, the residence of children clearly affects the residence of adults, and vice versa. The point is that in societies of type 2, the physical circulation of members begins at an earlier phase in the developmental cycle and hence has different implications.

Any attempt to explain the incidence of these two clusters of interlocking variables must also take into account non-kinship factors, such as we have listed at the beginning of this chapter. We note that all the 'bilateral' groups form part of a complex stratified state, and that these states have all been influenced in varying degrees by Islam, whose family law greatly modifies the organization of descent groups (Greenberg 1946; Trimingham 1959). The advent of Islam had important social implications: paternal parallel cousin marriage and diverging devolution modifies the system of descent groups, making them 'weaker' in some senses. But here we would give more weight to the nature of the centralized systems. These are conquest states, established by one ethnic group over another, under a situation of open connubium (free and frequent intermarriage between status groups).

Given the incorporation of structurally diverse groups associated with frequent intermarriage, discussed in chapter 6, the result is a mutual adjustment of domestic institutions (the area most directly influenced). This tends to produce a kinship system based on the lowest common denominators and results in the kind of 'bilateral' system found (for much the same reasons) in other centralized poly-ethnic African states; the Hausa and Nupe of northern Nigeria, the Dagomba of northern Ghana and the Ngoni, the Nyakyusa and the Lozi of Zambia, all of these have incorporated groups of widely different social structures. Indeed the evidence on these state systems suggests the presence of a set of kinship variables very similar to those that we have isolated among the Gonja.

NOTES

We are grateful to Susan Drucker Brown and Christine Oppong for information on the Mamprusi and Dagomba; other material for this paper was gathered during the course of our work in Ghana. Jack Goody is indebted to the Nuffield Foundation (1957) and the Leverhulme Foundation (1965–6) and Esther Goody to the Ford Foundation (1956–7), the Wenner-Gren Foundation (1964–5) and the Social Science Research Council (1966–7).

1. The mechanism at work here has something in common with the attempt of friends in some western cultures to perpetuate their necessarily evanescent relationships by acting as godparents to one another's children, and by joking references to marriage between their offspring. See Chapter 8.

2. In respect of the selected variables there is little difference between the LoWiili and the LoDagaba (whom we refer to collectively as the LoDagaa); but since our recent information was collected from Birifu (LoWiili), we will draw the contrast with this latter group.

3. While ideally a ratio of sibling to conjugal residence would be calculated for each woman over her lifetime and would represent the time spent with 'brothers' and with husbands, this ratio 'A' is in practice difficult to obtain and for comparative purposes virtually impossible to extract from published data. Less satisfactory (because of the assumptions entailed), but more practical, is ratio 'B', which compares the number of women living as wives and as 'sisters' in N households at a given time. In calculating ratio 'B' it is necessary to do so separately for each of several significant age cohorts in order to take into account differences in circumstances affecting young, middle-aged and old women.

4. By pattern we refer to the relative frequency of divorce at different periods of a woman's life. The assumption here is that there may be different factors affecting stability of marriage at different times (see Fortes 1949*a*; E. Goody 1962).

5. Residence with a husband in old age is slightly more common in eastern Gonja than in the central or western part of the country. But here women are at pains to explain that although they may live in the same house, they are no longer 'married', that is, they no longer sleep with or cook for the 'husband'. There is, for women, something incongruous about being old and being married.

6. A LoWiili girl will sometimes go to help her elder sister as a nurse girl (*biyaal*) to look after a young child, if there is no one else in the house to help. The same institution is reported for the Kusase and the Kasena. For the purposes of this comparison (Table 14), we have not reckoned this practice as a type of fostering, partly because the girl goes in the capacity of sister rather than as child, partly because of the instrumental character of the institution and its relatively brief duration and partly because the crucial factor for our argument is whether or not boys are fostered, and if so, whether foster parenthood is a function of lineage membership or not; girls have to move in any case because of marriage.

A very young child whose mother has died is taken by her kinsfolk to be looked after until he grows up (J. Goody 1956*a*).

7. How widely marriage and fostering are spread is directly related to population density and the distance between villages. Population is thinner, villages more widely separated and the distances involved in marriage and fostering are greater in central Gonja than in the east. Western Gonja occupies an intermediate position in this respect.

8. In some groups in northern Ghana, e.g. the Builsa, the Kasena and the Kusase, the widow is encouraged to remain in her dead husband's house, but she cannot marry there; instead, she takes lovers from among his distant lineage 'brothers' and breeds children to the dead man's name in a form of widow concubinage.

9. Exceptions occur in two types of situation. Where the marriage was between kinsfolk, an elderly woman who has no nearer relations may remain in her dead husband's house, partly as widow, partly as kinswoman. Where the widow is of slave origin and has no kin, she also stays in the house.

10. Gifts of money to the parents of the bride are becoming larger in eastern Gonja. In the west the traditional scale of gifts still obtains. Throughout the area the fixed legal payment is 12s. and 12 kola nuts.

11. Where orphans are placed in the custody of the parent's heir we speak of proxy-parenthood, since the heir replaces the parent in a whole variety of domestic and descent group roles.

12. Ardener makes a useful distinction between demand-sensitive and demand-insensitive systems of marriage payments (1962: 78).

13. Tallensi divorce is clearly very high in the experimental phase. Fortes writes that 70 per cent of women had been married more than once, in some cases a subsequent marriage being leviratic (1949*b*: 85 f.n.); and that in a sample of over 100, no man over 30 'failed to experience one or more unsuccessful and usually short-lived marriages' (84). But if only fertile marriages for which bridewealth was paid are counted, the ratio of marriages ending in divorce to all marriages is 7 per cent, i.e. relatively low (85 f.n.). This figure corresponds to what we have called the middle and terminal phases of marriage. The figure of 7 per cent is not

entirely satisfactory as it excludes barren marriages. For comparative purposes it would be desirable to compare the percentage of all 'correct' marriages ending in divorce, in addition to the percentage of all fertile correct marriages so terminated. But the concept of a 'correct' marriage again raises analytical problems.

14. We have altered the rubric of section 5, since more work needs to be done on the inheritance systems of these groups before we can be certain about their position.

15. 'Grandparents are entitled to the services of the first-born son and daughter of their eldest son. These children will leave the home of their parents (supposing the eldest son to have "gone out" and built his own compound) as soon as they can walk, and go to live with their grandparents, until they marry. They will, however, visit their own parents from time to time' (Rattray 1932: 1, 263).

'It is not uncommon for Nankanse children to be brought up in the maternal uncle's compound, with the full consent of the natural parents. "Your mother's mother often loves you more than your mother. You may take anything you like at your uncle's compound and be familiar with his mother, calling her 'old grey hairs'. A child may continue to live at his uncle's house until he grows up, and may marry and continue to live with his uncle after marriage" ' (1, 273).

16. The high marriage payments of urban Ghanaians are basically wedding expenses; the high payments of the Kanuri are not 'jurally' high as they vary between 5 and 100 pounds (Cohen 1961) and the high payments in Egypt were an indirect dowry for the bride (Lane 1871: 1, 204).

17. These last two factors possibly help to explain the relatively high rates of divorce among the Fulani, the Bedouin, the Kanuri and the Somali. It was Evans-Pritchard who called attention to the interdependence of bridewealth and exogamy (1965: 186, first published 1934); but the relationship is rather between bridewealth and sibling incest. That is to say, it does not actually *require* exogamous unilineal descent groups to operate a system of what he called 'indirect exchange' in which a sister is sent outside the group in exchange for bridewealth to be used to obtain a wife for a brother. Exogamous descent groups do, however, tend to be associated with the use of bridewealth in this context.

18. This point is never mentioned in Gray's account of the Sonjo situation (1960). While he rightly corrects the emphasis on the purely 'symbolic' nature of marriage payments, he seems to raise other analytic problems of similar magnitude.

19. Following Radcliffe-Brown (who tended to use 'patrilineal' in a blanket way to include inheritance, succession and descent) Gluckman at times phrased his argument in terms of *father-right*, which, as Leach has pointed out, is of limited use as an analytic tool (1961: 115). But he states that 'I am myself uncertain whether it is the stability of people's attachment to specific areas, or patriliny or father-right itself, or the agnatic lineage, or all of these together, which, whatever the other variables are, tend to be associated with a strong marriage tie' (Gluckman 1950: 203). In summarizing Gluckman's hypothesis, Mitchell specifically associates a low divorce rate with 'corporate patrilineages' (1961: 318), and this seems to be the main variable with which Gluckman was concerned.

20. E.g. Cohen 1961: 1231; Gibbs 1963: 552.

21. Epainogamy is 'that condition of marriage which is societally supported, praised and sanctioned—indeed almost enforced' (1963: 553).

22. The relationship between specific variables is discussed by all these writers, but when they leave that realm of discourse they adopt the technique of explaining the less inclusive by the more inclusive, i.e. by raising the level of generalization.

REFERENCES

Amherst, H. W., 1931, 'Report on the Constitution, Organization and Customs of the Nanumba People', Ms., West African Research Unit, Cambridge.

Ardener, E., 1962, *Divorce and Fertility: an African Study* (Nig. soc. econ. Stud. 3), London.

Barnes, J., 1949, 'Measures of Divorce Frequency in Simple Societies', *J. R. anthrop. Inst.* **79**, 37–62.

Blair, H. A., 1931, 'An Essay Upon the Dagomba People', Ms., West African Research Unit, Cambridge.

Cardinall, A. W. n.d., *The Natives of the Northern Territories of the Gold Coast: Their Customs, Religion and Folk-lore*, London.

Cohen, R., 1961, 'Marriage Instability among the Kanuri of Northern Nigeria', *Am. Anthrop.* **63**, 1231–49.

Evans-Pritchard, E. E., 1965, *The Position of Women in Primitive Societies and Other Essays in Social Anthropology*, London.

Fallers, L. A., 1957, 'Some Determinants of Marriage Instability in Busoga: a Reformulation of Gluckman's Thesis', *Africa* **27**, 106–21.

Fortes, M., 1949a, 'Time and Social Structure: an Ashanti Case Study', in *Social Structure* (ed.) M. Fortes, London. 1949b, *The Web of Kinship Among the Tallensi*, London. 1950, 'Kinship and Marriage among the Ashanti', in *African Systems of Kinship and Marriage*, (eds) A. R. Radcliffe-Brown and D. Forde, London. 1959, 'Descent, Filiation and Affinity: a Rejoinder to Dr. Leach, 1 & 2', *Man* **59**, 193–7; 206–12.

Fortes, M. and Evans-Pritchard, E. E. (eds), 1940, *African Political Systems*, London.

Gibbs, J. L., 1963, 'Marital Instability Among the Kpelle: Towards a Theory of Epainogamy', *Am. Anthrop.* **65**, 552–73.

Gluckman, M., 1950, 'Kinship and Marriage Among the Lozi of Northern Rhodesia and the Zulu of Natal', in *African Systems of Kinship and Marriage* (eds) A. R. Radcliffe-Brown and D. Forde, London.

Goody, E., 1960, 'Kinship, Marriage and the Developmental Cycle among the Gonja of Northern Ghana.' Ph.D. thesis, University of Cambridge. 1962, 'Conjugal Separation and Divorce Among the Gonja of Northern Ghana', in *Marriage in Tribal Societies* (ed.) M. Fortes, Cambridge. 1966, 'Fostering in Ghana: a Preliminary Report', *Ghana J. Soc.* **2**, 26–33.

Goody, J., 1956a, *The Social Organization of the LoWiili*, London. 1956b, 'A Comparative Approach to Incest and Adultery', *Br. J. Soc.* **7**, 286–305. Reprinted as Chapter 2. 1962, *Death, Property and the Ancestors*, Stanford. 1967, 'The Over-Kingdom of Gonja', in *West African Kingdoms* (eds) D. Forde and P. Kaberry, London. 1968, 'Descent Groups', in *International Encyclopaedia of the Social Sciences*, New York. 1969, 'Marriage Policy and Incorporation in Northern Ghana', in *From Tribe to Nation in Africa* (eds) R. Cohen and J. Middleton, San Francisco. Reprinted as chapter 6.

Goody, J. and Goody E., 1966, 'Cross-cousin Marriage in Northern Ghana', *Man (N.S.)* **1**, 343–55. Reprinted as Chapter 8.

Gray, R. R., 1960, 'Sonjo Bride-price and the Question of African "Wife Purchase"', *Am. Anthrop.* **62**, 34–57.

Greenberg, J. H., 1946, *The Influence of Islam upon a Sudanese Religion* (Monogr. Am. ethnol. Soc. **10**), New York.

Labouret, H., 1931, *Les Tribus du rameau Lobi*, Paris.

Lane, E. W., 1871, *An Account of the Manners and Customs of the Modern Egyptians, Written During the Years* 1833, –34, *and* –35, 5th ed., London.

Leach, E. R., 1951, 'The Structural Implications of Matrilateral Cross-cousin Marriage', *J. R. anthrop. Inst.* **81**, 23–53. 1957, 'Aspects of Bridewealth and Marriage Stability Among the Kachin and Lakher', *Man* **57**, 50–5. 1961, *Rethinking Anthropology* (Lond. Sch. Econ. Monogr. soc. Anthrop. **22**), London.

Lévi-Strauss, C. 1963, *Structural Anthropology*, New York.

Lewis, I. M., 1962, *Marriage and the Family in Northern Somaliland* (E. Afr. Stud. **15**), Kampala: East African Institute of Social Research. 1965, 'Problems in the Comparative Study of Unilineal Descent', in *The Relevance of Models for Social Anthropology* (Ass. soc. Anthrop. Monogr. **1**), London.

Mackay, n.d., 'Essay on the Mamprusi', Ms., West African Research Unit, Cambridge.

Mitchell, J. C., 1961, 'Social Change and the Stability of African Marriage in Northern Rhodesia', in *Social Change in Modern Africa*, (ed.) A. Southall, London.

Nadel, S. F., 1952, 'Witchcraft in Four African Societies', *Am. Anthrop.* **54**, 18–29.

Radcliffe-Brown, A. R., 1930, 'The Social Organization of Australian Tribes', *Oceania* **1**, 34–63, 206–46, 323–41, 426–56.

Rattray, R. S., 1932, *The Tribes of the Ashanti Hinterland*, Oxford.

Richards, A. I., 1950, 'Some Types of Family Structure amongst the Central Bantu', in *African Systems of Kinship and Marriage*, (eds.) A. R. Radcliffe-Brown and D. Forde, London. 1956, *Chisungu: a Girl's Initiation Ceremony among the Bemba of Northern Rhodesia*, London.

Schneider, D. M., 1953, 'A Note on Bridewealth and the Stability of Marriage', *Man* **53**, 55–7.

Stephens, W. N., 1962, *The Oedipus Complex: Cross-cultural Evidence*, Glencoe, Ill.

Stenning, D., 1959, *Savannah Nomads*, London.

Tait, D., 1961, *The Konkomba of Northern Ghana*, London.

Tauxier, L., 1912, *Le Noir du Soudan*, Paris.

Trimingham, J. S., 1959, *Islam in West Africa*, Oxford.

Wilson, M., 1951, 'Witch Beliefs and Social Structure', *Am. J. Sociol.* **56**, 307–13.

CHAPTER EIGHT

Cross-cousin Marriage in Northern Ghana

(WITH ESTHER GOODY)

IN recent years the discussion of cross-cousin marriage (XCM)[1] has concentrated upon the prescribed forms, and much ink has flowed in arguments about preferences and prescriptions, about the differences between normative rules and rates of occurrence (statistical 'norms'), and about the relation between these two aspects of social behaviour, and exactly what it is that prescriptive marriage prescribes (i.e. is it marriage with a particular person, sibling group, descent group, or category of kin, for in each case the social implications will differ?). The concentration on prescriptive forms is linked with the central role that Australia has played in the comparative study of kinship. This antipodean dominance derives partly from the timing and nature of European expansion in the area and partly from certain assumptions about the value of the Australian material as providing evidence for the origins of man's social institutions. Technologically, the Australian aborigines have the simplest living (or recently living) culture, so that those social institutions that are closely entailed with technology might be expected to reflect this fact. But Australian societies (as we have often been reminded) have had as long a past as any other human group, and when one compares certain aspects of their kinship institutions and religious beliefs with those of other parts of the world, one is impressed not so much by their 'elementary forms' (*pace* Durkheim and Lévi-Strauss) as by their highly specialized, morphologically complex nature.

Be this as it may, it is possible that an examination of the more widespread and flexible institution of preferential cross-cousin marriage may throw some light upon the more rigid and formalistic systems to which theoretical attention has been largely devoted.

This chapter forms part of a series of studies of kinship variables among the peoples of northern Ghana and follows the method of limited comparison discussed in Chapter 7. We start by examining a few groups in which intensive fieldwork has been carried out, namely the Tallensi, Konkomba, LoDagaa, and Gonja, in order to set out the problem. We then go on to consider all the available data on the peoples of northern Ghana in order to see how far the associations derived from the intensive studies are valid over the wider area. Finally, we discuss why the practice of cross-cousin marriage should take the form it does in these societies.[2]

In addition to preferred cross-cousin marriage, we also want to focus attention on a related, but neglected, institution, that of prohibited cross-cousin marriage. Prohibitions are usually treated in the context of asymmetrical cross-cousin marriage, where one type (MBD or FZD) is allowed and the other forbidden. In dealing with preferential systems it is necessary to treat prohibitions as varying independently of prescriptions or preferences.

There are many societies in which all cross-cousin marriage is actively prohibited. Rattray (1932: 350) remarked upon this feature among the Tallensi of northern Ghana and he obtained the following explanation, which he describes as 'ingenious rather than convincing'. 'If you married your MBD, and quarrelled about the cows paid to your *ahen* or *asen* (maternal uncle; Nankane: *asiba*) for *sull* (Nankane: *sulle*),[3] this would lead to trouble. Suppose you quarrelled with your wife after marriage and she returned to her father, who is your maternal uncle, you would ask him to return the cows. Should he not do so, you would be entitled to seize cows belonging to any person from his, that is from your own mother's, town; you would descend into the valley . . . After doing so you could no longer perform sacrifices to your mother or to her mother; you would not sleep; your children would die, and your uncle would also suffer.'

A somewhat similar explanation was offered for the avoidance of marriage with the FZD. 'You cannot marry her because of the cows. If she went back home you would claim the cows back from her father, who is your own "father", and this would interfere with the sacrifices to your father and father's father' (Rattray 1932: 351).

Rattray tended to interpret this incompatibility as a matter of relationship terms, but it is clear that his informants view the difficulties of cross-cousin marriage as related to the incompatibility of one man (or woman) filling both a kinship and an affinal role, not because of any mystical opposition between the two, but because of the pragmatic difficulties that arise when a parent's sibling becomes a spouse's parent. Were the marriage to represent a single and complete act—a sale between two males involving a transfer of the woman—then a temporary affinal element might be swallowed up in the persisting relationship between kin. But this is not the case, as the reference to the cows suggests. The transactions are conditional and the difficulties between affines are likely to be most intense at the break-up of the marriage, especially when the wife's parents have to return the bridewealth they had earlier received.

While Rattray's informants refer mainly to the final dissolution of a marriage, it is clear that any quarrel arising out of the union of kin may lead to a chain reaction within the whole network of kin relations, particularly when the transactions involved mean the transfer over time of a heavy bridewealth payment. Hence the likelihood exists that kinship marriages are jurally more stable (i.e. less easy to break) than other marriages within the same society.[4]

As in the rest of northern Ghana, marriage among the Tallensi has its religious facet; the ancestors are deeply interested in transactions which secure the continuity of their line. Moreover, the sort of quarrels which the dissolution of marriage so often entails—disputes over the custody and care of children, over property used in the domestic enterprise, over the relative culpability of husband and wife—these disputes are unwelcome to the ancestors. It is particularly dangerous for men engaged in such discordant activities to participate together in sacrifices to the ancestors, since both may well be making an appeal to the same set of forebears to help them in their quarrel. These dangers emerge not only from Fortes' analysis of the Tallensi, but just as explicitly from the statements of Rattray's informant among the near-by Nankanse and Kasena. Of the latter, he writes: 'The circle within which marriages are prohibited was described as follows: "A man may not marry into any group with whom he meets and sacrifices", and again "you cannot marry into your 'small mother's' group, i.e. among mother's, or father's mother's relations. Marriages with cross-cousins are prohibited" ' (1932: 539).

The prohibition on cross-cousin marriage, then, performs the manifest function (i.e. explicit to the actors) of preventing role incompatibility (i.e. encouraging role segregation) or more concretely, of protecting certain kin relations from the added troubles to which marriage may give rise. At the same time it prevents the groups with which one sacrifices to the ancestors (i.e. kin groups) from becoming involved in affinal quarrels.

The ban on marriage within one's unilineal descent group (UDG) is already given by the system of clanship that obtains in much of northern Ghana. It is significant here that the additional prohibitions on marriage with the MBD (and sometimes with the FZD) are often phrased not in terms of cross-cousins at all, but in terms of the groups (unilineal descent groups, or more usually segments of them) to which a person is linked through women. Examples of the extent and elaborateness of such prohibitions are given in the work of Fortes (1949b) on the Tallensi and Tait (1961) on the Konkomba; they also emerge in Rattray's account of the Kasena, Dagaba, and Isala, though, since he was engaged in surveying a large area, his questions were obviously phrased in a limited way and hence often refer more specifically to cross-cousins, although in local terminology these are often not distinguished (except descriptively) from siblings and other cousins. It is clear that one of the latent functions or consequences of such prohibitions is to force a man to separate his ties of kinship and in-lawship, or, more specifically (since agnatic kinship is already separated by clan or lineage exogamy), matrilateral ties from affinal ones.

In addition to the set of prohibitions phrased in terms of segments of patrilineal unilineal descent groups, many of these societies have unnamed descent groups of the *soog* type, based on the female line (e.g. the Tallensi *soog*), within which marriage is forbidden. Where such groups (which have elsewhere been called complementary or secondary) are absent, restrictions may be expressed in terms of a prohibition on intermarriage among the descendants of a common ancestor, a number of generations removed: two among the Konkomba (Tait 1961), four in the case of some southern Yoruba groups, e.g. the Ondo (Lloyd 1962: 102), and among the Tiv the incest taboo extends to those individuals who have a common grandparent (Bohannan 1953: 27). In these cases the range of prohibited kin forms in effect what has been called a descending kindred,[5] essentially bilateral in its definition.

The uterine or bilateral ban ('You cannot marry the offspring of the same grandparents') is not inconsistent with the 'unilineal' one mentioned above ('You cannot marry e.g. your mother's people'); among the Konkomba both formulae seem to be used in different contexts. For the particular prohibition on co-descendants may be part of a more general one on particular unilineal descent groups or on a segment of them. In the patrilineal societies of northern Ghana such an extensive prohibition is common for the group to which a man is linked by ties of complementary filiation (the mother's patrilineage), but less common for the more particularistic ban on marriage with the FZD or MZD.

In any case, one effect of the prohibition is to force a man to extend his ties at each generation and hence maintain as wide a web of kinship for his children as he has enjoyed himself. Instead of repeating the pattern of alliance over each generation, he is forced to establish new partnerships at each marriage, though it should be remembered that in one sense these only replace (in number, not in each particular) the ties with matrilateral groups which are continually contracting.

One aspect of this forced extension of marriage is identical with that assigned to exogamy in Tylor's well-known statement of the alternative that faced the human race, marry out or be killed out (1889: 267). By prohibiting close marriages, you prescribe distant ones. The advantages here are often quite explicit to the actors. The Tiv of central Nigeria, for instance, state that they prefer socially distant marriages because these widen the field of support upon which the offspring can draw (Bohannan 1953: 25).

The prohibition on cross-cousin marriage is, then, part of a more inclusive ban on marriages between near kin; agnates are prohibited by clan exogamy, and even where we do not find an exogamous *soog*, there is a ban on marriage with the MZD.[6] Nor is this simply a feature of the group of societies we have used as our universe;[7] for, as Murdock (1959: 83) has pointed out, cross-cousin marriage is prohibited among most of the Mossi- and Grusi-speaking peoples in the Voltaic area, as well as among the Konkomba (Tem) and among the patrilineal Kwa-speaking groups of southern Nigeria.

We have pointed to some of the gains that this system offers from the actor's point of view. Such an argument would apply to many, if not all, societies. Yet, when we look around the peoples of northern Ghana, we find that some prohibit, some allow, and some encourage cross-cousin marriage. Do we find any significant concomitants here?

In fact, there is a striking association between the system of unilineal descent groups and the system of cross-cousin marriage or other kinship marriage. In Table 16 we categorize the societies in northern Ghana according to the presence or absence of various kinds of unilineal descent group. We do not here wish to elaborate upon this classification except to point out that, however unsatisfactory it may be from other points of view, it was not manufactured for the present purpose. Elements of it have appeared in earlier publications (J. Goody 1961; E. Goody 1960), and the information comes largely from Rattray's 1932 survey, supplemented by our own field notes. We should add that, unlike many writers on northern Nigeria, we have made a distinction between unilineal descent groups of the usual kind (e.g. Tallensi, LoDagaa) and dynastic descent groups (see J. Goody 1966); all the states listed in Section 6 appear to have the latter. Otherwise they are without unilineal descent groups in the more usual sense and are characterized by one of the different forms of kin range or kin group, e.g. the *dang*, or descending kindred of the Dagomba (Manoukian 1951: 28), normally referred to under the blanket term 'bilateral'.

Table 17 shows the correlation between systems with patrilineal UDGs and prohibited cross-cousin marriage on the one hand, and double descent (J. Goody 1961) plus 'bilateral' (or non-UDGs) and cross-cousin marriage on the other.[8] The Tallensi and other societies with patrilineal UDGs plus *soog* group have the same system of marriage as societies with patrilineal UDGs alone.[9]

To try and explain this correlation, we need to examine the particular advantages of cross-cousin marriage in societies belonging to Categories 4 and 5. We begin by noting the tendency—one cannot put it more strongly than that—for a stated preference for FZD marriage in the double descent systems (or rather among the LoDagaba, which is the only one to have been examined in any detail) and a similar preference (anyhow on the part of the senior generation) for MBD marriage in the bilateral group (Category 6).

TABLE 16

UNILINEAL DESCENT GROUPS IN NORTHERN GHANA

1. *Patrilineal UDGs*
   Konkomba
   Isala
   Awuna (Fra)
   Awuna (Nagwa)
2. *Patrilineal UDGs, plus complementary (secondary) uterine groups (i.e. weak matrilineal UDGs).*
   (a) *unnamed*
   Tallensi
   Namnam
   Nankanse (Gorensi)
   Kusase
   Builsa
   Dagaba
   Kasena
3. (b) *named*
   LoWiili
4. *Fully-fledged double descent (i.e. patrilineal UDGs, plus matrilineal UDGs, plus double inheritance).*
   LoBirifor
   LoDagaba
   Chakalle (?)
5. *Weak, named patrilineal UDGs, plus double inheritance.*[1]
   Tampolensi
   Vagala
   Safalba
   Degha (Mo)
   Choruba
6. *Bilateral systems (UDGs absent, except for patrilineal dynastic descent groups).*
   Gonja
   Dagomba
   Mamprusi[2]
   Wala[3]
   Nanumba

---

[1] On the basis of earlier observations the Vagala and Safalba were classified as fully fledged double-descent systems (J. Goody 1961). Further research in 1965 shows that the Vagala belong to a category of societies that includes the Degha (Mo), Safalba, Choruba and probably the Chira, Nome and Batige, where inheritance is split in the usual manner (movable in the uterine, immovable in the agnatic line) but where the only unilineal descent groups are weak patrilineal groups.

[2] The Mamprusi royals appear to give somewhat greater stress to unilineal descent groups than the other societies in Category 6.

[3] Rattray's material on the Wala appears to refer mainly to the commoners (Wala Dagaba) who are similar to the Dagarti (or, more properly, Dagaba).

The reason behind the association of double descent with FZD marriage is clear. We here define as fully fledged double descent systems (for empirical purposes) those societies with 'corporate' (i.e. property-holding) UDGs based on both lines. The difficulties of defining a preference are manifest, and even where one can state this, one may find a contradiction between an expressed and a statistical preference. Among the LoDagaba, people will point out the material gains to be had from FZD marriage. When a man dies, his property is split between an agnatic and an uterine heir (except where it is inherited by a full brother), but by FZD marriage, his grandson (his ZDS) becomes a member of the same patrilineal and matrilineal clan and hence a potential heir. Rattray made the same point with regard to the Ashanti where, although there is no splitting of the jural inheritance (though property does go to the son by gift), there is a similar splitting of a man's social personality, since neither his sons nor his sister's sons belong to the same *ntoro* and the same *abusua*; but his ZDS does, at least when his son makes a FZD marriage.

There is yet more important element in this unification of the children of siblings of opposite sex which emerges from Fortes' discussion (1949a: 76) of the Ashanti. There he writes: 'They describe cross-cousin marriage as a device by which men try to unite their love of their children with their loyalty to their maternal kin.' In other words, the division between children of opposite sex siblings which unilineal descent groups and sex-linked inheritance inevitably create (what in Chapter 3 was called the problem of the residual sibling), is healed by a marriage between the children of those siblings. The same expressed attitudes appear among the LoDagaa; in the LoWiili village of Birifu, when Bonyiri was asked for his daughter in marriage one day, he replied, 'That's up to her mother', and her mother, when asked, wanted her to marry back into her own lineage to one of her brother's sons (FZD marriage). The return of a daughter was implied in the marriage contract and had some effect on bridewealth transactions, for marriage to a FZD seems to have meant that the final bridewealth payment (the *nabaara*) was cancelled. Because of the long-term nature of these marriage payments, and the fact that a debt here is probably balanced by a service there, it would be well-nigh impossible to make any exact statement on this matter.

TABLE 17

CROSS-COUSIN MARRIAGE IN NORTHERN GHANA

	MBD	*FZD*	*References*
1.			
Isala	o	o	R.503
Awuna (Fra)	o	o	R.528
Awuna (Nagwa)	no information		
Konkomba	o	o	Tait 1961
2.			
Tallensi	o	o	R.350; F.
Namnam	o	o	R.373; G.f.
Nankanse (Gorensi)	o	o	R.278
Kusase	o	o	G.f.
Builsa	o	o	G.f.
Dagaba	o	o	R.410
Kasena	o	o	R.539
3.			
LoWiili	†	†(P)	G.1956: 48
4.			
LoBirifor	†	†	Labouret 1931
LoDagaba	†	†(P)	R.436; G.1962: 349
Chakalle (?)	†	†	G.f.
5.			
Tampolensi	†(P)	†(P)	R.519
Vagala	†	†	R.521; G.f.
Safalba	†	†	G.f.
Degha (Mo)	†	†	G.f.
Choruba	†	†	G.f.
6.			
Gonja	†(P) (1st disapproved)	† (1st disapproved)	G.f.
Dagomba	†(P) ,, ,,	† ,, ,,	Oppong f.
Mamprusi	†(P) ,, ,,	† ,, ,,	Brown f.
Wala	†(P) ,, ,,	† ,, ,,	G.f.
Nanumba	no information		

Legend o: prohibited. †: permitted. P: preferred.
Sources R: Rattray (1932). F: Fortes (1949b). G: Goody. f: fieldnotes.

In the LoWiili case we have mentioned, the unification of the split siblings through cross-cousin marriage is not a matter of inheritance (although this was probably the case in former times), but of unilineal descent groups and, perhaps most importantly, of households (residence). Because of the incest taboo, most marriages involve the spatial separation of those people who have been brought up together as children. This, of course, is the case in bilateral societies, too, such as the Gonja of northern Ghana; cross-cousin marriage may perform the same role as kinship fostering, that is, preventing the disappearance (or, anyhow, dispersal) of kinship ties. The Gonja encourage cross-cousin marriage, but give no preference to FZD marriage (there is no inheritance advantage). Indeed, there is a limited preference for MBD marriage, as in the case of the Dogon (Marti 1957: 39), the Bambara (Murdock *et al.* 1962: 122, 125), the Mende (Murdock *et al.* 1962: 387), and, indeed, the whole of the Mende-speaking area, an area characterized by patrilineal UDGs.[10] As in the Mende area (and as, to some extent, among the LoDagaa, where both forms of cross-cousin marriage are permitted), the marriage with a MBD is part and parcel of the total relationship with the mother's brother; and for a woman, as scarcely needs pointing out, FZD marriage is marriage to the son of her mother's brother. A man's relationship with his sister's son may involve more than the limited transfer of property *inter vivos*—which is epitomized in the snatching of the flesh of sacrificial animals—or in the building up of a man's first independent wealth by the gift of a chicken, what the LoDagaa call the 'fowl of rearing' (Fortes 1949b: 194; J. Goody 1956: 58). It may also involve a contribution towards bridewealth which, of course, assumes greater importance, the 'heavier' the payment. Among the LoDagaba (category 4), the mother's brother contributes in this way, though his help is specifically tied to reciprocal assistance on the farm. Here, farming for the mother's brother can be regarded as a kind of bride-service, even though the reward is not the farm-owner's daughter. The LoWiili, on the other hand, who can be regarded as struggling against the pulls of matrilineal inheritance and UDGs, consider that if a man gets all the bridewealth from the mother's brother, then the children should belong to the benefactor. A way round this problem of the filiation of the children of a procreative union, which societies in Africa resolve in a variety of different ways (there are always forms of secondary recruitment), is for the mother's brother to provide not the cash but the girl herself.

This is the situation among the Gonja of northern Ghana (category 6). Here, both forms of cross-cousin marriage are allowed, and a few Muslim marriages occur with FBD as well. Moreover, the dynastic descent groups (as in northern Nigeria) are not exogamous, and the agnatic descendants of the founding ancestor, Jakpa, marry among themselves, although they would avoid first-degree FBD and MZD unions. A man has special call upon his mother's brother in the business of taking himself a wife. This general obligation comes out specifically at the Fire Festival of Jentige, the Muslim Ashura, held on the tenth night of Muharram. On this day, there is a lot of horseplay, and boys and girls will go to sweep the houses of their maternal uncles of varying degrees of relationship.[11] At this time, an uncle is supposed to reward his 'sister's sons' with a few pennies or perhaps a shilling, and only the ill-natured set more than token tasks. At this time, too, people will talk, though not very seriously, about the obligation of a mother's brother to provide them with a wife.

This general obligation gets translated into action where a nephew has been particularly punctilious in his greetings, and has either lived with and farmed for his uncle, or made time for extended visits during which he has worked for him. It is often said that the uncle may one day summon such a youth and ask 'Do you want a wife, money or a horse?' In other words, it is usually the dependent sister's son who wins a bride in this way, and this situation is a reflection partly of the residual claim a man has on the property of his maternal uncle and partly of his inability to acquire a bride from other sources. However, although a man has in theory the power of disposal over his daughter (or, rather, the father is one among the occupants of four roles, the parents and their siblings, who have a say in this matter), he very seldom hands her over to his sister's son. The obligation is to provide a wife (the equivalent of bridewealth, which does not here exist) rather than a specific woman, and this wife may come from anywhere in the family; anywhere, that is, where he has a say in the disposal of a girl in marriage. The bride seldom comes from one's closest kin, however, so that first-degree cross-cousin marriage is rare; the tie is considered too close. Above all, the parents of the pair must not have been born of one mother. Should they be related through a common father this is less dangerous, although in fact only one such case was encountered. Much more frequent is marriage between the grandchildren of two siblings or half siblings. These are still termed cross-cousins as long as the parents of the spouses are of the same generation and of the opposite sex. When kinship marriage involves such relatively distant relationships, the mother's brother is not likely to have direct control over the girl whom he wishes to marry to his nephew. Hence he must himself 'beg' the girl from her parent or guardian.

The girls over whom a man does exercise a strong authority are the daughters of his 'sisters'. These nieces, like their brothers, owe respect to, and attendance on, their mother's brother. It is he, the Gonja repeatedly assert, who can sell them into slavery or pawn them to pay a debt, a prerogative which their father does not have. At Jentige, when dutiful sisters' children greet their uncles and perform some small service for them, a mother's brother may seize his sister's daughter to sell or pawn, or to present to a friend or benefactor as a wife. The daughter of a full sister, however respectful she may be during the rest of the year, is therefore loth to approach her uncle on this day, lest he exercise that prerogative.

A man's authority over his sister's children diminishes with the distance of the relationship. Nevertheless, it is from these classificatory sister's daughters that he may seize a wife for his own son. While the pawning of a distantly related niece or nephew might be resisted, such giving in marriage would not, as long as the girl had not been promised elsewhere.

In Gonja, cross-cousin marriage forms only a small part of the total number of marriages between kin and is largely submerged in this wider category, both in thought and practice. Indeed, since they have a Hawaiian-type kinship terminology (like the Tallensi and most other groups in northern Ghana), people do not really think specifically in terms of cross-cousin marriage.[12] To them, a cross-cousin is a distant 'sister'; but whereas the Tallensi forbid marriages between close kin, the Gonja encourage it.

Putting together the material we have on northern Ghana, we find three kinds of association between cross-cousin marriage and unilineal descent groups (+ or −).[13]

1. Patrilineal UDG with no XCM, or, rather no close kinship marriage (e.g. Tallensi, Konkomba, Dagaba).

2. Double descent (i.e. patrilineal UDG and matrilineal UDG, plus double inheritance) with XCM, especially with FZD.

3. Bilateral with XCM, especially with MBD.

If we widen our horizon to include other areas of west Africa, we need to add:

2a. Matrilineal UDGs (e.g. Ashanti, LoWilisi etc.) with XCM, especially with FZD marriage (but in matrilineal systems, the type of XCM is much influenced by the residence pattern, and the Ashanti actually have more MBD marriage). Here, as in other respects, double descent systems bear some strong resemblances to those where matrilineal UDGs are found with virilocal post-marital residence.

4. Patrilineal UDGs plus preferential matrilateral XCM (MBD), e.g. Dogon, Mende.

5. Patrilineal UDGs plus XCM and parallel cousin marriage (PCM), e.g. Ewe.

6. Patrilineal UDGs, plus preferential MBD marriage and proscribed FZD, e.g. Ga (Field 1940).

We elicited some of the reasons for the differences in kin marriages between 1, 2, and 3. Two further problems remain. If we look at the savannah peoples outside northern Ghana, we find that in another group of societies with patrilineal UDGs, MBD marriage is preferred. Second, even in those systems where XCM is preferred and obviously beneficial, it occurs less frequently than its advantages might suggest. In Ashanti it is 8 per cent (Fortes 1950); among the LoDagaa it is perhaps 5 per cent;[14] among the Gonja there were undoubtedly many 'family marriages' (approx. 40 per cent in our first sample), but comparatively few of these were with cross-cousins.

Why is this so? Why is there conflict between ideal and actual marriages? Why are there not more of these preferred marriages? They are clearly very useful in the manipulation of kin relationships, and it is the manipulative advantages that we must keep in mind when trying to explain these relatively flexible systems as against the rigidity, real or assumed, of prescriptive XCM.

The apparent lack of any obvious concomitants of the Tallensi-Dogon dichotomy (patrilineal UDGs, minus XCM, or patrilineal

UDGs plus matrilateral XCM) and the comparative infrequency of preferred XCM are probably related, and we shall attempt to suggest an explanation.

The Gonja situation throws some light on the problem. Here there is great pressure towards tying relationships together and keeping in touch with siblings. The obvious way of doing this is through cross-cousin marriage, and yet it does not often occur. In fact, the Gonja are much more likely to transfer offspring to their siblings as foster children than as brides or grooms. The explanation seems to lie in some observations of Gonja marriage that were made in another context (E. Goody 1960). For while cross-cousin marriage in many ways is desirable, it is also seen as dangerous, because the inevitable disputes of married life are liable to bring about supernatural intervention. If the dead kinsfolk of the pair see that there is quarrelling or infidelity, they may chastise them, usually by harming the children. Indeed, the dead may act even if there is nothing more serious than muttering or angry unspoken thoughts. Good behaviour is expected of the partners in cross-cousin marriage at all times; in particular, they ought never to separate, though divorces do in fact occur.

Not all the dead are felt to be equally dangerous. It is said that while your dead father can make you ill, the ghosts on your mother's side can kill you and your children. Thus women, and the ancestors traced through them, are seen as threatening in many circumstances. Where, however, a couple shares some of the same ancestors (as in cross-cousin marriage), the two sources of mystical danger are combined and the risks are doubled. Added to the general threat from maternal ancestors is the specific fear of retribution for the maltreatment of one descendant by another.

The general anxiety which surrounds cross-cousin marriage seems to focus upon the wife's ancestors. If these are also a man's maternal ancestors, that is, if he has married his MBD, then they are seen as doubly dangerous, so that the marriage that is most discussed is also the marriage that is most feared. Conversely, his wife's ancestors continue to appear relatively benign to a man who has married his FZD, for he is accustomed to expect support rather than threats from the dead among his father's kin. For women the picture is, of course, reversed; but, probably because men have a latitude of choice in arranged marriages that is not permitted to women, the male view of things is made explicit in the assertion that it is more dangerous to marry a matrilateral than a patrilateral cross cousin.

That MBD marriages still occur is due firstly to the fact that a balance exists between gains and costs in unions with close kin. Kinship marriages may also be differently valued by the junior generation (who are wed) and by the senior generation (who arrange, or promote the wedding). In Gonja the ideal exists that a man should present a favoured sister's son with a wife in return for the services he has rendered. From the point of view of the man who bestows his 'daughter' on such a nephew, the possible wrath of his, and their, ancestors is not seen as a threat. The dead involved are too close to him—his own parents, their siblings, his own siblings, and eventually himself—and, in any case, the anxiety of the partners in such a marriage may well be largely a projection of inter-generational hostility which the parental generation might be expected to recognize with respect to its own parents, but not to acknowledge towards its children.

The analysis of preferential cross-cousin marriage among the Gonja demands a recognition not only of the ambivalence to which it is subject, both on a 'structural' and on an individual level, but also of the different viewpoints of the generations involved. The question 'whom would you prefer your daughter to marry?' does not necessarily produce the same answer as 'whom would *you* prefer?' When we speak of an expressed preference among the Gonja, we refer to the usually unfulfilled obligation of a man to find a wife (a 'daughter') for his sister's son.

It is not only the Gonja who view cross-cousin marriage in an ambivalent way. The LoDagaa do the same; for one of the partners, both forms of cross-cousin marriage are bound up with the potency of the curse possessed by the mother and the mother's brother. The LoDagaa see this in supernatural terms, but the use of such sanctions arises out of quarrels between spouses and other affinal relatives. If there are no ancestors in common (or only distant ones), then quarrels will not matter; if they are close, then marital disputes will affect the whole order of life. Kinship marriages are consequently seen as harder to break, although whether this is reflected in differential divorce rates we cannot tell from the data collected.

In other words, even where cross-cousin marriage is permitted or preferred, people still have the same doubts about its effect on existing kin relationships as the Tallensi give for forbidding it altogether. Thus, whatever the structural consequences of the change may be, the shift from preference to prohibition (or vice versa) does not require a radical re-orientation of views on the actors' part.

Conclusion

When one looks at the traditional societies of northern Ghana, a correlation can be found between prohibited and preferred marriages on the one hand and the system of unilineal descent groups and inheritance on the other. Despite their advantages in some social systems, such unions never comprise a high proportion of all marriages. The reason for this apparent anomaly is that all cross-cousin marriage is treated as dangerous because the actors see vital relationships between close kin as being disturbed by the introduction of affinal disputes. Kinship relations are not, of course, always smooth, but they are a good deal rougher when overloaded with marital problems. So the tendency is to separate the fields of kinship and affinity. Somewhat tentatively we suggest that (in this area) one finds cross-cousin marriage where one finds specific incentives; hence one would expect a direct link between cross-cousin marriage and other aspects of social organization, including the religious ones. These specific arrangements arise from a more generalized base in which the desirability of maintaining the bonds between siblings of opposite sex separated by marriage is linked to the difficulties of doubling roles (or rather doubling the conflicts centring on inter-personal relationships). So that, even where the social system may confer substantial benefits on cross-cousin marriage, there is still a reluctance to marry in this way, certainly as far as very close kin are concerned. Yet, it is close kin from whom one inherits, so that where property is a factor, one reduces the advantages the further out one's bride. There may, of course, be some correlation here with those systems of transmission (J. Goody 1962: 347) which place a premium on distant rather than close inheritance, but this is a question for much more research.

We have discussed some aspects of kinship marriage of a manipulative (or optative) rather than a prescriptive kind, and have also considered the opposite of prescriptive cross-cousin marriage, namely the proscribed system of the Tallensi. Neither of these institutions has received much attention in recent years compared with that spent seeking out (and demolishing) systems of a more rigid kind. A change of direction is perhaps called for; the more 'elementary' forms of cross-cousin marriage could well be the preferential rather than the prescriptive, the latter being a more highly specialized form. But our point here is not concerned so much with the establishment of evolutionary sequences or a morphological framework as with the analysis and comparison of particular systems. Here, we suggest, the discussion of cross-cousin marriage might well shift from the evanescent world of solidarities to a more mundane consideration of the profit and the loss.

NOTES

1. For reference to the accumulated discussion on cross-cousin marriage, see Schneider (1965); for the terminology employed, see J. Goody (1968).

2. This encroachment upon the work of our colleagues (the topic out of Leach, the people out of Fortes) is not altogether accidental, since it testifies to the continual stimulation we have had from both.

3. *Sull* means 'to espouse', 'to pay bridewealth for'.

4. Among the Lozi of Zambia, marriages of kin to anyone whose genealogical relationship can be traced are said to be unbreakable, although otherwise divorce is common (Gluckman 1950: 173–4).

5. Or what Goodenough refers to as 'unrestricted non-lineal descent groups', and Bohannan as 'omnilineal descent groups'.

6. This prohibition on MZD marriage, which is virtually universal in our area, arises, we presume, from the relative intimacy of the mother-child bond, combined with the very close identity of full and half-sisters.

7. Our universe is the culturally arbitrary one of northern Ghana. We hope later to extend our study more systematically, firstly to the Voltaic peoples.

8. The minimum typology for an examination of cross-cousin marriage has to be fourfold in order to take into account prohibited, prescribed, preferred and permitted forms.

9. This was essentially the simple and obvious point of the attempt to classify systems of double descent (chapter 4), i.e. that for most analytic purposes the complementary or secondary (the term used is arbitrary) descent groups of the Tallensi (and to a lesser extent of the Ashanti) are of peripheral importance and it only becomes confusing to group them with societies of the Yakö-LoDagaba type.

10. In Murdock *et al.* (1962) the Bambara are listed as Cm,* i.e. cross-cousin marriage with a matrilateral preference. The note remarks that this varies, and in some districts cross-cousin marriage is permitted but not preferred, while in some districts cross-cousin marriage is forbidden. The Mende are classified as Mm, i.e. as having preferred matrilateral cross-cousin marriage.

11. A similar custom at Ashura (there known as Bugum) exists in Mamprusi, Dagomba and Wa. A man had a general obligation to provide his sister's son with a wife; this is rarely, if ever, his own offspring, but rather someone who falls within the general category of 'daughters'.

12. The significance of the kinship terminologies in northern Ghana is discussed in a forthcoming paper in this series of studies.

13. FBD marriage is found in many Muslim groups (occasionally in Gonja) and among the Fulani. Unilineal descent groups can, of course, continue to exist under such conditions, but they are obviously weaker than they would otherwise be.

14. A subsequent analysis of data collected in 1966 shows 34 per cent of marriages were with classificatory cross-cousins; this is a much higher figure than I give above, where I was thinking of marriages to first cousins.

REFERENCES

Bohannan, L. and P., 1953, *The Tiv of Central Nigeria* (Ethnogr. Surv. Afr., W. Afr. 8), London.

Durkheim, E., 1915, *The Elementary Forms of the Religious Life* (transl. J. S. Swain), London.

Field, M. J., 1940, *Social Organization of the Ga People*, London.

Fortes, M., 1949a, 'Time and Social Structure', in *Social Structure*, M. Fortes (ed.), London. 1949b, *The Web of Kinship Among the Tallensi*, London. 1950, 'Kinship and Marriage Among the Ashanti', in *African Systems of Kinship and Marriage*, (eds) A. R. Radcliffe-Brown and D. Forde, London.

Gluckman, M., 1950, 'Kinship and Marriage Among the Lozi of Northern Rhodesia and the Zulu of Natal', in *African Systems of Kinship and Marriage*, (eds) A. R. Radcliffe-Brown and D. Forde, London.

Goody, E., 1960, 'Kinship, Marriage, and the Developmental Cycle Among the Gonja of Northern Ghana', Ph.D. thesis, Cambridge University.

Goody, J., 1956, *The Social Organization of the LoWiili*, London. 1961, 'The Classification of Double Descent Systems', *Curr. Anthrop.* 2, 3–25. Reprinted as chapter 4. 1962, *Death, Property and the Ancestors: a Study of the Mortuary Customs of the LoDagaa of West Africa*, Stanford. 1966, 'Circulating Succession among the Gonja', in *Succession to High Office*, (ed.), J. Goody, Cambridge. 1968, 'Descent Groups', in *International Encyclopaedia of the Social Sciences*, New York.

Labouret, H., 1931, *Les tribus du rameau Lobi*, Paris.

Leach, E., 1951, 'The Structural Implications of Matrilateral Cross-cousin Marriage', *J. R. anthrop. Inst.* 81, 23–53.

Lévi-Strauss, C., 1949, *Les structures élémentaires de la parenté*, Paris.

Lloyd, P. C., 1962, *Yoruba Land Law*, London.

Manoukian, Madeline, 1951, *Tribes of the Northern Territories of the Gold Coast* (Ethnogr. Surv. Afr., W. Afr. 5), London.

Marti, M. P., 1957, *Les Dogon*, Paris.

Murdock, G. P., 1959, *Africa*, New York.

Murdock, G. P. et al., 1962, 'Ethnographical Atlas', *Ethnology* 1, 113–34, 265–86, 387–404, 533–45.

Rattray, R. S., 1932, *The Tribes of the Ashanti Hinterland*, Oxford.
Schneider, D. M., 1965, 'Some Muddles in the Models: or, How the System Really Works', in *The Relevance of Models for Social Anthropology* (Ass. soc. Anthrop. Monogr. 1), (ed.) M. Banton, London.
Tait, D., 1961, *The Konkomba of Northern Ghana*, London.
Tylor, E. B., 1889, 'On a Method of Investigating the Development of Institutions: Applied to Laws of Marriage and Descent', *J. anthrop. Inst.* **18**, 245–74.

CHAPTER NINE

Indo-European Kinship

Two general articles dealing with the reconstruction of 'Indo-European' society repeat the often made assertion that it was of a 'patriarchal' character. Crosland writing on 'Indo-European Origins' maintains that 'they had a developed patriarchal society',[1] while in his article on the 'Indo-European Language', Paul Thieme states that: 'the family system of the Indo-Europeans was of a patriarchal character, that is that the wife married into her husband's family, while the husband did not acquire an official relationship to his wife's family as he does where a matriarchal family system exists'.[2] This statement is in line with Meillet's conclusion to his examination of 'Indo-European' kinship terms, where he states:

> Tout ceci indique un état social où la femme entrait dans la famille du mari, mais où le mari n'avait pas avec la famille de sa femme une parenté. Il s'agit de ces 'grandes familles' à parenté masculine, telles qu'on les observe encore chez les Serbes (*zadruga*) et chez les Arméniens.[3]

I am in no position to judge the validity of the linguistic evidence which Thieme and Meillet bring forward, whether for example the words they isolate indeed have common roots. I merely want to comment on the deductions made from the terms which they suggest belong to the 'Indo-European language'.

My point is simply that the sort of evidence accepted by Thieme, Meillet, Crosland, and others can be used to reach quite opposite conclusions. The system put forward by the philologists has no parallel in the kinship systems known anywhere else in the world. If it were true, as they argue, that no terms existed for the wife's kin, this could be as consistent with a matrilineal as with an extreme patrilineal system of the type they imply.

Both Meillet and Thieme claim that because there are terms by which a woman refers to her husband's kin and no terms at all by which a man refers to his wife's family, the wife 'entered' (Meillet) or 'married into' (Thieme) her husband's family, while the husband had no relationships ('official', says Thieme; 'kinship', says Meillet) with his wife's family. Meillet speaks of this system as displaying 'parenté masculine', while Thieme translates this as 'patriarchal'.

It is not easy to decide what Thieme means by 'patriarchal' since it is a concept which has played little part in analyses of kinship systems in the present century, largely owing to its ambiguity. The term was used for example to designate a certain mode of reckoning unilineal descent (patriliny), as well as the vesting of household authority in males. I take it that the philologists are referring to the former rather than the latter, as 'patriarchal' domestic authority may be found in conjunction with matrilineal descent groups, where it could hardly be said that the woman 'entered' the family of the husband, except in the purely spatial sense of joining him on marriage.

However, if we assume that the reference is to patrilineal descent, and this is explicitly what Meillet was thinking of, the difficulties if anything increase. For there is no patrilineal system known to me in which there are no terms whatsoever employed by men to address or refer to their wives' kin. In his list of 137 kinship terminologies, Morgan (1871) reports 13 without giving the term for 'wife's father', but in each case the particular terminologies are incomplete in many other respects.[4] For example, in seven of these cases there is no term for the 'husband's father' either, producing a situation difficult to reconcile with any sort of organization in which the family is a residential unit. It is true that, in systems which involve more or less compulsory 'kin marriage', affinal terms may also be kinship terms. For example, among the Murngin of Australia, when a man marries the daughter of his mother's brother, the term for father-in-law (man speaking) and for mother's brother is one and the same. But whether or not distinctively affinal terms are available, terms always exist by which a man may refer to or address the kin of his bride. Moreover this would appear to be just as true of matrilineal and cognatic (bilateral) societies as of patrilineal ones. The philologists have posited a system that would be possible only if a society provided for no recognition of a woman's natal kin at or after marriage. And although recognition may be absent in certain types of marriage ('slave' marriage), no known society fails to provide for marriage of a higher status where the woman's relationships with her natal kin continue to be recognized after marriage, at least terminologically, and hence provide a link between the kin of the groom and those of the bride.

There are three possible solutions to this difficulty. Firstly, we may accept the implications of the philological evidence and insist that the 'Indo-Europeans' did in fact have a system of marriage entirely by 'capture', or by 'purchase', or by some other means which involved completely separating the bride from her natal kin, to the extent that the husband required no term of reference for his wife's kin. I have remarked that no such kinship system has to my knowledge been found, and some scholars would maintain that it was sociologically impossible. The second possibility is to seek some alternative explanation of the 'absence' of specific in-law terms for a man. And the third is to reject the kind of philological deductions which bring us to this impasse.

The Murngin example suggests a possible reason for the 'absence' of these terms, namely that such relatives were referred to by some more inclusive word. I am not suggesting a terminology which assumes kinship marriage, for this would operate in the same way for members of both sexes; i.e. there would be no specifically in-law terms for a woman as she too would be marrying a kinsman. We should recognize the further possibility of inclusion within some more comprehensive term. The most obvious category with which, for example, affines of senior generation might be associated is that of parents of senior generation. Indeed, in the English system, affines are referred to by terms similar to those used for kin, but with the addition of that curious phrase, 'in-law'. Moreover, this qualification too may occasionally be dropped as when the 'mother-in-law' is sometimes addressed simply as 'mother'.

In English this use of a kinship term for an affinal relationship simply represents an alternative usage, perhaps not a very common one at that. But there are systems in which this is not an alternative usage but the standardized form. According to Morgan, in Platt-Deutsch the term for husband's father is *vader* (also 'father'), and for wife's father, *frauen vader*. Here in-law usage is asymmetrical, that is, different for each spouse, one of the terms being identical with a kinship term. Morgan records a somewhat similar system in Armenian; the husband's father is *geshire* ('half-father') while the wife's father is *ahnare*, a quite different form. 'Half-father' resembles the English 'father-in-law' as against the Platt-Deutsch *vader* in that it is a modification of, rather than identical with, a kinship term. On the other hand, its use resembles the German instance as against the English, for it is asymmetrical rather than symmetrical.

The terminology which Meillet and other philologists suggest obtained among the 'Indo-Europeans' might possibly represent such an asymmetrical affinal type, where one set of terms is identical with a kin term such as 'father'. But whereas the systems we have discussed provide examples of one asymmetrical pair of terms, the philologists assume a system in which there are no special terms for any of the husband's affines. In all of Morgan's 137 kin terminologies, there is not one fully recorded system which fails to provide some distinctive affinal terms, for spouse's siblings if not for spouse's parent. Indeed, even if we confine our attention to spouse's father, there are only five examples of an asymmetrical kinship pair, other than Platt-Deutsch. Of these, three are like the German in that the kin term used by the woman refers to her husband's kin (Omaha, Kaw, and Crow). Only the other two, Dakota (Ogalalla) and Laguna, resemble the supposed Indo-European system in this respect. Of these, the first is one of eight Dakota lists, and the significance of the special usage difficult to determine. Morgan's Laguna list does not record the terms for the wife's siblings, so this might be considered the closest of any to the philologists' reconstruction. Laguna is one of the Western Pueblo groups and its social organization is based not only on matrilineal descent groups but upon uxorilocal residence, i.e. the husband joins the wife on marriage.[5] Thus, as in the Platt-Deutsch terminology (and also the Crow and Omaha cases; I do not know about the Kaw), the in-marrying spouse uses for 'father-in-law' the kinship term already employed by the spouse who does not change residence. Logically, residence would appear to be an important factor here. Indeed it might be suggested that where kinship terms are used asymmetrically, either exclusively or as alternatives, for a spouse's parent, it is likely to be done by the incoming rather than by the stationary spouse. Thus, if we assume that the 'Indo-European' terminology is of this asymmetrical sort, it would appear to indicate that our linguistic forebears had a matrilineal, uxorilocal system rather than a patrilineal or patriarchal type, as is usually asserted.

I do not seriously suggest that this was the case. But I do suggest that, firstly, the whole theoretical basis on which this sort of analysis rests needs a good deal of re-examination, and that those interested in reconstructing cultural history from such material should meanwhile treat it with considerable reserve. Secondly, more attention should be paid to developments in the analysis of non-European societies over the last fifty years. As we have seen in the many studies of 'myth and ritual' in the religions of the Near East, proto-historical studies are too often encumbered by the incorporation of the discarded hypotheses of social anthropology as part of their academic tradition. Setting aside the whole problem of whether it is possible to isolate a single 'Indo-European' culture, and acknowledging that there may be other reasons for supposing that these hypothetical people were 'patrilineal' (or 'patriarchal'), an analysis of their supposed kinship terms does nothing to confirm a theory which appears to be accepted as established fact in so many accounts of the prehistoric past.

NOTES

1. Crosland, R. A., 1957, 'Indo-European Origins. The Linguistic Evidence', *Past and Present*, 12.

2. Thieme, Paul, 1958, 'The Indo-European Language', *Scientific American* **199**, 4, 68.

3. Meillet, A., 1934, *Introduction a l'Étude Comparative des Langues Indo-Euro-péennes*, 7th ed., Paris.

4. Morgan, Lewis H., 1871, *Systems of Consanguinity and Affinity of the Human Family*, Smithsonian Contributions to Knowledge **17**, Washington.

5. Eggan, Fred, 1950, *Social Organisation of the Western Pueblos*, Chicago.

CHAPTER TEN

On Nannas and Nannies

SOME years ago, when I was living in a Cambridgeshire village, I overheard a young boy speak of his grandmother as his *nanna*. I later heard the word used very frequently in this kinship sense, not only by the villagers in these parts but also by townsfolk such as college bed-makers, who are themselves often grandmothers.[1]

Shortly after I first heard the word I was writing a paper on kinship in England for a seminar and I started to search in written sources for any references.[2] I could not remember having come across this usage in any play, novel, or other literary work, so I turned to the dictionaries. The original edition of *The New English Dictionary* (1888–1928), later called *The Oxford English Dictionary* (*O.E.D.*), failed to list the word at all. However, in the supplement, issued in 1933, it did appear, but with a different meaning, namely, 'a child's form of address to a nurse; hence, a children's nurse', an alternative form of the more familiar *nanny*, the first use of which is given as occurring in *Chambers's Journal* for September, 1864. I should add that, like *nanna*, *nanny* was also absent from the main dictionary, except as 'elliptical for nanny-goat' and in the compound form of *nanny-house* (or *nanny-shop*), which appeared in the *New Dictionary of Cant* in 1720 and meant bawdy-house.[3] In the *O.E.D.*, both these words, *nanna* and *nanny*, are tentatively derived from the girl's name *Nanny* (or *Nan*, *Ann*, or *Anne*).

Dictionaries of American English were scarcely more rewarding. Webster (1961) gives *nana* ('probably of baby-talk origin') as meaning 'a child's nurse or nursemaid';[4] *nanny* is the same but 'chiefly British'. *Nana* also appears as the Arabic for 'mint' and the Tupi for 'pineapple'. And finally there is yet another *nana* recorded, the Latin for a female dwarf, 'probably akin to Greek *nanna*, *nenna* female relative, aunt—

240

more at NUN'. While the connection with the Cambridge grand-mother seemed tenuous (though intriguing), here at least was a suggestion of kinship.

Although it was apparently a 'dialect' word, dialect dictionaries were of little or no help. *The Vocabulary of East Anglia* (edited by Robert Forby, London, 1830–58) has no such entry, although on p. 227 it does mention *nanny* as nursemaid in another context (thus providing an earlier instance of this usage than the *O.E.D.*). Edward Gepp in *An Essex Dialect Dictionary* (second edition, London, 1923) says that *nanny* means 'head', but gives no other usage. Even in his general survey of English dialects, Joseph Wright (*English Dialect Dictionary*, 1903) gives no *nanna*. Under *nanny* (alt. *nunny*) appear a whole variety of compound words, such as *nanny-wiper* (an imaginary snake supposed to inhabit the bellies of sick people), and for the word by itself he has she-goat, whitethroat, heron, stingless humble-bee, the stomach, and a small three-wheeled cart. But not a nursemaid, let alone a grandmother, among them. A search through Harold Wentworth's *American Dialect Dictionary* (New York, 1944) was a little more helpful. In New Orleans, *nannan* was recorded as meaning 'godmother' (1917); here at least was a usage of a quasi-kinship (or ritual kinship) kind. And one further entry from the South was of some interest: in Kentucky an alternative to the proper name *Nannie* is *Ninnie* and in the same general region *ninny* means 'a breast, or milk from the breast'.

It was dictionaries of slang that turned out to be most fruitful of the written sources. In his *Dictionary of Slang and Unconventional English* (third edition, 1949), Eric Partridge gives quite a different etymology from Webster for the word *nan*, a maid-servant, which was used by Shakespeare in 1596. Like the *O.E.D.*, he derives this usage from the proper name *Nan*, a by-form of *Anne*; the thesis is elaborated in his *Name into Word* (London, 1950), where he writes: '*nanny*, a nurse, and *nanny* (or female) *goat*, often shortened to *nanny* (contrast *billy goat*), are common-propertyings of *Nanny*, a diminutive either of *Nan* or directly of *Nancy*, a given-name more usual perhaps in the "lower" than in the "higher" strata of society.' Nancy, it should be remarked, is also the name for an 'effeminate male', or pansy.[5]

In sum, while these entries contain no direct reference to grand-mothers, they do show that the words *nanny*, *nanna*, and *nan* are closely linked with women and with women's tasks, especially the care of children; and that they are used particularly of persons hired to do the job. The role of the Victorian and Edwardian *nanny* as a proxy mother is well illustrated in many memoirs of the period,[6] and the alternative *nannna* (or rather *nana*) was of course the name of the Newfoundland dog which acted as the Darlings' nurse in *Peter Pan* (1904).[7]

But while *nanny* and *nanna* as 'children's nurse' are only recorded as nineteenth-century usages, *nan*, as 'serving-maid', dates from the late sixteenth century. And it is perhaps no coincidence that, royalty apart, one of the earliest nurses of whom we have much information (she looked after various children of the Verney family in the middle of the seventeenth century) was called Nann Fudd.[8]

Indeed remembering that the word *nan* for serving-maid and *nanny-house* for brothel were both current at the same period, the very end of the sixteenth century, it would appear that these maids might 'serve' in more senses than one and that such nannies represented the Bad Mother as well as the Good. In *Slang and its Analogues* (7 vols., London, 1890–4), Farmer and Henley give the following terse entries for the words in which we are interested:

Nan = A Maid (1596, Shakespeare, *The Merry Wives*, I, iv, 160).
Nanny = 1. a goat.
    2. a whore.

A slightly earlier compilation (*A Dictionary of Slang, Jargon, and Cant*, edited by Albert Barrère and Charles G. Leland, London, 1889)[9] suggests an explanation of this Jungian paradox, and at the same time supplements the etymology of Partridge and the *O.E.D.* (which, as we have seen, itself supplemented the baby-talk theory of Webster). *Nanny shop* '(common)', they write, means 'a brothel',[10] and *Nanny* '(common)', a prostitute. 'Probably from nun, meaning the same.'[11] This curious entry is explained under *Abbess, lady*, a word which was used for the mistress of a brothel, a procuress; the inmates were known as 'nuns' or sometimes 'Sisters of Charity', and her fancy man as the Abbot.[12] A crozier'd abbot, or abbot on the cross, referred to the rather specialized role of a man who kept a brothel 'more for the purpose of robbery and extortion rather than that of prostitution'. This derivation receives some confirmation from the fact that Elizabethan writers such as Thomas Nashe (in *Christ's Tears over Jerusalem*, 1593) and John Fletcher (in *The Mad Lover*, 1617, IV, ii) use *nunnery* for brothel; and of course Hamlet repeats the word to Ophelia five times in the course of only 30 lines (*Hamlet*, III, i, 121–52), each time with this 'common' implication. Thus the 'bad' sense of *nanny* would seem to be a direct inversion of the 'good' meaning of *nun*; sexuality masquerades as asexuality, the wanton as the virgin, and the Bride of Christ is the mistress of all.

As for etymology, the 'good' meaning of *nanny* is derived by Webster from baby-talk and by Partridge from the proper name Ann (the Biblical Hannah), or rather from variants associated with the 'lower' social strata. But this is not the whole picture by any means. For the good and bad meanings, with their seemingly distinct etymologies, are much closer than at first appears. The clue is given in one of Webster's entries under *nana*, the Latin for a female dwarf. For, as we saw, the authors go on to say, a little cryptically, 'probably akin to Greek *nanna*, *nenna* female relative, aunt—more at NUN'.

Turn to *nun*, and you find that it comes from the 'Old English *nunne*, from the Late Latin *nonna* nun, child's nurse; of baby-talk origin like Greek *nanna*, *nenna* female relative, aunt, Welsh *nain* grandmother, Albanian *nanë* mother, child's nurse, Russian *nyanya* child's attendant, Sanskrit, *nana* mother, little mother'. The *O.E.D.* also gives the word *nun* a classical root, but one of a slightly different, though apparently cognate form. 'The ultimate source is ecclesiastical Latin *nonna*, feminine of *nonnus* monk (in late Greek *nonna*, *nonnos*), originally a title given to elderly persons, whence Italian *nonno*, *nonna* grandfather, grandmother, Sicilian *nunnu*, *nunna* father, mother, Sardinian *nonnu*, *nonna* godfather, godmother.'[13] The relevant Greek roots, it should be added, are given by Liddell and Scott (1925–40) as '*nannas* or *nanna*, maternal or paternal uncle or aunt'; '*nanne*, maternal aunt'; '*nennos*, mother or father's brother, uncle, mother's brother or (in poetry) mother's father'; '*ninne* perhaps grandmother or mother-in-law'; '*nonnos* = *pater* (cf. *nennos*)'.

At the outset, there are two points to be made about these entries in Webster and the *O.E.D.* First, they suggest that the analysis of Greek kinship terminology has not been carried very far. And secondly, they show that a surprising number of apparently cognate words have different meanings in closely related languages. Nevertheless, there seems some grounds for suggesting that the English *nanna*, child's nurse or grandmother, may be linked to words found in various Indo-European languages for a kinswoman (or ritual kinswoman) belonging to the first or second ascending generation. If this is the case, the grandmother usage of *nanna* is probably not new to English. Yet the first and only dictionary reference which I could discover did not appear until the supplement to Partridge's *Dictionary of Slang and Unconventional English* issued in 1961.[14]

One possible reason for the way in which the compilers of dictionaries have neglected the kinship as distinct from the servile use of *nanna* is that the former is largely confined to the 'lower' social strata. The only written references that I know are in two recent surveys of 'working-class' communities, Young and Wilmott's report on their work in Bethnal Green (*Family and Kinship in East London*, 1957, pp. 28, 41) and Madeleine Kerr's study of a Liverpool slum, *The People of Ship Street* (1958, p. 46). For in Britain, kinship usage, like many other aspects of culture, is heavily stratified; the usages of the lower levels often seem 'common' to those above, while from below those of the upper echelons appear 'soft' or 'affected'. *Grannie* sounded wrong to some of my 'lower' informants; *mum* (but not *mummy*) was frowned upon by the others.

I have used the terms upper, middle, and lower classes (or upper and lower strata) in a rather loose sense, to indicate rough position in what is for most purposes a hierarchical continuum (or parallel series of continua). There is doubtless more than one significant breaking point in the differentiation of English kinship usage, but the limited survey which I have already carried out suggests that the most important is attendance at a public school, rather than, for example, occupational status calculated on the Hall/Jones scale. In her urban study Margaret Stacey notes that 'Public-school education is, in fact, of so great importance as a class factor that it is used . . . as a primary definition of the traditional upper class in Banbury and district' (*Tradition and Change: A Study of Banbury*, London, 1960, p. 141). The dividing line, which is by no means as rigid as some self-conscious analysts of the stratified differences (or 'class-indicators') in English speech have tended to suggest,[15] roughly corresponds to Ross's U and non-U speech, or what

Chapman sees as the usage 'in good society', Walker as 'correct' and others as 'standard' or 'Oxford' English.[16] However, the terms used by these authors reflect the fact that, explicitly or implicitly, they adopt the upper-class point of view and it is to counterbalance this tendency that I prefer to phrase the distinction as one between 'popular' and 'genteel' English.[17]

While the class factor might well account for the absence of this usage from compilations such as the *O.E.D.* that reflect U speech (ordinary speech is 'common'), it hardly explains its omission from dictionaries of dialect and slang. Perhaps this is just a case of the literary specialists who collect the entries overlooking the close and familiar (kinship) in favour of the strange and exotic (thieves' cant and bawdy).[18] For there can be no doubt of the very widespread use of the term *nanna, nan, nanny, nin*, for grandmother, not only in southern England and the midlands, but also in the northern counties, southern Scotland, South Wales, New Zealand, New England, and Canada.[19] Indeed several persons have told me that they knew the word *nanny* only in the kinship sense until they began to read novels and discovered that other people paid *nannies* to look after children. Moreover this 'popular' usage seems to be holding its own, despite the standardizing pressures of radio and television in favour of *granny* and *granma*, which have the advantage (from one standpoint) of being closer to the term of reference.

One reason for this persistence may be that although the term *nanna* for grandmother is lower status from one point of view (in that it is not used by the speakers of genteel English—the products of the public schools), it is often highly valued as a popular usage and given preference over the main alternative of *granma*. 'All my thirteen grandchildren (sons' children and daughters' children) call me *nanna*,' Mrs. King (65, of Cambridge) told me. 'I don't like this "granma" at all. Yes, comes from the tele. One of my grandchildren called me Kate the other day. Said his mum did so. I told him off proper. And her too. What if he called you that in the street?'

So highly is the term valued, that in some cases the two female grandparents compete for the right to use it. Miss Christie (22, of Yorkshire) told me that in her family it was the mother's mother who was called *nanna*. She had lived with them during the war and had been 'like a second mother'. The father's mother, who was not so close, was called *granma*. But with Miss Christie's mother's sister's children, the situation was different. There the father's mother also insisted upon being called *nanna*, so that the two grandmothers had to be differentiated as *nanna* (Smith) and *nanna* (Jones). In another case where both grandmothers were called *nanna*, the mother's mother (London) was so called 'because all her other grandchildren did', but the father's mother (Northumberland) insisted on being addressed in the same way 'because granma and granny made her sound so old'.[20]

The situation is perceived in much the same way by the junior generation. In explanation of her own usage, Miss Horton (26, of Blackpool) volunteered, 'I don't like Granma Jones; that's why I use the formal name. I call Nanny that because I like her.' Others thought that *nanna* was more appropriate for a grandmother who was living in the same house, and hence part of the family (i.e. household). In view of these statements, it is not surprising to find that of my respondents who addressed one of their grandparents as *nanna*, the majority used the term for their mother's mother.[21] For as recent surveys have shown, both in working-class and in suburban communities, the closer grandmother is the mother's mother;[22] she it is who is the likelier to be living with a married couple and hence having the closest relationship with their children. Usually, then, the *nanna* is the mum's mum.[23]

There are two reasons I think why high value is placed upon the term. In the first place, like other alternatives (such as pet names) that seniors encourage, the use of *nanna* is seen as fixing them less firmly in the hierarchy of generation than the more formal term.[24] For individuals are often reluctant to accept the full implications of 'grandparenthood', and an alternative label enables them to cling to earlier roles. The dilemma of the males of this age group was recently brought out by Bing Crosby when he (or his script-writer) remarked of himself and Bob Hope, 'There's just one trouble for us now. We're too old to get the girl and too proud to play grandfathers.'

But it is not simply that the grandmother is trying to avoid her new role. She is in fact continuing to act in her earlier capacity when she becomes 'a second mother', nursing (in the wider sense) her children's children, and thus allowing the mother to go out to work, to help on the farm, or just to get on more freely with her household tasks. Miss

Kerr records an instance where the children addressed their maternal grandmother as 'mother' and called their real mother 'mum', a situation which recalls that reported by R. T. Smith for the Negro population in the rural areas of Guyana. Motherhood, he notes, is not simply a matter of biological relationships. 'When a daughter bears a child whilst she is living in the household controlled by her mother, the child frequently grows up calling its maternal grandmother by the term "Mama", and its own mother by her christian name.' And he goes on to add that 'This is particularly true when the grandmother has small children of her own towards whom the child adopts a sibling relationship.'[25] For it is when the grandmother is both young and near at hand that she plays a significant part in the domestic activities of the wider kinship group, which she cannot so easily do in those social strata where at this point in the domestic cycle the generations are more widely scattered, owing to the nature of their work and to the wider range of their social contacts. But even in these strata, many women make considerable efforts to be present at the birth of their grandchildren, and thus to participate in the most critical of the domestic activities of their children.

These child-caring functions the upper classes could delegate to their nannies. But the less affluent also have their proxy mothers, their nannas, although recruited by ties of kinship rather than on the labour market,[26] and relieving the mothers themselves for work rather than for leisure. Indeed, as incomes tend to become more equal and domestic help more scarce, it's these kin-based ties that have the edge here, both on the middle-class family that has to move around and on the upper-class family that can no longer get servants. Which is perhaps some recompense for the fact that over the last few centuries their 'popular' usages may have sometimes escaped the notice of the 'genteel' scholars who compile the dictionaries.[27]

NOTES

1. In view of my later discussion I should explain that I myself only knew my mother's mother, who lived far away in north-east Scotland and was always known as 'grannie' which is I believe the usual term in those parts. Moreover as I spent my early years in what was then a very new town in Hertfordshire, grandmothers appeared to play little part in the lives of my age mates. On this point, see the interesting analysis of the cycle of domestic groups in suburban

England in Peter Wilmott and Michael Young, *Family and Class in a London Suburb* (London, 1960). In 'middle-class' Woodford elderly parents live with their children (generally their daughters) almost as frequently as in 'lower-class' Bethnal Green, but there is not the continuous association with Mum throughout a woman's life that characterizes family ties in the East End.

2. A seminar run by W. Lloyd Warner, Visiting Professor in Social Theory at Cambridge, 1954–5.

3. In full, *A New Dictionary of the Terms Ancient and Modern of the Canting Crew In its several Tribes of Gypsies, Beggars, Thieves, Cheats, etc., With An Addition of some Proverbs, Phrases, Figurative Speeches, etc., Useful for all sorts of People, (especially Foreigners) to secure their Money and preserve their Lives; besides very diverting and Entertaining, being wholly New*, B.E. (Gent.), London, 1720? (first edition 1699).

4. The middle 'a' in this word is rather longer in American English than in the English of Southern England, i.e. *naana* rather than *nanna*.

5. Partridge, 1949, *A Dictionary of the Underworld*, London, is rather more specific. *Nancy* means 'the posteriors' and 'in the derivative (?) sense "an effeminate man; especially a passive homosexual." ' Barrère and Leland derive the name from Nancy Dawson, a prostitute celebrated in song. According to Jamieson (*An Etymological Dictionary of the Scottish Language*, new edition, 1880), these personal names may be derived from Agnes; Partridge follows this different suggestion in another book (*Origins*, London, 1958). In American slang, *Nancy* carries the same meaning; and in East Anglia, Forby reports, it also means 'a small lobster'.

Attention should also be drawn to the fact that *ninny* is a long-established word (1593) for 'a simpleton; a fool,' and the O.E.D. tentatively suggests that it is an abbreviated form of 'innocent'; related compound words are the synonyms *ninny-hammer* (1592) and *nincompoop* (abbrev. *nincom*), of which the dictionary reports 'etymology unknown; probably fanciful' (but see also Joseph T. Shipley, *Dictionary of Word Origins*, New York, 1945, 243). The word *ninny* is in frequent use today, and so too is the form *naana* (see Partridge, *Dictionary of Slang*, where 'a right nana' means 'a real softy' and a 'nana-cut' is a woman-like hair-cut). This use of *ninny*, and possibly *naana*, may be connected with those discussed earlier in this paper; the use of a female term for a male may indicate not only 'effeminacy' but also general incapacity in the performance of male tasks, a meaning associated with the man's view of the woman's role.

The word *nanny* also appears in *The American Thesaurus of Slang* (edited by Lester V. Berry and Melvin Van Den Bark, London, 1954, 551) as 'a tone that flutters rapidly back and forth over a range of two to three notes'.

6. For example the Nanny Sibley of Baroness Ravensdale's autobiography, *In Many Rhythms* (London, 1953, 24f.), who broke her engagement to continue to look after her three charges when their mother died; 'The real prop and backbone of my life was our Nanny Sibley'. But of course even when the mother was alive the nanny often played the main part in bringing up the children. In her account of how to manage a Victorian home, Mrs. Beeton speaks of the daily visit paid by a busy mother to the nursery (*Beeton's Book of Household Management*, London, 1861, 103ff.), the rest of the children's care being left to the Nursemaids (Upper and Under), whose roles are to be distinguished from that of the Monthly Nurse (who looks after the mother) and the Wet Nurse (who feeds the child). The

following remark gives some idea of the complexity of the household organization: 'In higher families, the upper nurse is usually permitted to sup or dine occasionally at the housekeeper's table by way of relaxation, when the children are all well, and her subordinates trustworthy' (1014). On nannies and nursemaids, see Mary Ann Gibbs, 1960, *The Years of the Nannies*, London. The increased use of *nanny* for children's nurse may be linked with the specialization of nurse for a trained (and registered) sick nurse which followed the establishment of training schools in the mid-nineteenth century; in London, Mrs. Fry (of the Society of Friends) started the Institution of Nursing Sisters in 1840. The term nurse, which had referred especially to the nourishing of infants, came to be linked with the care of the sick and it was the *nanny* who now looked after the 'kids' (though in fact this usage for children goes back to 1690).

7. Those who have not read Barrie's whimsy on the domestic life of Bloomsbury since their childhood may need reminding that Nana displayed to perfection all the characteristics that the upper middle class could wish of its servants; she demanded little keep (the Darlings could not really afford to have a nurse), kept silent in the face of ill treatment and was completely faithful. The children were also devoted to Nana and flew away because she was chained up by the bad-tempered father; when they return, Nana walks 'with the importance of a nurse who will never have another day off' (1928, 153). One of the play's most insistent concerns is the search for mother.

8. *Memoirs of the Verney Family during the Seventeenth Century* (eds F. P. and M. M. Verney), London, 1925, I, 304. The term nurse was then used to refer not only to the children's nurse, who in this case looked after more than a single generation of the family, but also to the wet nurse, necessarily a temporary employee. The wet nurse often looked after the child in her own home. It was this practice of boarding out which encouraged the great fear of the changeling, a dread epitomized in Sir Ralph Verney's comment upon his son's choice of a village nursem aid; 'tis greate odds his child would be changed for one of the Nurse's Sister's children' (2, 276). On 3rd June 1647, Sir Ralph's wife, Mary, who was then living in London, gave birth to a son; three weeks later the wet nurse, who came from near the Verneys' country seat, set off to take the child to her home. When Mary Verney went there in August, the child was ill; a new wet nurse had to be found and the mother returned alone to London. (The new nurse was given 4*s.* a week and two loads of wood, 'being she had nott ye cristening, for nurses are much dearer than ever they were ...' (I, 380). The wet nurse was normally entitled to the christening money; Mrs. Brough, wet nurse to Edward VII, received a thousand pounds.)

In royal households of the same period, although wet nurses were of lowly status, the children were subsequently looked after by titled gentlewomen. Earlier, during the middle ages, male children were often sent away from court to be brought up by strangers, as when Henry II entrusted the education and fostering of his heir to the Chancellor, Thomas Becket, son of a London burgess. Such fostering was also a common practice in the Scottish royal family. In the late sixteenth century the future James VI was brought up away from his mother, by the Earl and Countess of Mar in the royal castle of Stirling; and, despite the protests of his Danish wife, he insisted that his eldest son, Henry, be treated in a similar manner; their second child, Elizabeth, was placed under the care of Lord and Lady Livingstone and the third, the future Charles I, in the charge of Lord Fife. While the reasons behind such fostering certainly included dynastic security, the rearing of children by proxy parents was well established in Britain among this and other social strata long before the coming of the Foundling Hospital for the poor and the Public School for the rich.

9. *Embracing English, American, and Anglo-Indian Slang, Pidgin English, Tinkers' Jargon and Other Irregular Phraseology.*

10. For a further 50 English variants of brothel, see Farmer and Henley (1890–4).

11. In *A Dictionary of the Underworld*, Partridge derives *nanny house* from *nanny goat* ('Lit., a house for containing female goats'); there is sometimes no great etymological consistency from one book to another, even when they are written by the same author.

12. *Abbot*, like *pope* (*papa*), comes from a word meaning 'father' (Aramaic, *abba*; Arabic, *abu*).

13. See also Ernest Weekley, 1921, *An Etymological Dictionary of Modern English*, London. This etymology apparently derives from Weekley; see his *Adjectives—and Other Words*, London, 1930, 89f., in a chapter entitled 'Baby's Contribution to Speech.'

14. Weekley remarked that although *nanna*, a nurse, was not admitted to dictionaries, it was nevertheless 'entitled to rank among the few vocables that have an uninterrupted life of some thousands of years' (ibid., 89); so the suggestion that *nanna* for grandmother has similarly led a sub-literary existence over a considerable period (Welsh *nain*? or a Latin-derived source?) is perhaps not beyond the realms of possibility. As Weekley observes in another essay, 'What we regard as vulgarisms are usually older pronunciations which have been gradually expelled by the printed word. *Waps* is not a corruption, but the legitimate descendant of Anglo-Saxon *wæps*' (ibid., 143).

15. Nancy Mitford, 1955, 'The English Aristocracy', *Encounter*, September, 5, maintains that between the upper middle and middle classes 'there is a very definite border line, easily recognizable by hundreds of small but significant landmarks.' See Evelyn Waugh's pertinent criticism 'An Open Letter . . . on a Very Serious Subject', *Encounter*, December 1955, 13.

16. Alan S. C. Ross, 'Linguistic Class-Indicators in Present-Day English', *Bull. de la société néophilologique de Helsinki*, 55, 1954, 20–56, part of which is a commentary on R. W. Chapman, *Names, Designations and Appellations*, Society for Pure English, Tract No. 47, 1936, and upon J. Walker, *Critical Pronouncing Dictionary and Expositor of the English Language*, London, 1791. See also H. C. Wyld, *The Best English*, S.P.E. Tract, No. 39, 1934, and R. W. Chapman, '*Oxford' English*, S.P.E. Tract, No. 37, 1932.

17. Weekley avoids this particular bias and points out that 'standard English' is really what the literary specialists look upon as 'corrupt dialect' (*Adjectives—and Other Words*, 140).

18. Chapman remarks that neither dictionaries nor works of reference tell us much about modes of address, even in 'good society'; which is one of the reasons why they can be so useful as class-indicators (1936, 231).

19. From Canada I have a printed card with the words 'Happy Birthday, Nana'. I should add that in English-speaking countries overseas, the less rigid system of

stratification means that the term does not appear to have the same class significance as in England.

20. The same point was made to me by much younger people, e.g. Mrs. Arthur, 23, of Wellington, New Zealand.

21. Based upon the figures obtained in a preliminary survey; the numbers are not large but I hope to extend them.

22. On the other hand inheritance considerations may counteract the tendency to reside with maternal kin since the preference is for the means of livelihood (farms, estates, shops, factories) to be transmitted from father to son. See also Margaret Stacey, *Tradition and Change*, 125, note ii.

23. On the subject of *nan*, Miss Kerr remarks: 'No constant rule has been found about which name is given to which grandmother' (48). This is so; there is certainly no strict rule. But it should be noted that in the particular instance which she records it is the maternal grandmother who is called *nin* (49); in Young and Wilmott's study of Bethnal Green, two families use *nan* for the maternal grandmother (Wilkins, 28; Cole, 41) and one family for both (Tawney, 41).

24. Writing of genteel usages in the mid thirties, Chapman remarks, ' "*Father*", "*Mother*", "*Grandfather*", "*Grandmother*" are in common use. They have however a certain formality or solemnity which is often evaded by the use of less aweful substitutes . . " *Dad(dy)*" and "*Mummy*" hold the field. "*Granny*" is well established.'

Of course, while kinship terms differ according to position in the status hierarchy and also appear to conserve their general structure over long periods of time, actual usage is always undergoing small but important changes. This affects not only special modes of address (no English child, I believe, would still address his father as 'sir') but also the form of the familiar kinship terms (*mummy* as against *mamma*). It is possible that such changes occur more frequently in upper-status groups; with class mobility and mass communications, the usage of the upper classes inevitably tends to spread downwards and, as with other 'fashions', the retention of exclusiveness demands the adoption of new forms.

25. *The Negro Family in British Guiana*, London, 1956, 143. This is not I think simply an example of tekeisonymy (identification of children with parents, see Yih-Fu Ruey, 'Parent-Child Identity in Kinship Terminology', Engl. summary, *Bull. Ethnol. Soc. China*, 1955, I, 45–62), although there are instances of the related practices of spouse-and-child identification in English usage. A husband for example may refer to his mother-in-law as 'mother', differentiating her terminologically from his own mother (see Ross, 'Linguistic Class-Indicators', 30). Chapman however solved the delicate problem of addressing in-laws by the use of teknonymy (child-identification): 'If I am obliged to name my mother-in-law direct, I call her, by invitation, "*Granny*"; a solution not wholly satisfactory, but made possible by a nursery atmosphere' (*Names, Designations* . . . , 234).

26. Or of course acting in a maternal role when the real mother (or grandmother) is dead. The difference between the upper and lower usage is illustrated by the two instances which I came across where a mother's mother died leaving young children. In the first (upper) case, my informant called his mother's upbringer *nan*, knowing that she was an employee; in the other instance, my informant called his mother's foster-mother *nan*, thinking that she was his true grandparent.

27. The divergence between what Samuel Johnson called 'regular and solemn' forms on the one hand and 'cursory and colloquial' ones on the other fully crystallized only in the last two centuries; as Ernest Weekley observes in his essay 'Mrs. Gamp and the King's English', it was to a large extent a creation of the printing press, of the development of a literary language in Elizabethan times and of the rise of professional orthoepists in the seventeenth and eighteenth centuries. At the end of that period, with the composition of Walker's *Pronouncing Dictionary* (1791), 'educated speech had been more or less standardized and assimilated to the literary language' (*Adjectives—and Other Words*, 142). Differences in pronunciation increasingly reflected social stratification rather than regional distribution. But the different connotations of *nanna* appear to be linked with role differences in the class hierarchy which long antedate the changes that Weekley is writing of.

Index